The Way Literacy Lives

THE WAY LITERACY LIVES

Rhetorical Dexterity and Basic Writing Instruction

SHANNON CARTER

STATE UNIVERSITY OF NEW YORK PRESS

Published by
STATE UNIVERSITY OF NEW YORK PRESS, ALBANY

© 2008 State University of New York

Printed in the United States of America

For information, contact
State University of New York Press, Albany, NY
www.sunypress.edu

Production, Laurie Searl
Marketing, Anne M. Valentine

Library of Congress Cataloging-in-Publication Data

Carter, Shannon.
    The way literacy lives : rhetorical dexterity and basic writing instruction / Shannon Carter.
        p. cm.
    Includes bibliographical references and index.
    ISBN 978-0-7914-7355-9 (hardcover : alk. paper) 1. English language—Composition and exercises—Study and teaching. 2. Literacy—United States. 3. Education—Standards—United States. I. Title.

LB1576.C31793 2008
808'.042071—dc22

                                                                            2007024995

10   9   8   7   6   5   4   3   2   1

Contents

Acknowledgments

In the three years since I began writing it, this book has taken a number of forms: course syllabi and materials, grants, conference presentations, a textbook for students enrolled in our basic writing program, a training guide for instructors working with these students called basic writers. Each version and each new audience demanded further reading, reflection, and observation; each incarnation better articulated the theoretical framework I required—as a scholar, teacher, and administrator—but could not have anticipated. Like most new things, this is not the book I intended to write; like most things, I could not have possibly written it alone.

In that sense, the writing of this single-authored manuscript was an intensely collaborative experience. The students enrolled in our basic writing program over these last few years and the graduate assistants assigned to teach them deserve much credit for the book this turned out to be. Through them, I learned so much about writing and the teaching of writing.

Without the freedom to experiment, however, this collaborative relationship would not have been possible. Thus, I am eternally grateful to my colleagues Gerald Duchovnay, Bill McCarron, Bill Bolin, Dick Fulkerson, and Donna Dunbar-Odom for giving me the trust and the space necessary to try things out. In particular, I want to thank Donna Dunbar-Odom; her support, encouragement, guidance, and innovative leadership and scholarship have had a significant impact on this project and its approach. Through its many incarnations—as a graduate-level course, as a basic writing textbook— Donna has read almost every word. In every way, Donna has been an invaluable mentor, colleague, and friend. I also with to thank Dick Fulkerson for reading and responding to the earliest versions of this project; his rigor as a scholar and enviable skill as a debater forced me into tighter arguments and more responsible prose. Thanks, as well, to Texas A&M-Commerce for granting me the sabbatical (called here "Faculty Development Leave") that gave me the time I needed to complete this book.

Beyond A&M-Commerce, I want to thank Susan Naomi Bernstein for inviting me to become a part of the basic writing professional community in more formal and service-oriented ways. At home, I am grateful to my mother (Danielle Carter), my brother (Eric Carter), and my dear friend and partner Stephen Foote for expanding my own understanding of literate practice through their tireless engagement with rigorous, intellectually challenging out-of-school literacies. All three have given me much of their time, encouragement, and support as I interviewed them about video gaming, electronic music, and comic books and, where possible, they taught me how to make use of the texts associated with these social spaces. From his brother Michael, Stephen even provided access to an artifact created to guide their use of the text-only adventure game *Raaka-Tu* (circa 1981). I am grateful to Michael Foote for granting me permission to include in this manuscript a copy of this map (see Figure 1). As always, my father, John Carter, and grandmother, Grace Carter, also deserve much of my admiration and gratitude.

Portions of chapter 6 appeared in the 25th anniversary issue of the *Journal of Basic Writing* (2006, as "Redefining Literacy as a Social Practice"). I wish to thank *JBW*'s co-editors Rebecca Mlynarczyk and Bonne August for supporting this endeavor. In particular, I wish to extend my warmest appreciation for Rebecca Mlynarczyk, whose tireless support, encouragement, and enthusiasm enabled me to condense this book-length project into a workable article and, in the process, strengthened the book from which the article emerged.

Thanks, as well, to Larin McLaughlin, Laurie Searl, and the anonymous reviewers of this project. Without their insight, feedback, and guidance, this project would not have been possible.

ONE

The Way Literacy Tests

Without testing, reform is a journey without a compass. Without testing, teachers and administrators cannot adjust their methods to meet high goals. Without testing, standards are little more than scraps of paper. Without testing, true competition is impossible. Without testing, parents are left in the dark. . . .

    Testing is the cornerstone of reform. You know how I know? Because it's the cornerstone of reform in the state of Texas. (George W. Bush in the first of the presidential debates of 2000, qtd. in Hillocks 11)

In education reform circles these days, Texas is everywhere. If Governor George W. Bush is elected president, the Texas school reforms—and particularly the state's whips-and-chains accountability system—are likely to become a model for national education policy, as they already are in a large number of states. (Schrag 2000)

THE WAY LITERACY LIVES offers a curricular response to the political, material, social, and ideological constraints placed on literacy education, particularly basic writing, via the ubiquity of what Brian V. Street calls the "autonomous model of literacy" and instead treats literacy as a social practice. According to Street, the autonomous model

disguise[s] the cultural and ideological assumptions that underpin it so that it can then be presented as though they are neutral and universal and that literacy as such will have the . . . benign effect of . . . enhancing the . . . cognitive skills [of those marked "illiterate,"] . . . improving their economic prospects, making them better citizens, regardless of the social and economic conditions that accounted for their "illiteracy" in the first place. ("Autonomous and Ideological Models" 1)

Rather than perpetuating this problematic treatment of literacy—through which "testing" can be easily accepted as the "cornerstone of reform" (Bush)—Street urges us to embrace "the alternative, ideological model." An ideological model of literacy

> posits . . . that literacy is a social practice, not simply a technical and neutral skill; that it is always embedded in socially constructed epistemological principles. It is about knowledge: the ways in which people address reading and writing are themselves rooted in conceptions of knowledge, identity, being. It is also embedded in social practice, such as those of a particular job market or particular educational context and the effects of learning that particular literacy will be dependent on those particular contexts. Literacy, in this sense, is always contested, both its meanings and its practices, hence particular versions of it are always "ideological," they are always rooted in a particular worldview and a desire for that view of literacy to dominate and to marginalise others (Gee 1990; Besnier and Street 1994). ("Autonomous Model" 2)

Thus, according to Street's ideological model, standardized tests of literacy must be understood as not only inappropriate but largely unethical in that they privilege particular contexts, identities, and knowledge while marginalizing all others.

Accepting that a curricular solution to the institutionalized oppression implicit in much literacy learning is necessarily partial and temporary, I argue that fostering in our students an awareness of the ways in which an autonomous model deconstructs itself when applied to real-life literacy contexts can empower them to work against this system in ways critical theorists advocate. The primary objective of the current study is to offer a model for basic writing instruction that is responsive to multiple agents limiting and shaping the means and goals of literacy education, agents with goals that are quite often in opposition. Doing so requires that I not offer a curricular solution in isolation as any responsible pedagogical decisions must take into account the layers of agents influencing any and all social, political, material, and ideological conditions for learning. Thus, I will situate this new model for basic writing by drawing attention to the local context from which this program emerged; it is a context with national implications because, as Peter Schrag has pointed out, "in education circles these days, Texas is everywhere."

TEACHING TO THE TEST

> It is not valid to suggest that literacy can be 'given' neutrally and then its 'social' effects only experienced afterwards. (Street 2)

I came of age in Texas during the 1980s, an era of major educational reform in response to the National Commission on Excellence in Education's controversial report *A Nation at Risk* (1983). Laced throughout with the Cold War rhetoric that was so much a part of our culture at the time, its analysis of the state of American education was scathing:

> If an unfriendly foreign power had attempted to impose on America the mediocre educational performance that exists today, we might well have viewed it as an act of war. As it stands, we have allowed this to happen to ourselves. We have even squandered the gains in student achievement made in the wake of the Sputnik challenge. Moreover, we have dismantled essential support systems which helped make those gains possible. We have, in effect, been committing an act of unthinking, unilateral educational disarmament.

Following this report, politicians throughout the nation made education a "top priority," and Texas was no exception. Then-Governor Mark White enlisted the help of Dallas billionaire Ross Perot and the result was House Bill 72 (in 1984) that mandated, among other things, "a new statewide curriculum and minimum skills test" (Watson). Thus began the culture of testing from which the much more recent *No Child Left Behind Act* would eventually emerge.

For the most part, that means my public school experiences were largely dominated by "standards" shaped and measured by state-mandated testing as "[c]entral to the Texas accountability system has been the use of a standardized test to assess student achievement" (Toenjes et al. 3–4). Each incarnation of that test (first the "Texas Assessment of Basic Skills" [TABS], then the "Texas Educational Assessment of Minimum Skills" [TEAMS], next the "Texas Assessment of Academic Skills" [TAAS], and—most recently—the "Texas Assessment of Knowledge and Skills" [TAKS]) has measured "literacy" via student responses to a generic writing prompt and multiple-choice questions about grammar and usage. Each incarnation of that test has violated the principles of good writing assessment, stated most emphatically and clearly by the Conference on College Composition and Communication Position Statement on Assessment (1995): "no one piece of writing—even if it is generated under the most desirable conditions—can ever serve as an indicator of overall literacy, particularly for high stakes decisions" ("Writing Assessment"). Each incarnation has placed students of color and, especially, those from poorer neighborhoods at an even greater disadvantage (see Haney; Valenzuela, Schrag).[1]

My junior class (1987–1988) was among the first the state would require to pass a standardized test before being approved for graduation. I began college the year the TASP Law (Texas Academic Skills Program) was enacted (September 1989), a test—again via multiple-choice questions and a single writing sample generated under "standardized" conditions—that, for the next fourteen years, would be used to determine college-readiness and—for those deemed "not ready"—state-mandated remediation.[2] With the implementation of each standardized test and the increasingly high stakes associated with them, the campus climate began to shift. Students and faculty alike were scared and angry. We discussed little else. We did little else.[3] Our "compass"—to invoke George W. Bush's metaphor—was always "the Test," and this compass took us right back to the test yet again, a circular journey that defined literacy for us as singular, autonomous, and devoid of any context or purpose beyond separating the "good" students from those who must be, ironically enough, "left behind." Even as teenagers, many of us understood what George Hillocks Jr. would assert nearly fifteen years later: "If assessments limit the kinds of writing taught or the ways they are taught, or the thinking that good writing requires, then the assessments may be of questionable value" (17). As one basic writer[4] in our program put it, "[a] person is more likely to write better about something they know or are passionate about, not about stupid subjects like, why there should be uniforms in public school. To more creative people like myself, it's like a road block . . . a vacuum sucking all inventive thought, [making writers more likely] . . . to stick with the softer ideas than anything radical" (Holly, WA2, 3–4).

After college, I decided to teach English at the secondary level, again in Texas and both times at schools marked as "low performing" or "at risk" by their overall performance on TAAS (the Texas Assessment of Academic Skills), designations that, as I would soon learn, indicated little more than the darker color of our students' skin and the lower socioeconomic status of their caretakers. Rather than spending our time developing innovative curricula that required our students to think critically and "write to learn," we wasted hour after hour of our planning period sitting at the dining room table of the home economics department and poring over charts that we were to shape into "proof" that our curriculum was aligned with the requisite TAAS objectives—or suffer the wrath of the upper administration who were no less victims of these same standardized tests and the state laws that held them "accountable" for the results. "The only way to survive," said my wise colleague who'd experienced fifteen years of award-winning, creative teaching before the rise of standardized testing, "is to 'fit in'" any and all "real" teaching (those activities that may actually engage and challenge students) "after March"—often the month when TAAS-testing officially ended for the year. Until that time, she said, "simplify, simplify, simplify!"[5]

My third and final year as a Texas public school teacher I had the opportunity to build a visual arts program. I soon found myself shackled by TAAS once again, however, despite the fact that TAAS measures "math," "reading," and "writing," and the testing culture rarely allowed any overlap among or beyond these "skill-sets." Late in the spring semester in preparation for adding a second class to our newly implemented art program, the upper administration asked me to "frontload" TAAS objectives there too. Frustrated and disillusioned, I quit—beginning a PhD program with the certainty that college teachers did not have to struggle under such oppressively standardized conditions. In fact, my first tenure-track position was directing a writing center and a basic writing program at a public university in Texas. I should have known better.

TESTING STANDARDS

From the Texas Higher Education Coordinating Board in 1985:
It is obvious that the first step in solving the basic skills problem is to identify those students who need help.
The only way to do this is to test them. (*A Generation of Failure* 8)

Susanmarie Harrington and Linda Adler-Kassner's review of basic writing scholarship (1998) reveals two distinct trends within the field: a "focus on the writers themselves and what happens in the act of composing" (9) and a "focus . . . on a sense of institutional or social culture" (12). As you may have already guessed, the current study is most concerned with the "institutional" and "social culture" surrounding the activity system that is basic writing. I am interested in helping to change the way literacy education functions and the way "basic writers" are defined, but I understand the limits of my own power to effect change, as Richard Miller insists I must. As he explains in *As If Learning Mattered*, "educational systems . . . have assumed a historically produced character that manifests itself in our time as an immensely complex bureaucracy with an inherent resistance to structural change" (23). Our situation is not altogether depressing, however, even in Texas, despite our regular diet of poisonous fare like standardized testing and "accountability" rhetoric. Teaching in the academy is fundamentally an activity shaped by and constrained by bureaucracy, particularly in basic writing programs, as we shall see. Thus, in order to affect change within this context, "students, teachers, and administrators must develop a sufficiently nuanced understanding of how power is disseminated in bureaucracy to see that *constraining* conditions are not *paralyzing* conditions" (Miller 211, emphasis in original). That's what I will attempt to do here.

Educational reform is a complex activity from any perspective, but it is a particularly complex one for those of us teaching in and otherwise responsible for basic writing programs. According to Keith Rhodes,

Bound up in curricular processes normally designed to retard changes, basic writing usually suffers further from being one of the few subjects in which nearly everyone has a stake, so that several layers of administrators often feel empowered to make decisions about it. As a site of complicated struggle, basic writing can be unusually difficult to change in small increments, and unusually subject to large-scale makeovers. It is highly likely that the current basic writing program at your school was put in place as part of a revolution of some kind, retaining in part the detritus of earlier revolutions. It can seem at times that no method can align all the stars and planets in such a way that any gradual improvement is possible. Further, writing professionals can't always integrate the revolutions they want, nor guide the results once things get going. (86)

Worse still, the mere existence of basic writing may signify changes the university culture and the general public may find difficult to accept, as Mina Shaughnessy and rest of the SEEK Program at City College discovered more than forty years ago. Adrienne Rich describes the program's precarious position thus:

> When I first went to teach at SEEK in the late sixties, conditions were better, less crowded: there was more money for SEEK itself. After Open Admissions, the overcrowding was acute. In the fall of 1970 we taught in open plywood cubicles set up in Great Hall; you could hear the noise from the other cubicles; concentration was difficult for students. I also remember teaching in basement rooms, overheated in winter to a soporific degree. My feeling was that the message was being sent that the new students were being no more than tolerated at CCNY; but also, of course, I could only respect their tenacity, working part time, with families, traveling for hours on the subway, and with barely any place to sit and talk or read between classes, none of the trappings of an "intellectual life" such as the Columbia students enjoyed a few miles downtown. (qtd. in Maher 109)

In fact, "Mina fought for space in every way she could" (qtd. in Maher 109). She fought for everything related to this program and continued access for writers denied admittance under the previous system. Despite her tremendous abilities as a persuasive writer and public speaker, despite her charm and unbelievably rigorous work ethic, despite the fact that she, as Mary Soliday explains, "lavishly documented student need in terms of error . . . Shaughnessy's program was radically downsized" (*The Politics of Remediation* 143). By 1976—in the wake of major budget cuts that led administrators to, among other things, fire nearly sixty faculty members (the majority of whom taught in Shaughnessy's SEEK program) and end the 125-year tradition of free tuition—SEEK was all but gone. As Janet Emig put it in her poignant obituary that appeared in the February 1979 issue of *College Composition and Communication*, "Mina lived long enough to watch [at] CUNY, her university, what many of us are watching at our own—the quite systematic dismantlement of what she had so laboriously built, to which she may have quite literally given her life. She was even asked to participate in the demise and destruction; for the Savage Seventies are nothing if not thorough in trying to divest us of our most hard-won beliefs and actions" (38).

Nearly twenty years later, City University's "remedial" population again gained national (and negative) attention, this time with James Traub's hugely popular *City on a Hill* (1994). As he explains, "City . . . has set itself the task of raising standards up to the level required for a college education [but] the promise not only to admit but to transform woefully undereducated students presses City to kneel down rather than to lift up" (191). From his study, he concludes that "City shouldn't be admitting these students because the experience isn't helping *them* [the students] enough. Perhaps City hasn't figured out how to help them, or perhaps, as I thought, their problems are too profound to be addressed in a college setting" (343). More recently, we have begun to hear echoes of the same rhetoric of exclusion, most clearly in response to the Secretary of Education's "Commission on the Future of Education" (2005). In the first "Issue Paper . . . released at the request of Chairman Charles Miller to inform the work of the Commission," Charles Miller and Cheryl Oldham "set the context" for this "National Dialogue" by declaring the very existence of basic writing as a major reason for American postsecondary education's "diminished capacity" (2006). As they explain, "[s]everal institutions of higher education are admitting students who lack adequate preparation for college-level work, thus expending precious resources in remediation." As our own institution struggles with the retention rates of our first-year students, faculty and administrators have begun to ask whether they should even be here. They are not, after all, "college material." In this climate, I fear that Secretary Spellings's "Commission" may soon force us to exclude an even greater number of minority and poor students in order to raise retention rates, in much the same way that Texas public schools raised test scores and graduation rates by dubious means: retaining students, moving at-risk students to special education, or perhaps even "suggesting" they attain General Education Diplomas (GED) instead. As Walt Haney, Linda McNeil, and others have revealed, such moves have not been uncommon as students in special education programs are not required to take and pass TAAS and those who drop out but obtain GEDs within a year will not be counted as "dropouts" on the school's performance record.

As Deborah Mutnick has argued, "To sanction 'low standards' is not the same as advocating for students located at the margins of society" (189). Neither is admitting and supporting students "located at the margins of society" the same thing as lowering standards. But still the debate between standards and access rages on. According to Mary Soliday, that persistent debate and its irreconcilability may be key reasons for the very existence of basic writing as an institution. In keeping with Miller's assertion that the institution itself is a sociohistorical construct that must be taken into consideration when advocating change, Soliday suggests that it is necessary for us to "understand the relationship between the politics of representation and access" and to recognize that "our courses have to perform a delicate balancing act . . . remaining mindful of the historically constricting role that skills instruction plays while also responding to a course's gatekeeping function within an institution" (*The Politics of Remediation* 144, 145).[7]

William Mayo founded the university where I teach on the promise that, as David Gold explains in his recent archival history of our early years (1889–1997), "any student [shall be] allowed to enter, despite his or her previous lack of training or ability to pay," and though we are not currently "Open Admissions," many of our students are first-generation college students from similar backgrounds. Thus, understandably, my colleagues often look to the basic writing program and the writing center I direct to "fix" those writers they understand to be "appallingly underprepared," and we feel compelled to do so. Our very existence grew from a philosophical framework most basic writing scholars cannot endorse, yet we leave ourselves vulnerable if we don't focus on "changing the writer" to meet the standards and codes of the academy.

Basic writing teachers and tutors in similar circumstances abound in community colleges and universities across the nation and are similarly charged with fixing the basic writing students' tendency to, as Mina Shaughnessy puts it, "leave a trail of errors behind him when he writes"—to teach them to perform in ways that take the shape their accusers assume literate ability should mimic. Even so, we understand that real writing instruction is not about repair work anymore than real writing is about rules. In her autoenthography "Writing on the Bias," Linda Brodkey makes a fascinating distinction between "school writing" and actual "writing":

> [S]chool writing is to writing as catsup is to tomatoes: as junk food is to food. What is nutritious has been eliminated (or nearly so) in processing. What remains is not just empty but poisonous fare because some people so crave junk food that they prefer it to food, and their preference is then used by those who, since they profit by selling us catsup as a vegetable and rules as writing, lobby to keep both on the school menu. (31)

The Way Literacy Lives explicitly challenges any sale of "rules as writing" by drawing attention to "the way literacy lives" in real-life contexts that extend far beyond the artificial ones often promoted in our schools and in political constructions of educational "reform."

TESTING THE TEACHER

Like so many writing program administrators (WPAs), I often find my quest to subvert problematic representations of literacy disrupted by the reality of my daily work and the fact that such representations far outnumber the ones composition scholars might endorse. While this experience may be a common one among WPAs in general, however, the distance between these perceptions seems all the more significant for those of us who direct basic writing programs, writing centers, and similar learning spaces. Despite the multiple and persuasive arguments against the validity of doing so, many "basic writers" continue to be identified by standards-based assessments of their reading and writing "skills," and basic writing classrooms continue to be dominated by skills-based instruction (Del Principe). Unfortunately—and, in my case, even by state mandate—those of us who know better are often no less constrained by the ubiquity of current-traditionalism in public representations of literacy learning. From 1989 to 2003, all Texas public colleges and universities were required to assess (via a "state-approved" test) every incoming first-year student in reading, writing, and math; writers failing the reading and/or writing sections were subsequently labeled "not ready for college-level literacy" and those of us directing basic writing programs at these institutions were required—again, by state law—to "remediate" them accordingly.[8]

Scores on these standardized tests are, in fact, improving ("The Texas Miracle")—even among minority populations in the state; however, critics like Stephen Klein (et al.), Angela V Valenzuela, and Linda McNeil insist that such "improvements" mask the material realities of student learning and achievement. According to McNeil and Valenzuela,

> TAAS is widening the gap between the education of children in Texas' poorest (historically low-performing) schools and that available to more privileged ones. . . . Our analysis reveals that behind the rhetoric of rising test scores are a growing set of classroom practices in which test-prep activities are usurping a substantive curriculum. These practices are more widespread in those schools where administrator pay is tied to test scores and where test scores have been historically low. These are the schools that are typically attended by children who are poor and African American or Latino, many are non-English-language dominant. These are the schools that have historically been underresourced. In these schools, the pressure to raise test scores "by any means necessary" has frequently meant that a regular education has been supplanted by activities whose sole purpose is to raise test scores on this particular test. Because teachers' and administrators' job rewards under the TAAS system of testing are aligned to children's test scores, the TAAS system fosters an artificial curriculum. It is a curriculum aimed primarily at creating higher test scores, not a curriculum that will educate these children for productive futures. The testing system distances the content of curriculum from the knowledge base of teachers and from the cultures and intellectual capacities of the children. It is creating an even wider gap between the curriculum offered to children in traditionally high-scoring schools (white, middle and upper-middle class) and those in typically minority and typically poor [schools]. . . . In the name of "alignment" between course curricula and test, *TAAS drills are becoming the curriculum in our poorest schools.* (5, emphasis mine)

And they are widening the gap between high school and college for those graduating from our poorest schools. Since Texas law requires only those students who do not score high enough on the TAAS[9] test to even take the TASP[10] exam and since TASP is very similar to TAAS, it seems only reasonable that much of the "damage" of the TAAS system of testing among college-bound students would show up in our basic writing classrooms as well. The same conditions that hijacked student opportunities for learning in high school are placing basic writers at an even greater disadvantage when they come to college.

Even though the TASP law was repealed in 2003, the logic that placed these writers via this system remains.[11] According to Deborah Mutnick (1995, 2000), making major changes in placement procedures seems unwise in an environment in which raising admission standards might be a more popular and likely choice than any placement procedure I might advocate. Recently, many colleges and universities across the nation have experienced such threats more directly—even those housing some of the most important programs in the history of basic writing (like City University of New York and the University of Minnesota-General College of Minnesota). These difficulties are likely to continue, making literacy instruction all the more complicated. As Richard Miller explains, nothing we do in the academy ever takes place "under conditions of complete freedom," as much as we'd like to believe otherwise. In fact, there are many "material, cultural, and institutional constraints that both define and confine all learning spaces" (7). It is in this environment that I continue to find myself asking how one can possibly effect change in a system so profoundly shaped by and dependent upon maintaining the status quo.

In *Basic Writing as a Political Act: Public Conversations about Writing and Literacies* (2002), Linda Adler-Kassner and Susanmarie Harrington examine just this question in their attempt to make sense of the very real "tensions between making basic writing a political act and doing so within institutional and social constraints that essentially work against politicizing the act of literacy development" (8). In their exploration of (1) how basic writers are portrayed in key scholarship, (2) how basic writers perceive themselves and their position as "basic" writers," (3) how they are portrayed in mainstream media, and (4) how their teachers represent them in their syllabi and other course materials, the authors reveal the complex ways in which the confusing "problem" of basic writers is generated and perpetuated by multiple artificial and conflicting narratives with narrators who seem largely unaware of one another. They contend that a more practical and at once more politicized solution is to bring all these conflicting narratives into conversation with one another, reminding ourselves "that basic writing, no matter how theorized or studied, is fundamentally a classroom-based enterprise" (97). I argue that this conversation must begin in the classrooms and other learning spaces over which we have some control, even when we may feel ourselves without the power to determine who should populate those spaces. Thus, at the levels of curriculum, tutor training, and teacher training, the basic writing program at Texas A&M-Commerce attempts to circumvent problematic representations of literacy in ways that "politicize" basic writing without making it unnecessarily vulnerable[12] to the arbitrary systems of institutionalized oppression that claim to "identify" those "not ready for college-level literacy."

PLACING BASIC WRITERS

High-stakes testing has been an integral part of Texas education for some time, so many accept it as a given (and unchangeable) part of the power landscape. As explained above, at A&M-Commerce, not unlike most Texas state colleges and universities, "basic writers" are those who have failed either the "reading" or the "writing" portions of the state-mandated, "objective" test *Texas Higher Education Assessment* (THEA), formerly the *Texas Academic Skills Program* (TASP).[13] As I've already pointed out, the test that places students in basic writing works from a very different set of assumptions than the courses that make up the program itself.[14] As explained on the *THEA Test Home Page*, "The purpose of the test . . . is to assess the reading, mathematics, and writing skills first year students should have if they are to perform effectively in undergraduate certificate or degree programs in Texas public colleges and universities." The literacy skills deemed necessary to function in college include the following: (1) "determine the meaning of words and phrases," (2) "understand the main idea and supporting details in written material," (3) "identify a writer's purpose, point of view, and intended meaning," (4) "recognize effective organization in writing," (5) "recognize effective sentences," and (6) "recognize edited American English usage." These skills (among others) are determined by multiple-choice, "objective" questions participants are expected to answer in a timed environment (five hours for all three sections), despite the fact that, as the CCCC Position Statement on Assessment reminds us, "choosing a correct response from a set of possible answers is not composing" ("Writing Assessment"). In addition to these multiple-choice questions, students are expected to develop a "writing sample" that must exhibit high levels of "competency" in the following areas: (1) appropriateness, (2) unity and focus, (3) development, (4) organization, (5) sentence structure, (6) usage, and (7) mechanical conventions ("Section II: TASP Skills").

Each of the items listed here represents literacy as what Lauren B. Resnick calls "a bundle of skills." Of course, motivations for assessing writers according to their ability to "recognize effective sentences" and "identify a writer's purpose, point of view, and intended meaning" are based on an understanding that those who fail to do so on a "standardized" assessment in decidedly sterile conditions will not be able to do so in a college classroom, where circumstances are much more variable and problematic. Logically, then, these writers and readers should be marked "basic writer" and "remediated" until they are able to "recognize edited American English usage" and the rest. As Resnick explains,

> If literacy is viewed as a bundle of skills, then education for literacy is most naturally seen as a matter of organizing effective lessons: that is, diagnosing skills, strengths, and deficits, providing appropriate exercises in developing felicitous sequences, motivating students to engage in these exercises, giving clear explanations and directions. (3)

Before I arrived on our campus in 2001 to direct the writing center and the basic writing program, a rather progressive curriculum was already in place—one deeply informed by border pedagogy and the basic writing program model at the University of Pittsburgh as portrayed by David Bartholomae and Anthony Petrosky's *Facts, Artifacts, and Counterfacts* (1986). Students were required to work with complex texts like Mary Shelly's *Frankenstein* and Neil Postman's *Amusing Ourselves to Death* and to produce sophisticated essays in response to these texts via sequenced assignments organized around a course theme like "identity" or "growth."

In almost every way, the basic writing program worked directly against the problematic representations of literacy I have attempted to challenge in the previous pages. However, despite the fact that the curriculum itself was rooted in a pedagogy of liberation, standardized testing remained an integral part of outcomes assessment. Students were required to pass a TASP-like examination in reading and writing before they would be allowed to "pass" English 100. Much like the TAAS system in the public schools, students who failed to pass the exit test would "fail" basic writing and be required to repeat it, even if their scores on everything else were excellent. They had many chances to retake the test, both at midterm and again near the end of the term, but that flexibility, though admirable, meant that in the meantime these students lost about three weeks of "real" instruction. Those responsible for implementing this exit criteria argued that because these students' scores on TASP placed them in basic writing in the first place, it only seemed appropriate—and, it turns out, the previous directors assumed it to be state law (as did I)—that such writers be assessed again at the end of the course to ensure their work in the course was worthwhile. And that their experiences in basic writing were, in the words of the Commission on the Future of Higher Education, of "added value." It was also assumed that since the course itself was much more intellectually demanding than the TASP test could ever hope to be, those students doing well with the rest of the course activities should easily pass TASP. The problem with this logic is, as Dennis Baron points out in his response to the Commission on the Future of Higher Education, standardized testing presumes a standard body of skills and knowledge that's being tested. In writing, this is certainly not the case. It's not in reading either. By all assessments, literacy practices are those which are situated in actual school and out-of-school contexts, not those gleaned from asking students to pick out the grammatical errors or to reorder the sentences in paragraphs that only exist on standardized tests or in study guides for taking standardized tests.

Applying a national "standard" as exit criteria for a specific course is inappropriate, but I can certainly see why my predecessors felt they had no other choice. In fact, our reading of the TASP law presumed the very same thing and thus required that all students "retake" TASP until they passed it, regardless of their performance in the classroom.

The year before I arrived, I'm happy to say, the State of Texas had already begun to offer public universities a little more freedom than previous administrators had experienced. In 2000, TASP law was supplemented with the "B or better rule." That meant that students earning a "B or better" in a handful of preapproved, college-level, writing-intensive courses would *not* be required to retake and pass TASP. I took that opportunity (after only one semester under the old system) to remove the TASP-like exit exam from our basic writing program and implement instead an exit portfolio graded by a panel of readers, thus preserving the credibility of true standards offered under the previous system but regaining some levels of pedagogical consistency between curriculum and assessment measures.[15] Thus today, even as these students were placed in our basic writing program according to assessment measures representing literacy as a "bundle of skills," the program itself deliberately circumvents the validity of such representations.

THEORETICAL JUSTIFICATION

It is from within this politically and ideologically charged space that the curriculum driving our basic writing program at A&M-Commerce emerged. Over the past few years, my teaching and administrative work have become increasingly affected by regular attempts to circumvent current-traditional representations of literacy and my growing appreciation of vernacular literacies—video game literacies, Star Trek literacies, and comic book literacies, among others—as represented not only by our students but also in, among other things, Deborah Brandt's *Literacy in American Lives* (2001), Cynthia Selfe and Gail Hawisher's *Literate Lives in an Information Age: Narratives of Literacy from the United States* (2004) and *Gaming Lives* (2007), Steven Johnson's *Everything Bad Is Good for You: How Today's Popular Culture Is Actually Making Us Smarter* (2005), and, especially, work in the New Literacy Studies (like James Paul Gee's *What Video Games Have to Teach Us About Literacy and*

Learning [2003] and *Situated Language and Learning: A Critique of Traditional Schooling* [2004]). According to these and similar studies in multiple literacies, even the most conservative readings of literacy have to accept that literacy itself has changed and, as the world moves from a print-based culture to a digital one, it will only continue to change. All this makes teaching writing much more complicated than ever before, but knowing this better enables me to make deliberate use of the literacies my students already possess, even those students populating our basic writing classes. The trick is helping these writers figure out how to use what they already know to learn what they don't yet know: often the language of the academy. That's the primary objective of the current study and the basic writing program on which it is based.

As I continue to take vernacular literacies seriously, I have been amazed to find the intellectual rigor and rhetorical sophistication embedded in rhetorical spaces that extend beyond the academy, especially those spaces rarely understood to have anything to do with the kinds of writing students are expected to do at school. This growing knowledge and the conservative political climate in which those of us committed to representing literacy differently often find ourselves have led me to develop what I call a "pedagogy of rhetorical dexterity"—that is, a pedagogical approach that develops in students the ability to effectively read, understand, manipulate, and negotiate the cultural and linguistic codes of a new community of practice based on a relatively accurate assessment of another, more familiar one.

CONTEXT AND RELEVANCE

What's original about a pedagogy of rhetorical dexterity is not the basic assumption that, as Katherine Schultz and Glenda Hull put it, "literacy is not literacy is not literacy" (19), or that academic literacies (standard edited English) have much more academic and social currency than vernacular ones (Street; Gee; Purves and Purves; Lu "Redefining"). I'm not the first to assert that basic writers have their own expertise and should be encouraged to draw from them (Soliday, "Toward a Consciousness"; Eleanor and Zamel; Mahiri; Marinara), nor am I the only scholar to argue that basic writers are only "basic writers" within the system that identified them as such (Fox; Horner; Soliday, *The Politics of Remediation*; Lu and Horner; Hindman; Hilgers; by implication, Huot; Bartholomae, "The Tidy House").

The innovation of this approach is in the ways I propose to teach those writers labeled "basic" to value their expertise, abilities Eleanor and Zamel have called "competencies" but that I will call here "literacies." In doing so, we pay particular attention to our students' experiences with more vernacular literacies like those associated with work (waiting tables, styling hair, building homes, designing webpages) and leisure (quilting, painting, hunting).[16] A pedagogy of rhetorical dexterity thus enables us to represent literacy differently—to basic writers, to tutors, to basic writing teachers, and, through them, to those representing literacy beyond our learning spaces. Via a pedagogy of rhetorical dexterity, I have chosen to shape "instruction that enables students to understand how definitions of literacy are shaped by communities, how literacy, power, and language are linked, and how their myriad experiences with language (in and out of school) are connected to writing" (Adler-Kassner and Harrington 98).

External, state-mandated measures mark these writers as "basic" writers, and our basic writing program accepts this designation—not because we agree with it but because Texas law demands it. Not unlike many composition teacher-scholars, rather than quietly submitting to such arbitrary standards, we make the political dimensions visible by treating literacy differently, not as a "bundle of skills" but as a situated, people-oriented activity governed by "rules" established and maintained by insiders—members of the target community of practice. In doing so, we treat literacy not as an abstract set of rigid "standards" and "rules" but rather as a blend of mutable, social forces that are deeply situated in time and place.

GOALS AND THEORETICAL FRAMEWORK

In training tutors and teachers to work with basic writing students and in speaking with colleagues about what these writers need, I have found myself frustrated time and again with the ways in which this culture of testing seems to have contributed to what activity theorists Jean Lave and Etienne Wenger call "the commoditization of learning," a phenomenon they argue

> engenders a fundamental contradiction between the use and exchange values of the outcome of learning, which manifests itself in conflicts between learning to know and learning to display knowledge for evaluations. . . . Test taking then becomes a new parasitic practice, the goal of which is to increase the exchange value of learning independently of its [real] value. (112)

According to Brian V. Street, literacy itself has been treated in much the same way, a phenomenon he calls the "pedagogization of literacy." By this he draws attention to the ways in which "literacy has become associated with educational notions of Teaching and Learning and with what teachers and pupils do in schools, at the expense of the many other uses and meanings of literacy evident from comparative ethnographic literature." In this sense, "pedagogy . . . has taken on the character of an ideological force controlling social relations in general and conceptions of reading and writing in particular" (Social Literacies 106, 107). Adler-Kassner and Harrington discovered something similar in their survey of public attitudes of literacy, something they call the "school-success narrative."

> At its heart is a familiar theme: A college education is the stepping-off point for entrance into middle-class society, and obtaining this education will ensure that students will participate in the perpetuation of that society and its values. A central requirement of getting this education is amassing and reproducing objective literacy skills, which help to ensure that students are learning the appropriate material to facilitate participation in middle-class life. (62)

Working against this "school-success narrative" perpetuated by the "pedagogization of literacy," this book has been quite deliberately influenced by my attempts to circumvent the literacy myths that lead to so many misconceptions about what basic writing students can do and what they need, especially inasmuch as the writing center and the basic writing program I direct are charged with "fixing" these problem writers, just as nearly every other writing center and basic writing program across the country is similarly charged.

This is a book, then, that attempts to force to the surface the intellectual viability of alternative literacies. *The Way Literacy Lives* works consciously against standards-based assessments of literate practices dominating most commonsense approaches to literacy learning while recognizing that such assessments and perspectives are always already a major part of any attempt to teach and learn school literacies. By recognizing and making explicit to students the ubiquity of autonomous models of literacy, the current study promotes a more context-based understanding of the multiple literacies available to writers—a more realistic picture of the way literacy lives.

In other words, if "literate ability" is something that's context-dependent (as many argue it is), then what's it take to be literate in contexts that may be more familiar to our students than they are to us? For example, what's it take to be *video game literate*? There are certainly some "skills" that most gamers possess, including, at the very least, the ability to punch the right buttons at the right times in order to achieve the appropriate and desired response (to jump, perhaps), "read" and comprehend the primary objectives of the game as scripted by the designer, and transfer (and often adjust) these literate practices to new video games with new objectives and new responses triggered by the same buttons used before (shooting rather than jumping, for example).

The Way Literacy Lives is based in part on our basic writing program, which is designed to help learners (1) recognize "other," "vernacular," or "marginalized" literacies as valid so they can begin to (2) draw from them as they learn what it means to write for college audiences—audiences far less unified or predictable than the literacy-as-universal-standard model allows.

The theoretical framework for this book relies on three, overlapping theoretical traditions: the New Literacy Studies (NLS), activity theory, and critical literacy. As Brian V. Street defines it,

What has come to be termed the "New Literacy Studies" (NLS) (Gee, 1991; Street, 1996) represents a new tradition in considering the nature of literacy, focusing not so much on acquisition of skills, as in dominant approaches, but rather on what it means to think of literacy as a social practice (Street, 1985). This entails the recognition of multiple literacies, varying according to time and space, but also contested in relations of power. NLS, then, takes nothing for granted with respect to literacy and the social practices with which it becomes associated, problematizing what counts as literacy at any time and place and asking "whose literacies" are dominant and whose are marginalized or resistant. (Street, "What's 'New' in New Literacy Studies?" 1)

In other words, NLS is primarily concerned with the way literacy manifests itself in various out-of-school contexts. To a great extent, the New London Group—especially as represented by James Paul Gee and Brian V. Street—is primarily concerned with exposing the artificiality of school literacies. According to New Literacy Studies scholars Cope and Kalanowitz,

Language discourse and register differences are markers of lifeword differences (work, interest and affiliation, ethnicity, sexual identity). As lifewords become more divergent and their boundaries more blurred, the central fact of language becomes the multiplicity of meanings and their continual intersection. Just as there are multiple layers to everyone's identity, there are multiple discourses of identity and multiple discourses of recognition to be negotiated. We have to be proficient as we negotiate the many lifewords each of us inhabits, and the many lifeworlds we encounter in our everyday lives. This creates a new challenge for literacy pedagogy. (17)

The NLS redefines literacy education as a matter of reading and negotiating various contextualized forces that are deeply embedded in identify formation, political affiliations, material and social conditions, and ideological frameworks. In doing so, it necessarily flattens hierarchies among literacies—where one literacy is inherently more significant or valuable than another—as the value of one literacy over another can only be determined by its appropriateness to context.

Relationships among those marked "illiterate" in one context and literate in another become increasingly important—as do those between agents marked "basic writer" in school contexts—when we understand that these same individuals are likely considered highly literate in one or more contexts *beyond* school. As NLS scholar Alan Rogers points out,

In the NLS, the relationships between the literate and illiterate become important. . . . It is a relationship of power; the "literate" have excluded the "illiterate" from their society and will only include them on the condition

> that the "illiterate" acquire the same literacy as the so-called "literate" pos-
> sess—attitudes which many of the non-literate members of society have
> internalized, so that they see themselves as deficient and excluded. (208)

The real problem, according to the NLS perspective, lies not in the basic
writer's inability to conform to standards or even their inability to develop
discourse academic communities recognize as appropriate, but rather in our
very definitions of what it means to be literate—how literacy functions in
society and how it comes to mean. The focus of rhetorical dexterity is not fixing deficits in these basic writers (as none are recognized as "deficit") or push-
ing forward a new world order (though I certainly wouldn't mind). Instead,
rhetorical dexterity attempts to develop in writers the ability to negotiate the
school literacies celebrated in the current social order in ways that are as ethical and meta-aware as possible. We begin this process by articulating the
ways in which what they already know well may help them learn what is, as
of yet, less familiar to them.

Building on Shirley Brice Heath's notion of "literacy events" as useful
foci in ethnographic studies of the social function of reading and writing,
Brian V. Street (2001) rearticulates the concept in ways I think new literacy
learners will find quite useful.

> If you were to observe this literacy event as a non-participant who was not
> trained in its conventions and rules, you would have difficulty following
> what is going on, such as how to work with the text and to talk around it.
> There are clearly underlying conventions and assumptions around the liter-
> acy event that make it work. (11)

However, he encourages us to consider these "underlying conventions
and assumptions" in terms of "literacy *practices*" rather than literacy "events":
"The concept of literacy practices attempts both to handle the events and the
patterns around literacy and to link them to something broader of a cultural
and social kind. . . . Literacy practices, then, refer to this broader cultural conception of particular ways of thinking about and doing reading and writing"
(11). As mentioned previously, it is important for us to expand the term "literacies" to encompass those social functions that extend beyond reading and
writing. In *Social Literacies: Critical Approaches to Literacy in Development,
Ethnography, and Education* (1995), however, Street warns us about stretching
the usefulness of this term "literacy" too thin as it may lead researchers "to
the reification of an autonomous model of literacy" (135). In terms of a
research model, Street may not like the way I am using "literacy" to determine "competence" or "skill" in a particular community, but I am focusing on
these "skills" and "competencies" as they are labeled and validated by other
members of the community; thus, I believe that this conceptualization of literate practice does not separate the language from the situation in which it is

used, which is Street's primary objection to this conceptualization.[17] I agree that such a use of the term "literate" may lead to the reification of an autonomous model of literacy if we are talking about a researcher (as an outsider or an insider) investigating a community in order to determine the terms of literacy in that community of practice when the "community" is drawn together by a particular activity (like chess, Star Trek, or composition studies) rather than broader and deeper social and political connections such as "home" or "family." However I don't think this would be so for a student acquiring new literacies. One may argue that the process of rhetorical dexterity is without immediate scholarly value but it does have immediate *pedagogical* value to new literacy learners.

Thus, the primary objective of rhetorical dexterity is to enable writers to make use of an ideological model of literacy as they negotiate ever-changing rhetorical situations rather than continue to force different rhetorical situations to conform to the autonomous model of traditional literacy education has trained them to accept. Doing so requires that we not only challenge the artificial binary between the "literate" and the "illiterate" but begin to understand literacy itself as an activity system.

Activity theory has its roots in Vygotskian psychology and is largely concerned with human practice as an "activity system." David Russell was the first to bring activity theory to composition studies, making clear the ways in which this theoretical framework may enable us to "create . . . a longer and wider network of disciplinary influence (power), [but] . . . only if we know more about . . . writing processes in many social practices, many systems of activity, many genres" ("Activity Theory and Process Approaches" 87). As Russell explains it in his earlier article, "Activity Theory and Writing Instruction" (1995),

> Activity theory analyzes human behavior and consciousness in terms of *activity systems*: goal-directed, historically situated, cooperative human interactions, such as a child's attempt to reach an out-of-reach toy, a job interview, a "date," a social club, a classroom, a discipline, a profession, an institution, a political movement, and so on. The activity system is the basic unit of analysis for both cultures' and individuals' psychological and social processes. . . . Activity systems are historically developed, mediated by tools, dialectically structured, analyzed as the relationship of participants and tools, and changed through *zones of proximal development*. (54–55, emphasis in original)

Whereas NLS focuses mostly on the *social* nature of literacy, activity theory emphasizes the goal-oriented behaviors that make up the activity system we call "literacy." When literacy is understood as a social practice, however, activity theory requires us to examine the social contexts in which these activities are mediated and reproduced. Thus, the current study examines the ways in which literacy is a social practice and, therefore, deeply situated and context dependent. Chapter 5, "The Way Literacy (Re)produces," offers a much more detailed discussion of activity theory and its implications for basic writing.

The third theoretical framework shaping the current study is critical literacy, which, like NLS and activity theory, emphasizes the social nature of literacy as "learning to read and write is part of the process of becoming conscious of one's experience as historically constructed within specific power relations" (Anderson and Irvine 82). "When we are critically literate," Ira Shor explains, "we examine our ongoing development, to reveal the subjective positions from which we make sense of the world and act in it." As C. H. Knoblauch and Lil Brannon describe it in *Critical Teaching and the Idea of Literacy* (1993), the primary concern of critical literacy education is "the issue of representation, the practices by which people name and rename the world, negotiate the substance of social reality, and contest prior naming in favor of new or different ones." In chapter 3, "The Way Literacy Liberates," I will offer a much more extensive discussion of critical literacy and its implications for basic writing

DEFINING LITERACY

The primary objective of this book and, in fact, the program on which it is based is this: to help our students develop the flexibility and skill necessary to negotiate multiple, always changing literacies, learning to hone and apply rhetorical dexterity to increasingly complex rhetorical situations. In doing so, we are clearly expanding the definition of literacy to include those activities not typically considered to be "reading" or "writing" in any traditionally "valuable" sense. "She is always reading," I recently heard a parent say of her daughter, "but never anything *worthwhile*. Those damn teen magazines all the time! Ask her anything about Britney Spears, and she's a virtual encyclopedia. Ask her about the Civil War, and she comes up empty! Ask her history teacher; he'll tell you. Her head is *filled* with useless facts!" The NLS scholar James Paul Gee calls this attitude the "content fetish."

> The idea behind it is this: Important knowledge (now usually gained in school) is content in the sense of information rooted in, or, at least, related to, intellectual domains or academic disciplines like physics, history, art, or literature. Work that does not involve such learning is 'meaningless.' . . .
>
> The problem with the content view is that an academic discipline or any other semiotic domain, for that matter, is not primarily content, in the sense of facts and principles. *It is rather primarily a lived and historically changing set of distinctive social practices*. It is in these social practices that "content" is generated, debated, and transformed via certain distinctive ways of thinking, valuing, acting, and often, writing and reading. (*What Video Games* 21, emphasis mine)

To understand the parameters of this more social conceptualization of literacy, David Barton and Mary Hamilton suggest we consider "literate" behavior in terms of "discourse communities" rather than universal standards, which they define as "groups of people held together by their characteristic ways of talking, acting, valuing, interpreting, and using written language." For our purposes, "communities of practice" seem more appropriate than "discourse communities" because the former stresses literacy as an *activity* rather than a state of being (via membership or ability to meet universal standards).

"Communities of practice" are relations of people who have in common a "shared competence and mutual interest in a given practice" (Choi 143), whether repairing Xerox machines (see Orr 1996 and Brown and Duguid 1991), recovering from alcoholism (see Lave and Wenger, 1990), teaching writing, or countless other activities in which a person may be involved. The concept first emerged in Lave and Wenger's study of the ways in which various communities of practice teach newcomers the practices valued and reproduced in those communities (midwives, meat cutters, tailors, and recovering alcoholics in Alcoholics Anonymous).[18] According to Lave and Wenger, a "community of practice is a set of relations among persons, activity, and world over time and in relation with other tangential and overlapping communities of practice." The term "impl[ies] participation in an activity system about which participants share understandings concerning what they are doing and what that means in their lives and for their communities" (98). Embedded in activity theory are two, complementary assumptions: (1) language, literacy, and learning are embedded in communities of practice rather than entirely within the minds of individuals; and (2) communities reproduce themselves through social practices. When these social practices become routinized and interrelated ("just the way things are done") within a community of practice, they may be understood as part of an activity *system*.

In any given community of practice—be it factory work or fishing, Xerox repair or midwifery, evangelism or a particular basic writing program or classroom—some activities will be understood as "appropriate" and others largely inappropriate, and the majority of these activities cannot be understood apart from the activity *system* in which these actions are perpetuated. That is, actions considered "typical" or otherwise valuable in a given community of practice become a part of the activity system representing that community. These systems are social and cultural rather than individual and objective in that any activity system is made up of groups of individuals who sanction and endorse particular ways of doing things and particular results, identifying some results and processes as innovative and valuable and condemning others as ineffective, inappropriate, or even unacceptable. Thus, Cindy may not be "literate" in terms recognizable to her history teacher and the relevant communities of practice with which he is associated, but she is highly literate in this aspect of preteen culture and the associated communities (those overlapping communities that may be affiliated with *Seventeen* magazine and television shows aimed at this viewing audience like *Degrassi* and other such shows on cable channels like *Noggin*).

Literate practices, at least the way I am using the term here, refer to those sanctioned and endorsed by others recognized as literate members of a particular community of practice. Like any community, the "literate practices" of preteen popular culture are "sanctioned and endorsed" by other literate members. Those of us who are not literate members of this particular community of practice are less likely to be able to tell the difference between someone who knows quite a lot about Britney Spears and her music and someone who is just pretending to know it.

Unless we are comparing very similar communities, however, the *points of contact* will likely be limited at first. *Points of dissonance* refers to those points of *difference* between two different communities of practice—points that confuse or disorient literacy learners. In learning new literacies, for example, Cindy is likely to find many characteristics of the new community that are at odds with those of her more familiar literacies. Specifically, as seems likely, the "ideologies" informing *Seventeen* are unlikely to mimic those of academic discourse—at least not at first glance, as we will discuss in later chapters.

Helping our students develop *rhetorical dexterity* is the primary objective of our basic writing program and the current project. I am not necessarily expecting these writers to develop full-blown, "objective" ethnographic studies of their familiar communities of practice, but I argue that we must routinely and explicitly validate the complex systems in which these students are already considered literate by taking them seriously and asking our students to do the same.

BASIC STRUCTURE

I began with a deep description of the local conditions in which our basic writing program functions and, in doing so, make the claim that such conditions must be understood when undertaking any new programmatic or curricular approach. Building on projects like Adler-Kassner and Harrington's *Basic Writing as a Political Act* that urge researchers and teachers to "reorient the work of the basic writing class toward collaborative action with teacher and student," the current study describes and analyzes a curriculum designed to "help . . . students understand how to determine the literacy demands of new contexts (in and out of school)," a function that, they argue "should be the primary goal of any writing course, especially basic writing." They continue,

> Asking students to consider what counts as "good" literacy practices in a
> given context is the key to traveling literacy skills. Students who can move

into a new classroom—or any new setting—and suss out what are the favored forms for writing, what are the favored forms for investigation, and what are the key conventions for discourse are well on their way to writerly success. (Adler-Kassner and Harrington 102)

Given that much of the current project rests on an assumption that this autonomous model is pervasive and extremely problematic for basic writers in particular, I will spend the next chapter ("The Way Literacy Oppresses") exploring the ways in which the autonomous model of literacy shapes both public discourse about literacy education and the basic writer's perception of her own needs as a writer. In doing so, chapter 2 will attempt to illustrate the reasons why this perspective is both politically/ideologically oppressive and pedagogically unsound.

Chapter 3, "The Way Literacy Liberates," explores the various ways in which basic writing scholars have revised basic writing curricula in response to critical theories, a philosophical perspective that has become quite common among teacher-researchers in basic writing. According to Deborah Mutnick, "the point of composition instruction, including basic writing, is to equip students with literacy skills along with a critical-historical perspective on reading and writing in school, work, and everyday life" (xii) by teaching them to, in the words of Paulo Friere, "read the word and the world." I conclude chapter 3 with a description of a basic writing curriculum designed and executed via an explicitly critical framework, where the goal was to develop critical consciousness among those writers I believed to be constructed as "oppressed" and thus in need of liberation through critically aware literacy education. Student responses to the curriculum are included, especially as represented through the experiences of Ana, a blind student immigrant from Mexico—experiences that have led me to question the viability of critical literacy as a primary framework for basic writing.

In chapters 4–6, I articulate a new pedagogy and basic writing curriculum in which the primary goal is not "liberation" in any general sense but replacing the autonomous model of literacy with an ideological one—socially situated, people oriented, contextually bound. Here I offer illustrations of a variety of communities of practice seemingly unrelated to academic discourse and its practices. By articulating the anatomy of literacies associated with video games like *Halo 2* and jobs like bagging groceries, especially as they are described by students in our basic writing program, I hope to redefine expertise in ways students and teachers alike might find relevant to the academy.

More specifically, chapter 4, "The Way Literacy Stratifies," focuses on the unequal value of various literacies as the dominant, autonomous model reconstructs them, as well as the inequity of access to those literate strategies perpetuated by this autonomous model. The next chapter, "The Way Literacy (Re)produces" further establishes the theoretical framework of rhetorical dexterity by articulating the ways in which various communities of practice (re)produce themselves through literate actions. Chapter 6, "The Way Literacy Lives," describes a basic writing curriculum shaped by rhetorical dexterity, as well as various student responses to this curriculum.

Finally, in the concluding chapter, I will examine again our tendency to separate orality from literacy, often privileging the latter over the former, the "literate" over the "illiterate." Such separations are perpetuated by assumptions that a "Great Divide" exists between the literate and everyone else, and this myth places new literacy learners, like our basic writing students, at an unfair disadvantage. According to Brian V. Street, this myth is perpetuated by anthropologists like Goody (1968, 1977) who have "replace[d] the theory of a 'great divide' between 'primitive' and 'modern' culture . . . with the distinction between 'literate' and 'non-literate'" ("Autonomous Model" 3). When we close that Great Divide between the literate and the nonliterate— between the basic writers and everyone else—we can begin to understand how to readjust literacy education in ways that are much more equitable to all learners.

TWO

The Way Literacy Oppresses

So absolute is the importance of error in the minds of many writers that "good writing" to them means "correct writing," nothing more. . . .

Much about the "remedial" situation encourages this obsession with error. First, there is the reality of academia, the fact that most college teachers have little tolerance of the kinds of errors BW students make, that they perceive certain types of errors as indicators of ineducability, and that they have the power of the F. Second there is the urgency of the students to meet their teachers' criteria, even to request prescriptive teaching they have had before in the hopes that this time it might "take." Third, there is the awareness of the teacher and the administrator that remedial programs are likely to be evaluated (and budgeted) according to the speed with which they produce correct writers, correctness being a highly measurable feature of acceptable writing. (Shaughnessy, *Errors and Expectations* 8–9)

This is my very first sentence and I don't know how to begin it. (opening line of Lamonda's first formal essay)

SINCE THE VERY BEGINNING, basic writing has been an activity system charged with fixing "deficient," "deviant," or otherwise "broken" writers; however, unlike more traditional literacy models, Mina Shaughnessy's approach—like many who followed this basic writing pioneer—locates the basic writing students' problem not in the "trail of errors" they leave behind but in the potential causes of those errors. According to Shaughnessy, such errors are not the result of carelessness but rather evidence of a complex system of logic that conflicts with the one perpetuated in standard academic discourse. A few years later, Sondra Perl located the basic writer's difficulty not in the logic that yields surface-level errors but in his or her truncated writing process, an assertion Mike Rose extends in his study "Remedial Writing Courses: A Critique and a Proposal" (1983). As Rose explains, "remedial writing courses" frequently perpetuate the problem Sondra Perl's study uncovers, not only by offering writing activities that, in fact, often force these writers to abbreviate their writing processes but also by asking them to complete isolated tasks on simple topics, requiring few, if any, writing practices likely to be relevant to writing experiences beyond the remedial course itself.

When we understand basic writing as an activity system according to the theoretical framework offered by these early basic writing scholars, literacy becomes a matter of applying to a given writing project a more appropriate logic (according to Shaughnessy) or procedure (according to Perl and Rose). Thus, in an effort to make sense of basic writing as an activity system, it seems useful to identify the input, output, and tools used to accomplish said output. Accordingly Shaughnessy's model basic writing program might identify the *input* as an educable writer currently unfamiliar with the systems of logic that determine "correctness"; the *tools* might be the variety of exercises she offers in *Errors and Expectations* guided by a teacher who "grants students the intelligence and will they will need to master what is being taught" (292), and the *output* becomes a writer with "a readable expository style that will serve for courses and, later, for professional or civic writing assignments" (280). According to the model offered by Perl, the input is a writer obsessed with getting things right and, therefore, one who truncates the writing process; the tools are lessons in invention and other process-based activities; the output is a writer with a more sophisticated understanding of the writing process and an ability to apply it in a variety of rhetorical contexts.

More recently, according to Joseph Harris (1995), metaphors like "growth," "initiation," and "conflict" have dominated basic writing scholarship. The "growth" metaphor "involves a shift in focus from the language the writer" must master to the student herself who is "somehow stuck in an early stage of language development, their growth as language users stalled" (29). The "initiation" metaphor, on the other hand, suggests that the basic writer's problem is not her immature language use but rather language choices that, while quite appropriate in communities with which the writer may have greater familiarity, are largely inappropriate for this new, more academic context (Ferrell; Bizzell 1984, 1986; Bruffee 1984). In other words, the "academy form[s] a kind of 'discourse community' with its own distinctive way of using language" (30). Thus, according to David Bartholomae, basic writing teachers should help writers "invent the university," or a piece of it, in ways academic readers can hear, understand, and take seriously. In this initiation model, then, the *input* becomes a writer who "invents the university" in problematic ways and the *tools* a curriculum that—as described in the introduction to the popular textbook *Ways of Reading*—helps students understand how the work of an author can be used as a frame for reading and inter-preting the work of another, demonstrating the basic principle of a liberal arts education: students should be given the opportunity to adopt different points of view, including those of scholars and writers who have helped them shape modern thought. These kinds of assignments give [the basic writer] the chance, even as a novice, to try [her] hand at the work of pro-fessionals. (Bartholomae and Petrosky 287)

The *output*, according to Bartholomae's model, should then be a writer who can, in fact, "invent the university" like an insider.

Metaphors like growth and initiation permeate basic writing discourse, yet, as Carol Severino suggests (1992), such metaphors are problematic: all "growth" here is confined to the student (not the teacher) and "initiation" to a basic writ-ing student joining the "in-group" (not the teacher making any move to learn about the discourse communities in which the writer is already a member). According to Severino, "the problem" with what she calls "transportation" and "club/in-group metaphors" "is that they are unidirectional and don't allow for the integration of home and school literacies" (9). The only traveler is the stu-dent; the only club worth joining is the one in which the teacher is already a member. As Mina Shaughnessy puts it, basic writers are "aliens . . . unacquainted with the rules and rituals of college life" (*Errors and Expectations* 40). Rarely are we as teachers placed in anything like the "alien world" Deborah Mutnick describes from the basic writer's point of view (*Writing in an Alien World*), yet we require this "alien" worldview from basic writers all the time.

At the root of much of the aforementioned scholarship is a series of assumptions about the way literacy functions, assumptions that some have argued work against warrants guiding the majority of current scholarship in basic writing, scholarship that openly resists arguments that fail to consider the material, social, political and cultural conditions shaping basic writers. These assumptions, which will be discussed at much greater length in chap-ter 4, include the following:

- Literacy is a fundamental prerequisite for individual progress.
- Literacy education is equally accessible and relevant to all who want it and, once acquired, all literate individuals hold equal value to society at large.
- Literacy has a constant value. In other words, once literate *always* literate.
- Literacy skills are autonomous and completely portable. When one is con-sidered literate in one context, one can expect those skills to serve one equally well in all other contexts.

An autonomous model perpetuates these myths, and I concur with the conclu-sions Adler-Kassner and Harrington draw from their analysis of key scholarship in the field: many of these same assumptions continue to guide our work with basic writers.

Conflict metaphors, most famously articulated and perpetuated in the scholarship of Min-Zhan Lu and Bruce Horner, work against several of these assumptions by drawing attention to the inequitable material and cultural conditions in which language operates. As Lu and Horner explain in *Representing the "Other"* (1999), "Basic Writing discourse has been trapped through its attempts to understand and justify the teaching of basic writing by imagining basic writers as beginners growing cognitively or as aliens becoming initiated into a specific discourse community" (xvii). Thus "growth" metaphors perpetuate an "'essentialist view of language, holding that the essence of meaning precedes and is independent of language (see Lu, "Redefining" 26), whereas "initiation" metaphors perpetuate "a view of 'discourse communities' as 'discursive utopias,' in each of which a single, unified, and stable voice directly and completely determines the writings of all community members (see Harris, "The Idea" 12)" (Lu 32). However, language is not neutral or innocent but instead political and deeply biased and "discourse communities" are not "discrete and autonomous entities . . . [but] rather . . . interactive cultural forces" (Lu 38). Therefore, rather than attempting to "'cure' all signs of conflict and struggle," Lu argues, "we need to find a way of foregrounding conflict and struggle not only in the generation of meaning or authority but of conventions of 'correctness' in syntax, spelling, punctuation, traditionally considered the primary focus of Basic Writing instruction" (55).

Carol Severino (1992), Mary Soliday, and Deborah Mutnick (1995), among others, offer some exciting, alternative ways we might conceive of the basic writing classroom and the work we do as basic writing teachers—not as a space to teach these writers to mimic the language conventions of the academy (perspectives guided by metaphors of growth and initiation) but to change academic discourse and ways of knowing. Thus, the *input* becomes not the writer but the language-use conventions of the academy; the *tool*, the marginalized or nonmainstream writer with double-consciousness (based on multiple, overlapping language and cultural experiences) and curricular choices that honor and extend into academic prose this double-consciousnesses; and the *output*, more flexible, relevant language-use conventions that accurately reflect the diversity entering our universities and making up the communities beyond the academy (see, especially, Soliday).

Despite the important ways metaphors of conflict challenge the inequitable power relations implicit in much literacy education, however, I continue to find such metaphors problematic in that they leave the autonomous model intact by treating literacy itself as an inherent good. The autonomous model is pervasive—in the academy, in the mainstream media, in our basic writer's literacy histories—and, as I will argue in the current chapter, this model, while inaccurate, is likely to continue shaping our students' approaches to literacy practices unless and until we draw their attention to its inaccuracy. Thus, following an exploration of landmark scholarship in literacy studies that illustrates the way literacy functions in several out-of-school contexts and a review of recent public discourse about literacy and literacy education, the current chapter builds on Adler-Kassner and Harrington's study by analyzing this autonomous model as an activity system in order to better understand the literate practices advocated in this scholarship and how they may be compared with those advocated in public discourse and invalidated by key findings in literacy studies. Finally, I will examine the ways in which an autonomous model of literacy education often shapes the basic writer's understanding of how literacy functions and, therefore, complicates and, at times, thwarts their abilities to acquire new literacies.

LITERACY IN OUT-OF-SCHOOL CONTEXTS

In Brazil, ten- to twelve-year-old, largely illiterate candy vendors with little or, for the most part, *no* formal education have devised rather complex mathematical systems for determining appropriate purchase costs from wholesalers and sale prices likely to offer adequate profit for the vendor while remaining competitive enough among other venders to attract new customers—and all of this within an infrastructure of wildly fluctuating inflation rates (see Saxe). Miles away and several years earlier, Sylvia Scribner and Michael Cole's study of the "literate" and cognitive activities among a small Liberian population find that in their everyday lives the literate "Vai people" had little reason to use their ability to encode and decode print, a conclusion directly in conflict with many Western arguments for the value of literacy education.[1] The study further proved that "there is not one literacy but many literacies, each acquired as a functional adaptation to a particular social need" (William 48). In America in the 1990s, Juliet Merrifield, Mary Beth Bingman, David Hemphill, and Kathleen P. Bennett deMarrais's profiles of twelve diverse individuals showed us how people with "limited literacy skills"[2] are able to negotiate a largely print-based society in many of the ways alarmist literature about the literacy crisis tell us they cannot—they hold jobs, pay taxes, value education, support their school-age children in their efforts to "improve" themselves; very few of the people profiled in this study take any form of government assistance; most pride themselves in being completely independent.[3]

Despite mounting evidence to the contrary, illiteracy is regularly promoted as a one-way ticket to a life of failure and dependency. Speaking of an upcoming "Celebration of Reading" in Dallas, Texas (2002), former First Lady Barbara Bush, "a longtime champion for family literacy," shares this about the consequences of illiteracy: "a lot of people in America can't read well enough to cope. They can't get jobs. And they don't have the dignity and the joy of reading" (qtd. in Thomas). A recent *Dallas Morning News* article offers this similarly chilling (though largely commonplace) argument:

> While most of us don't think about it, literacy determines how we interact with much of the world. People who can't read may not be able to obtain employment or may end up working in low-paying jobs with few or no benefits. Parents who can't read instructions on a medicine bottle may not be able to dispense medication to their children. . . . The examples of literacy's impact on our lives go on and on. (Pena)

Many of our basic writers agree with this assessment of literacy. For Gerrell, the difference between literacy and the alternative might be a matter of basic *survival*:

> If Ms. Fields [his fourth grade teacher] wasn't there to teach me literacy, I probably could have lost my life. . . . If there was a sign in public that said, "Take one and you will die" and I think it meant take one it's free, I would lose my life. Simply because I couldn't read or understand the sign and no one to help me understand or read it for me.[4] (WA3, 2)

In my home state of Texas, half the entire population of adults has been marked as unable to "cope" according to the data a national assessment of literacy was able to extract from their literate lives. According to the 2004 *Community Needs Assessment Update* (compiled and published by the United Way of Metropolitan Dallas), Texas is slightly above the national average in the percentage of individuals over sixteen years old with Adult Literacy Estimates at Levels 1 and 2 (49 percent United States, 51 percent Texas).[5] That means that according to the Adult and Family Literacy Indicators they used, more than half of the Texas population and nearly 47 percent of the Dallas County population would fall into the category of adults Mrs. Bush says "can't cope." This survey, conducted in 1992 by National Institute for Literacy, reports that "Level I and II individuals usually can sign their name, total a bank deposit slip, identify a country in a short article, [and] locate a piece of information in a sports article [or] . . . the expiration date on their driver's license." However, they usually cannot "locate eligibility from a table of employee benefits, total costs from an order, locate an intersection on a street map, fill out a government benefits application, locate two pieces of information in a sports article, [or] understand an appliance warranty" (IV–11).

As Arlene Fingeret's study "Social Network: A New Perspective on Independence and Illiterate Adults" (1983) implies, however, unemployed, functionally illiterate individuals are more likely to rely on someone who can read these ads (a friend or relative, a career counselor at the local unemployment office) rather than fail to look for a job; the parent is more likely to refer to the doctor who prescribed the medicine or the pharmacist who filled it to determine how "to dispense medication to their children" rather than to remain "unable" to do so.[6] According to this researcher,

> People do not need to identify literacy "problems" in order to get a friend to help understand a tax form or to have the railway official write out some train times. We all do this and there are particular people used for support who we can regard as brokers for literacy activities. It may be a neighbour or a friend who deals with figures or fills in the forms. It may be institutionalised, the railway officials who look up train times, the travel agents who fill in holiday forms for customers. (qtd. in Barton 202)

These are exactly the kinds of strategies one of my students (Stephen Williams) tells me his former coworker has been relying on for all of his working life. In his final paper for a basic writing course last fall (2006), Stephen introduced me to Randy, a "journey lineman that ran a bucket truck" with whom Stephen "once worked . . . at FEC Electric." As Stephen explains, "[Randy] was 'the Man' when it came to doing energized line work. He was also the man that was to teach us 'grunts' how to be lineman" (1). A whiz with mathematics—a particularly valuable trait given the fact that, according to Stephen, "Electricity is nothing but numbers"—Randy advanced through the ranks rather quickly and, by the time Stephen met him, this trait and his twenty years' experience in the field had made Randy the "best lineman that they had"—and the most highly paid.

But while he was, "by far, the most literate lineman the company had" (Williams 5), Randy could neither read nor write, at least not in the traditional sense of encoding and decoding print-based texts. Every night his wife completed his "time sheet" (a very detailed "daily record of activities"); every day Randy used the linemen with whom he worked (his "crew") to make sense of the "job order sheet" that outlined his duties for the day. As Randy explained it to Stephen one day when he asked him how he was able to make sense of the job order sheet when he couldn't read a word of it, "That's what I have you for!" Randy may have been illiterate when we measure these literacies via the "autonomous model" Brian V. Street tells us is artificial and largely irrelevant to daily life; however, Randy was, nevertheless, *highly* literate.

The conclusions Stephen draws from his experiences with Randy offer for basic writing students—and, by extension, their teachers—some rather telling advice: "Remember, you are good at a lot more than you are not good at. I'm sure a lot of the guys made fun [of Randy]. What he did was showed them a thing or two. By overcoming his shortcomings of not being able to read or write with being a literate lineman and a w[h]iz in math, he was able to surpass all of his coworkers on the pay scale" (5–6). Randy's story (through Stephen) makes a strong case against the myth that, as Barbara Bush puts it, the illiterate can't "cope." Literacy is not, in fact, a prerequisite for individual progress.

Even when defined as no more than the ability to encode and decode print in ways the school literacies so privileged in society mandate, however, "the *stigma* of illiteracy is a greater burden than the actual literacy problems evident in such cases" (Street, *Social Literacies* 19). Recently I spoke with a twenty-something gentleman from Vietnam who immigrated to America during high school. He told me he really wanted to go to college but he couldn't because he "can't write—my English is so bad, no one can understand me." I must have expressed surprise. "No," he said, "I can *speak* English just fine. It's just that I try to write it like I talk it and I get the commas all in the wrong places." "Really?" I said. "I can't imagine misplaced commas should keep you out of college." "Oh yes," he explained. "My high school English teacher told me I needed to learn where to put my commas because she can't understand me. My writing doesn't make sense, and I confuse my reader."

Surely his teacher is a very good reader of *published* prose, perhaps prose as confounding as that by poet Gertrude Stein[7] who writes this "on composing": "The composition is the thing seen by everyone living in the living they are doing, they are the composing of the composition that at the time they are living is the composition of the time in which they are living." It seems unlikely that this young man's prose is more confusing than this, certainly not so much so that his teacher should be unable to figure out what this young writer is trying to say. Should he really understand himself to be unprepared for college simply because he puts his commas in the wrong places? The New Literacy Studies (NLS) scholar Brian V. Street expresses further outrage at such measures of literacy, most especially the significant problems resulting from the "stigma" of being labeled "illiterate": "If . . . minor difficulties with spelling, decoding, sentence or paragraph structure (or simply non-standard pronunciation . . .) . . . are associated with the category "illiteracy" and that category is associated with lack of cognitive functions or with backwardness, the stigma is inevitable" (Street, *Social Literacies* 23). As we know, far too often that is exactly how the line between "illiteracy" and "literacy" is determined, much like the line between "basic writer" and everyone else is determined (see Harvey Graff, especially *The Labyrinth of Literacy*). "It is not only meaningless intellectually to talk of 'the illiterate'; it is also socially and culturally damaging" (Street, *Social Literacies* 19).

In her regularly cited article "Tropics of Literacy," Linda Brodkey challenges an earlier, "widely-cited study (1975) of Adult Performance Levels," a study in which those unable to read, fill out forms, and perform other "such literacy tasks as are considered essential to being an adult" (much like those cited by the 1992 National Adult Literacy Survey discussed above) were judged to be fundamentally illiterate (82). As a rather persuasive argument for how much (and what kind of) literacy is needed for one individual to "cope," this widely published scholar confesses her own illiteracies when judged according to measures like those she cites and the National Adult Literacy Survey cited previously.

I literally do not understand any of the literature sent to me by the benefits office at my university.

I suspect the difference between the members of APL1 [the "lowest levels of literacy" according to the study she cites] and me is that nobody seems to expect me to understand the forms and policies. To wit, my university insures my life and my health, I insure my car with a friend of a friend and I file my tax forms according to instructions from an accountant. This cadre of institutional and surrogate readers, who are supposedly comprehending these important documents on my behalf, is available to all members of the middle class, many of whom use them more extensively, of course, than I do, and some of whom would also include lawyers and brokers in their reading circle. The point I am making is really very simple. Functional literacy may be less a matter of decoding and comprehending official documents (since to do so requires specialized knowledge of law and economics as well as written language) and more the fact that I have ready access to the resources I need to use the documents. This is what separates the literate "us" from the illiterate "them." (83–84)

In a similar vein, Gemma Moss makes this argument: "An important resource within community contexts, networking allows those without the requisite literacy competencies on an individual basis to share in the competencies of the community as a whole when undertaking tasks such as form-filling or dealing with officialdom" (149). In my recent study of the highly literate inmates tutoring those judged "illiterate," I learned that prisoners regularly trade items (food, snacks, contraband), money, or protection for the assistance of those literate inmates who help them fill out forms, write letters home, and learn what their friends and family members have written to them.

Just as Brodkey relies on the accountant who is highly literate in tax law and procedures to take care of her income taxes each year, I rely on my mechanic who is highly literate in auto repair and maintenance to tell me my car shimmies not because I need to have it realigned (as I thought) but because I need new tires. Just so, the mechanic in the community in Fingeret's study relies on those "literate" members of the community to perform the various tasks required in a print-based society like ours.

Such a social view of literacy requires us to understand reading and writing not as a neutral skill set and an inherent good, but as a social practice that grows out of real living circumstances that dictate true need (see the NLS scholars like Barton and Hamilton, James Paul Gee, Brian V. Street, Cope, and Kalinovitz and work by literacy scholars like Shirley Brice Heath and Scribner and Cole). Neither Linda Brodkey nor I *need* to understand "the literature sent to [us] by the benefits office at [our] university[ies]" (84). Well, we do, but we do not need to be able to do so without assistance; that is the way literacy truly functions in a community. We share resources, where possible.

As Brian V. Street explains, if literacies "are located in a theoretical framework that assume there to be a variety of literacies in different contexts, no one line between literate and illiterate [or mainstream writer and "basic" writer], and a range of cognitive and social skills associated with orality and literacy equally, then the agenda shifts and the stigma" associated with a more skills-based model "becomes meaningless." In other words, every one of us is at once highly literate and entirely *illiterate*, but it is only those failing artificial literacy measures who suffer the stigma associated with that failure. Street continues, "Everyone in society has some literacy difficulty in some contexts. The classic 'middle-class' difficulty is with income tax forms, but in this context the emotional charge is drawn off through . . . jokes rather than reinforced through categorical labeling and stigma" (24).

That brings us to another important point: "literacy is not literacy is not literacy" (Hull 19). I'm "literate" in a number of spheres—as a writing teacher, as a viewer of *Law and Order*, as a reader of mystery novels, as a feminist—yet I am equally "illiterate" in a number of other social spaces—as a player of video games, a viewer of football, a reader of comic books, a mechanic, an accountant. I am not alone in this. We are all highly literate in some spheres at the same time we are equally illiterate in other spheres. Our "literate levels" in any given area may be based on aptitude, but they are much more empathically shaped by our experiences, interests, and current needs (see Street, Gee, and Brandt). The significance of our "deficits," however, is determined less by need and more by the value society places on the area in which we may be considered literate (or not), as well as the measures used to determine "literacy" (or illiteracy) in a given area, a subject to which I will return in chapter 4.

In the introduction to her collection *Writing Permitted in Designated Areas Only* (1996), Linda Brodkey warns us not to "fetishize illiterates,"

> to accept without comment representations of illiterates as an economic liability or a criminal threat to literates. Literacy does not literally defend people against unemployment. . . . Literacy is no defense against crime. . . . Fetishes of illiterates as "the problem" displace public interest in egregious systematic inequities in schooling, not to mention distracting us from examining and discussing the educational policies and programs that have historically produced illiteracy. (4)

Unfortunately, the mechanisms by which literacy education perpetuates inequities have much to do with this assumption that teaching students to "read and write" will make them more productive workers, better citizens, better *people*.

Inasmuch as this mandate to teach our students to "read and write" is tied to ensuring their success in the workplace and other public spheres, it often generates learning spaces obsessed with lessons about encoding and decoding print-based texts, leaving no actual, political, ideological, or practical space for critical thinking (especially cultural critique). According to Henry Giroux,

> Literacy within this perspective is geared to make adults more productive workers and citizens within a given society. In spite of its appeal to economic mobility, functional literacy reduces the concept of literacy and the pedagogy in which it is suited to the pragmatic requirements of capital; consequently the notions of critical thinking, culture and power disappear under the imperatives of the labor process and the need for capital accumulation. (*Theory and Resistance* 87)

The individuals and the various groups with which they most identify cease to matter in this educational model, serving instead the larger economic machine for which we are training these individuals.

In their ethnographic study cited earlier, Juliet Merrifield, Mary Beth Bingman, David Hemphill, and Kathleen P. Bennett deMarrais profile twelve diverse men and women with "limited literacy skills" in order to determine, among other things, "not . . . their literacy limitations—what they *cannot* do—but also . . . their *strengths*—what they can do" (2, emphasis mine). Their findings reveal that despite the assumptions that such individuals cannot "function" in society, they actually function quite well. Every person included in the study has developed multiple strategies for meeting the demands of "a print-based society," including a reliance on others to read to them and other strategies like guessing and "the extensive use of memory" (186).

"On the whole, [however], the literacy . . . levels . . . needed to 'get by' (figure out bills, use the bus, fix things, drive around, apply for work)" were quite "minimal." Even so, it is important to note that "literacy is only one factor in the complex social and economic interrelationships in the lives of poor and working people" (183, 86). In other words, a lack of literacy skills (as determined by conventional measures) will not, in fact *cannot*, in and of itself, ruin any single individual's life, but neither can an abundance of literacy save it, at least not by itself and when we define literacy as the ability to encode and decode print-based materials. In *The Violence of Literacy* (1991), Elspeth Stuckey makes this argument:

> The ways of literacy are reproductive of the material relationships of people, not the psyches of people. When and if literacy affects the psyche, the effect is fleeting, in both a historical and a developmental sense. Literacy is not a religious conversion. Indeed, if the moment of literacy produces some psychical change, *that change is a result of social forces, not literacy itself*. (93, emphasis mine)

An autonomous perspective is a highly problematic and, indeed, "violent" one. It is certainly a misleading one. As the authors of the study cited above explain,

> The reason for the discrepancy between their literacy skills and their ability
> to "function" in everyday life lies in their strategies for meeting everyday lit-
> eracy demands for learning. Even in a print-based society, there is more than
> one way to fulfill most everyday task. Competency-based assessments and its
> theoretical base, *functional literacy*, make a great leap: that if someone cannot
> read a bus timetable, they cannot use a transportation system effectively; if
> someone cannot read a want ad, they cannot find a job; if someone cannot
> read appliance instructions, they cannot learn to use it efficiently. (212)

In fact, as these researchers and many NLS scholars insist, *people* surround
many of these everyday tasks. Often these individuals with low literacy skills
in a particular context simply *ask* those same people or observe them or memorize the bus schedule based on previous experiences at that stop or countless
other compensation strategies. Actually, though "we might have expected
adults with limited literacy skills to have quite different literacy practices
from those with higher skills," they don't (185). When I purchase a new
appliance, I rarely read the instructions; instead I rely on a strategy Merrifield
et al. tell us was quite common among the adults they profiled: trial and error.
I do not live in an urban area, and the bus is not a part of my everyday life;
thus, I would likely have trouble figuring out the "bus timetable" and second-
guess myself even if I did, asking those around me when the next bus to my
destination would arrive.

BASIC WRITERS AND THE
PEDAGOGIZATION OF LITERACY

> The TAAS test is the first thing that comes to mind when I think about
> writing. English teachers were always assigning 3 types of essays: informative,
> persuasive, and the famous how to. It was all about getting a four on the
> writing portion of the test. I remember getting twos and at least one three
> while I was learning how to write these papers. You can only imaging how
> discouraged I felt while my peers were bragging about their threes and fours.
> Once I reached the fifth grade when I started to feel like I was not as good
> as the other students. I began to feel less and less confident because of my
> inability to produce high scores like the other children. Unfortunately, the
> teachers never noticed my problem or tried to help me individually, *which
> left me feeling left behind.* (Gretna, "Writing's Hold on Me" 1–2, emphasis mine)

> The biggest expectation in high school is to pass the scary TAKS test. (Ho
> Seung 1)

So pervasive in our public discourse and the culture of testing that sustains it,
the autonomous model of literacy cripples many of our basic writing students
as they find in each new rhetorical situation a need to, as one writer put it,

"start from scratch." One factor contributing to this perspective is, of course, the culture of standardized testing that so many of our students grew up with, as the vast majority of our student population received their schooling in the Texas public school system. However, even if we accept that a single test given in absolutely ideal circumstances could determine a student's ability to "function" in college-level classes, it is quite rare that such circumstances will occur. Jerron, a recent basic writing student, describes his response to the testing situation that identified him a "basic writer":

> Not doing well on a test is nothing new to me. I have always had problems with tests because I either go blank when the teacher passes out the test or I second-guess myself. There is always something that holds me back from doing good. Even when I have the subject down and make A's or B's on graded assignments, I have trouble with the test. (WA2)

In her second essay poignantly entitled "Writing's Hold on Me," Gretna describes a similar relationship with standardized testing. As she explains, "There are times when you are at a loss of words or have no idea what to write. It is really sad when it is held against you." She continues, describing her specific experiences with the testing context that placed her in basic writing:

> When I was given the writing portion of the T.H.E.A. test . . . [I learned] we were supposed to write about our favorite place. I had trouble because I could not decide on the place I would use. I spent half my time debating on whether or not I could use this place or that. At one point, I thought about giving up because I could not choose. *I had not been many places and the places I had been were not the types of places that I would recommend to anyone else.* After [several] minutes of debating, I decided to pick something that seemed somewhat clever and chose my dreams. . . . Unfortunately, people have to learn to pace themselves while writing, which is something I had to learn on the spot. As a result, I was not able to finish my essay and I failed the writing portion. This made me feel terrible because I knew I was capable of a much higher score than I did. If I would have had enough time to organize my ideas and add as many details as I possibly could, I might have been able to get a high enough score to pass it. (emphasis mine)

In his provocative argument about the ways in which national and state writing tests routinely truncate the writing process, Edgar H. Schuster shows us how all of us would be hard pressed to "demonstrate writing proficiency under such circumstances." It is not, in fact, a problem unique to inexperienced writers, as this well-published author proved to himself (and then to us) by "tak[ing] a simulated writing test" on five different occasions.

The semester in which Jerron was enrolled, our basic writing program curriculum, deeply informed by critical theory (and discussed at great length in the following chapter), asked students to offer their own definition of literacy in response to their experiences with it and their readings of, among other things, excerpts from Elspeth Stuckey's *The Violence of Literacy*. In his third essay, Jerron begins to critique the testing situation from a less individualistic and more sociological system of logic:

> [Elspeth Stuckey] would view this as a violence because when you take a standardize test you do not get any feedback, little chance to revise, and no knowledge in why you receive the grade you got. [As] Stuckey says in her article "Standardized literacy tests are tests of Standard English, and Standard English is held to be the benchmark of opportunity" (119). So by failing this test, this could have made me give up in my pursuit of literacy and be viewed as a violence of literacy because we do not know who is grading the test, how they graded the test, how they came to the assumption of given us the score we got, why I failed, what to work on, what to improve, what to correct, or even where my essay is now. *All of these questions go unanswered and can hurt me while they stay unanswered.* The THEA test (or even the TAAS test) also is a violence of literacy because throughout our four years in high school we were taught and molded into writing a certain way to pass the THEA or the TAAS test, but when we get to college *we have to start all over from scratch* and learn a new way. (emphasis mine)

As Jerrell explains it, the entire process of literacy testing leaves far too many "questions . . . unanswered" and this lack of information is harmful to him as it requires him to suffer the consequences of *not* knowing the answers he needs and, because literacy is presented via this autonomous perspective, he must "start all over from scratch" when he enters this new context. In her second essay, "No Rules, No Pass," Ashley argues that the rules, especially what she calls "the five paragraph rule," "limits my ability to express how I feel about the writing assignment." In fact, "I think that rule sucks and should be removed from wherever the rules of writing are made. I suggest that teachers of the future should: first, open children minds that there are many different ways of writing . . . and never teach a child that their teaching of the rules is the only way we should know" (2, 3).

The truth is, literacy is *not* a fundamental prerequisite for individual progress, nor does *il*literacy necessarily and always yield thwart individual progress—at least not when measured according to "standards" like those tested by state-mandated exams.

THREE

The Way Literacy Liberates

Reading does not consist merely of decoding the written word or language;
rather, it is preceded by and intertwined with knowledge of the world.
Language and reality are dynamically interconnected. The understanding
attained by a critical reading of a text implies perceiving the relationship
between text and context. (Freire and Macedo, *Literacy: Reading the World
and the Word* 29)

JACQUELINE JONES ROYSTER calls discourse a "people-centered enterprise." As she reminds us, "all language use . . . is an invention of a particular
social milieu, not a natural phenomenon" (21). In other words, "discourses
operate at the hands and the will of a *people*, rather than instruments or forces
of nature" (25, emphasis in original). This perspective is in direct opposition
to the ways in which literacy is defined via standardized tests and other vehi-
cles as described in the previous chapter. Such tests treat literacy and discourse not as a "people-centered enterprise" but rather as a "standards-cen-
tered" one.

Whether defined as a "people-centered enterprise" or one entirely neutral and autonomous of social context, literacy and language are most often
understood to be made up of symbols (alphabetic, visual, aural, and so on). In
the previous chapter, I argued that an autonomous model of literacy assumes
the symbols chosen should *represent* the world;[1] thus reading becomes a matter of decoding this representation of the world as it has been accurately represented by the writer and writing becomes a matter of determining how to
most clearly and persuasively communicate this representation to readers.
Versions of the more "people-centered" perspectives discussed in this chapter,
especially *critical* literacies, assume that the symbols themselves not only represent the world but actually help *generate* it and the way we experience it

(false consciousness); thus, reading becomes a matter of reading the world itself as the individual experiences it (how it comes to mean for her, how the symbols and codes the writer uses come to mean for her). Writing, then, is not a matter of representing the world as it truly exists—at least not in any generalizable, abstract, universal sense—but rather generating the writer's place within that world.

For those who define literacy in terms of people and the discourses they use rather than rules obeyed by the literate everywhere regardless of context and purpose, basic writing becomes much more complicated than merely "standardizing" irregular discourses. According to the New London Group,[2] "A discourse is a configuration of knowledge and its habitual forms of expression, which represents a particular set of interests" (Cope and Kalantzis 21). Accordingly, the "academy" comes to represent "a particular set of interests" that those new to it should learn and those already members must value and uphold in their everyday literacy practices. As suggested in the previous chapter, basic writing scholars like Patricia Bizzell (1984, 1986), Thomas J. Farrett, and Kenneth Bruffee argue that the goal of basic writing should then be to "initiate" those newcomers into the "academic community." Others, like Tom Fox, Mary Soliday, Jane E. Hindman, and Patricia Bizzell (in her later scholarship) work from a more critical perspective of literacy, making the goal of basic writing not "initiation" into *the* academic discourse community but rather a project of "liberation" from a "particular set of interests" represented by that academic community—a community that represents the more oppressive forces of society. As Bizzell explains, "because academic discourse is the language of a community, at any given time its most standard or widely accepted features reflect the cultural preferences of the most powerful people in that community" ("Introduction," *AltDis* 1).

As an activity system, the critical basic writing program treats literacy education as more complicated than "initiation" into a preestablished community of academic practices. According to the model established by Paulo Freire's work with "illiterate" peasants in Brazil, the goal of literacy education should not be *initiation* into a readymade discourse community but rather "conscientizacao," or "critical consciousness," which may be understood as "the ability to perceive social, political, and economic oppression and take action against the oppressive elements of society" ("Developing Consciousness in"). The privileged discourses are thus understood as "oppressive" to those not "literate" in them, an "oppression" that replicates a social order that keeps new members on the outside until they become willing and able to conform to preestablished codes and conventions.

The outcome of literacy education, according to this model, should not be a writer who can merely replicate the dominant cultural codes and conventions, but one who can, in fact, recognize the oppressive forces limiting and shaping daily life and work against them. As Henry Giroux explains, lit-

eracy is "a political phenomenon . . . [that] represents an embattled epistemological terrain on which different sociological groups struggle over how
reality is to be signified, reproduced, and resisted" (*Resistance* 237). For this
reason, "literacy can be neither neutral nor objective, and . . . for the most
part . . . is inscribed in the ideology and practice of domination" (225). In an
attempt to make the political and ideological dimensions of literacy and literacy education clear to students, I developed a curriculum designed to
emphasize the "people-centered" and political elements of literacy and literacy education. As Jacqueline Jones Royster explains, literacy is

> *embodied* and it is *endowed*. It is, in fact, a *people-centered* enterprise, and it is
> the fact of its people-centeredness that endows it so insidiously with the
> workings of social, political, and cultural processes. By such processes, we
> contend with the imposition of values, beliefs, and expectations through
> language; with the deployment of systems of power, control, privilege, enti-
> tlement, and authority through language; with the engendering of habits,
> protocols, systems of value through language. (25, emphasis in original)

In our basic writing program, I hoped that the sequenced approach advocated
in David Bartholomae and Anthony Petrosky's *Facts, Artifacts, and Counterfacts* might productively redefine literacy in social, people-centered terms,
thereby forcing students to read and challenge the system of signs that shape
the meanings and value-sets attached to literacy. I hoped these writers would
come to challenge the "culturally sanctioned beliefs that, regardless of good
intentions, defend the advantages of insiders and the disadvantages of outsiders" (Scott 47).

   In doing so, however, I also hoped to avoid forcing my leftist politics on
the large number of my students who were outwardly and deeply conservative
and religious and thus might understand my leftist politics to be just as oppressive as the forces I was attempting to get them to resist (see also Grobman,
Maxson, Fulkerson, Durst). In "Basic Writing in Context: Rethinking Academic Literacy," Lee Odell cites a particularly painful choice made by otherwise
well-meaning instructors. In an attempt to help reveal the oppressive forces of
institutionalized education at work in the students' lives, "students in this"
first-year composition course at his school "received the following assignment:
'Write an essay about the ways in which your education has arbitrarily
restricted the choices you may make as a student'" (51). In other words,
"instructors wanted students to reflect upon the ways their educational experiences may have limited their development as writers and thinkers." Put
another way, "Talk about how fundamentally naïve you are, how intellectually
inferior you are to your instructors, and how the institutionalized oppression
inherent in the American educational system made you that way." The irony
is that, as Odell explains it, "in the effort to liberate students from the arbitrary constraints of their education, these instructors arbitrarily constrained

students to develop a thesis that the instructors had already determined to be, in effect, the 'right answer'" (51).

But though I was worried about this, a carefully designed, sequenced curriculum seemed the way to keep the power in the hands of my students rather than my own. The curriculum I describe in the remaining pages of this chapter, then, employs a sequenced approach that complicates, builds upon, and forces students to engage with and then deconstruct the meaning of literacy as it functions in their lives with the assumption that doing so would lead to an awareness of the "embodied" and "endowed" aspects Royster articulates. In doing so, however, I took under advisement the many scholars who challenge (both directly and indirectly) the problematic assumptions Bartholomae and Petrosky's much celebrated curriculum perpetuates, and, in the process, built on more critically informed solutions like those offered by Mary Soliday, Martha Mariinara, and Jane Hindman.

THE CURRICULUM

Like the approach advocated in Bartholomae and Petrosky's model, each reading and writing assignment included in the sequence I describe (see Appendix A for sample assignments)[3] was designed to allow writers to take a very complex question, explore it from many different angles in many different ways, and build upon each response to this question by piling on yet another perspective. When most clearly shaped by the tenets of critical theory, our course sequence was ultimately concerned with literacy as a social and cultural construct; thus, the central question driving the course was "What is literacy? What does it mean to you and how did it come to mean for you?" Doing so required these students to "read the world" before (and after) "reading the *word*" (Freire). The students began exploring this question by reading their own literacy histories through the objects they felt best represented literacy for them. For Ana—the blind Mexican emigrant I will discuss in some detail below—it was "a slate and a stylus." As she describes it, "a slate is like a double-sided ruler that opens up and allows a piece of paper to fit in between two plates. A stylus is used to make Braille dots using the slate" (WA1, 1). For James, an African American student from Dallas, it was the "front pue [sic]" of his church, where he went from "a child that goes to church" to a "churchly child." (For more about James, see Carter, "Living Inside.") For Jessica, a Latina student for whom though she "was born in the US . . . the first language I learned to speak was Spanish," it was the "yellow notepad" she took to her first pre-K class because, as she explains it, "I would observe . . . teenagers on television [doing so], so I thought that this was what a student needed to have in order to go to school. It was my way of imitating what others were doing" (WA1, 1–2), particularly on the television show *Saved by the Bell*, the only program in English she watched (otherwise she watched only Spanish programming).

After describing the object that best represents literacy for them, they were asked to complicate this reading of literacy by examining it through what Deborah Brandt calls the "sponsors of literacy." Who is responsible for "enabling" and even "withholding" literacy in the lives of our students? What does this tell us about the meaning of literacy in their lives and the lives of those they care about? Next, we read excerpts from Elspeth Stuckey's *The Violence of Literacy*, which, of course, further complicated their readings of literacy by examining arguments that portray literacy and literacy education as "violent" and even oppressive. Then we watched the film *Central Station*, in which a former school teacher earns her living by writing letters for her "illiterate" customers to send to their family members. Here literacy is treated as the ability to encode and decode texts, but a reading of the world in which this version of literacy functions offers a detailed—and, at times, painful—portrait of the ways in which the functional perspective may oppress individuals considered "without" literacy and challenge the conceptualization of literacy as an "inherent good." Finally, we examine the meaning and function of literacy as a "people-centered enterprise" through George Orwell's novel *1984*, a chilling example of the seeming freedoms of some sponsorship activities and the devastating effects of others.

From all these explorations, each essay building on the previous one, my hope was that students in our program would develop a complicated, relevant, and productive response to the question of literacy and what it means to them. In doing so, I also hoped they'd adopt even more productive, flexible literacy strategies that should continue to make literacy more and more meaningful to them as they work to resist and engage with other readings of the various lifeworlds they currently inhabit, as well as those they strive to join. Ana would both fulfill and challenge these liberatory goals, a conflict that ultimately led me to rethink this approach and the practical consequences of a critical pedagogy.

ANA

Ana was a diligent, competent, "basic" writer who emigrated from Mexico only a few years earlier, and a blind student who took advantage of all the support services our university has to offer, including those available to students registered with Disability Services (DS). She acquired the novel *1984* as an audio book; the articles by Stuckey and Brandt were read to her by the same tutor (provided by DS) who helped her translate the texts she generated in Braille into texts legible to her sighted teacher, a graduate teaching assistant in our program. Ana also worked several times a week with tutors in our writing center—a support service separate from the tutoring services provided by Disability Services and the university's Trio Program. The film *Central Station* was quite a bit more complicated for her to access, a "violence" I will explore in just a moment.

According to my reading of Ana's world through her words, Ana's child-hood included many moments of the sort of violence Stuckey articulates in her book. The violence began in kindergarten in Mexico, at the hands of her very first teacher and, as a consequence, her classmates: "Each morning as soon as we came into class, the teacher would pass out sheets of paper with different shapes for us to color. Obviously this was very difficult for me to accomplish. Since I cannot see, I was not able to color shapes like everyone else." The other children would tease her ("Ana doesn't know how to color") or attempt to help her in ways that merely emphasized the "outlandishness," to invoke Patricia Bizzell,[4] she already felt (telling Ana what she needs to do to get it right: "The teacher told us to use a different color for each shape") (WA4, 2). As Ana explains, "I knew we were supposed to use a different color for each shape [but] in my case this was a very difficult thing to do. Since I could not see, I would just grab a crayon from the box without really know-ing if I had already used the same crayon to color a different shape" (WA3, 2). According to Ana, "I always felt out of place" (WA4, 3).

In the meantime, her family searched for, as Ana puts it, "a school for someone like me" (WA1, 1). "[B]ecause I was born blind in a rural town of Mexico, reading and writing were skills that at times seemed" inaccessible to her (WA2, 3). Ana's literacy (or *illiteracy*) was further "sponsored" by the Mexican government in that they "withheld" or otherwise made difficult her literacy acquisition. Quoting Stuckey,[5] Ana makes clear the consequences of her government's decision to offer few "services for people with disabilities":

> in my country the services for people with disabilities are very limited. "We promote greater literacy or we promote greater humility. The first choice is easy. The second is not. The second choice is infinitely more human, how-ever. Perhaps one of the consequences of literacy is its failure to end the vio-lence of an unfair society" (Stuckey 124). It's true that the government in my country promotes literacy, however the government of Mexico is not concern about promoting literacy for disabled people. (WA3, 1)

Her sister (Mireya) who was living in Mexico City at the time, however, was able to locate a place for Ana: the Institute for the Blind, also in Mexico City. Ana was then seven years old.

She was accepted, but her parents were told "they would have to find a place for me to live" (WA3, 3). Ana says that this mandate represented for her "a violent situation in literacy." She offers this from Brandt, followed by Ana's reading of her own world.

> "Throughout their lives, affluent people from high-caste racial groups have multiple and redundant contacts with powerful literacy sponsors as a routine part of their economic and political privileges. Poor people from low-caste racial groups have less consistent, less politically secure access to literacy

sponsors—especially to the ones that can grease their way to academic and economic success" ([Brandt] 170). This shows that when a family does not have economic resources to pay for education this presents a violent situation in literacy. (WA3, 3)

Luckily her sister "was able to locate a Catholic boarding home for [her] to stay in" while she attended the Institute for the Blind, but her need to rely on "charity" further complicated her chances of acquiring this literacy she so desperately wanted. This strict, rather cold environment, the rigorous schedule to which she was required to adhere, Ana's youth (she was only seven), and the distance from her family that she had to endure for four long years further complicated any notion that in order to get ahead one simply has to "work hard."

As a "poor, [disabled person] from [a] low-caste racial group [in a poor country, Ana had] less politically secure access to literacy sponsors" (Brandt 176), so any attempt to attain "higher" levels of literacy required suffering, levels that would be much more readily available to her richer, American, urban (or, as seems more likely, suburban), white counterparts. According to Ana's description, the very living conditions that granted her access to the literacy education she needed and desired were painful for a seven year old so far from home:

> [M]other Laura was in charge of the place. When I came to the boarding home [s]he explained to me that in order for me to do well I would have to follow the rules. . . . The schedule was as follows [sic] at 5 the bell would ring for us to get up. As soon as we got up, we were supposed to make our beds. . . . As soon as we got dressed, we were supposed to fold our pajamas and place them under our pillows. Then, we had to brush our teeth. At 6 the bell would ring for us to line up to go into the dining room and eat breakfast. Since this was a Catholic place, before we could touch our food we had to say a special prayer, to thank God for the meal. After this was done, we had to line up again to wash our dishes. When we were through, we had to go brush our teeth. The school bus would pick us up at 7. We were in school from 8 a.m. to 1:45 p.m.
>
> Since we had to wear a uniform, as soon as we came back from school we had to change into something different. The bell would ring at 3 for us to eat lunch. Once there we had to say a prayer before we could start eating. When we were through eating lunch, we had to say a prayer again to thank God for the meal. Again, we had to line up to wash dishes. As soon as we were finished, we had to brush our teeth again. (WA3, 3–4)

As Ana explains, "'the rules' weren't that hard, but I was only seven years old . . . I believe Stuckey would agree with me on the fact that is very sad that they would have all these rules, in order to acquire these two important skills" [reading and writing] (WA3, 4). In her fourth writing assignment (of five), following our reading and discussion of Orwell's *1984*, she begins describing her experience at the Catholic boarding home in much more painful terms, comparing her schedule to the Two Minutes of Hate Winston and the others are required to endure no less cheerfully and enthusiastically:

> I believe that the nuns had a way of manipulating everything we did. They had a schedule that we were obligated to following without complaining, not only did we have to follow the schedule we had to do it their way. The Two Minutes of Hate [in *1984*] can be related to the boarding home with the nuns because they held power over people. Like the [novel], the nuns are mind controlling and their purpose was to train us to do as they wished. (WA4, 4)

Twice that first semester, her mother visited; twice Ana cried and begged her "not to take me back with those nuns" (WA3, 5). Twice her mother "left without letting me know, which made me feel even worse. . . . I honestly believed that my mother didn't love me." She continues:

> The months passed and I felt very depressed. I really believed that no one in my family loved me and this was the only way for them to get rid of me. Clearly this is an example of violence in literacy. The fact that I had to be separated from my parents, to learn how to read and write, shows us that violence in literacy truly exists. (WA3, 5)

After spending "four and a half years . . . away from my parents," Ana's family brought her to America where she "once again . . . had to face another violent situation." As Ana explains, "though I knew Braille, I did not speak English. . . . Having to learn English meant I had to learn two different languages. I had to learn English and grade 2 Braille" (WA3, 5–6).

At college, the violence continued—this time at my hands. Even though I knew we had a blind student in our program, it did not cross my mind that the foreign film (with English subtitles) would be problematic for her. Had I considered it for even one moment, the problem would have presented itself to me quite quickly. However, as sympathetic as I thought I was and as I try to be with respect to student needs—particularly those with marginalized identity markers like Ana's (blind, Latina, nonnative speaker of English)—I was simply so caught up with the students in my own classes (and, perhaps, my own political agenda) that I didn't make other arrangements, at least not before Ana brought the problem to our attention.

In preparation for the film and the writing assignment that was to emerge from it, I asked the students to "pre-read literacy" as it may be represented in *Central Station* (see Appendix B):

> We've been reading and writing about your own literacy past for several weeks now. We've even traced what Deborah Brandt calls the "sponsors of

literacy" who have made literacy possible (or impossible). In *The Violence of Literacy*, Stuckey told us that literacy education itself may be said to commit the greatest acts of violence, perpetuating the inequities in society even while contending that education is the "great equalizer" in society.

In other words, sponsors of literacy may, in fact, be sponsors of a kind of "violence" against those who were promised access to the American Dream.

In this second part of our discussion (in preparation for WA3), I'd like for us to explore these issues in spaces that extend beyond the American context we've been examining thus far. What makes literacy an inherent "good"? Is the ability to write or read naturally better than an inability to read or write? Stuckey tells us we are committing "violence" when we treat literacy as more civilized behavior than we do illiteracy, thus privileging literate individuals over illiterate ones. What might be the consequences of literacy?

A brief synopsis of this film may be necessary before we continue. *Central Station* (1998) was filmed in Brazil and is set in Rio de Janeiro. Dora, the film's central character, is a former schoolteacher who makes her living by writing personal letters for those who cannot write but who have no other way to contact their loved ones. They line up in front of her folding table at the central railway station in Rio, dictate their messages to her, pay her, and leave their precious letters in her care with the expectation that she will mail them right away.

Business appears to be steady. At the end of each day, Dora leaves with plenty of money in her pocket and a stack of letters to circulate. Soon, however, we learn that Dora actually mails very few of the letters she writes on her customers' behalf. Apparently assuming her own literacy and background provide her with a better moral compass than that available to her illiterate customers, she makes judgments about their lives and decides which letters should be mailed and which should lay dormant in her dresser drawer in her home, joining years of other unmailed (unworthy?) correspondence. Dora makes these high-risk judgments based primarily on the data gathered as she encodes the text her customers dictate for her and decodes the text generated by her customers' loved ones. She even shares the unsent letters with her neighbor, for laughs and, it seems, to point out how much better off the lives of the letter "writers" will be as a direct consequence of the choices Dora has made for them, especially those wives trying to contact their husbands—husbands Dora often decides are "drunkards" and they are better off without. She has many repeat customers, so she may have years of letters written by and for the same individual—with increasing desperation—crammed into that drawer. Apparently, at least for Dora, the literate know best, certainly better than the illiterate.

But then the death of one of her repeat customers forces Dora to confront the reality that literacy itself does not equip or authorize a person to play god. Sight unseen, Dora had determined that the man the customer had been attempting to contact was a "drunkard," thus she never mailed the letters she wrote on his wife's behalf. The woman is subsequently hit by a bus near the station where Dora works, leaving her son Josue an orphan. Through a series of touching, rather painful events, Dora learns what her oppressive assumptions about the capacity of the "illiterate" have done to Josue and his family.

Since she grew up in Mexico, Ana, of course, speaks Spanish. The film is Brazilian and, therefore, in Portuguese (with English subtitles). She had no access to the film at all other than the few pieces she was able to make out due to a handful of similarities between the two languages (Spanish and Portuguese). Her instructor and I tried to track down the subtitles so perhaps her tutor could help her in the ways he had helped her with the other "texts" for the class, but we were unsuccessful. We described the film to her as best we could. Still, it was never quite fair and certainly very frustrating for Ana. As soon as she pointed out the problem (though she certainly shouldn't have had to), we asked her to skip incorporating the film into her WA3 and instead work with the texts she was able to access (Stuckey, Brandt) or perhaps make use of another film to which she had access. Ana wouldn't have it. She was a hard worker and, in her words, she didn't "want the course made easier" for her.

In a brilliant rhetorical and political move, Ana articulated the violence directly (and ironically) embedded in the sequence:

> To this day, I still experience violence in literacy. For example, now that I'm a freshman, I still feel many things are [in]accessible for blind people, like the moving "At Central Station." This movie was made in Portuguese. For me this is very difficult because I have to work with some scenes from the film. However, I am unable to obtain English subtitles for the film. This proves that even now disabled people still struggle to accomplish certain things. . . . Many things have changed in my life. However, as I sit here typing this assignment, I feel just as scared as I did when I was a first grader learning how to write. (WA3, 6)

Inasmuch as the curriculum (as Ana experienced it) "empowered" her to articulate a rather forceful challenge to that same curriculum, the program was a success for her—at least according to the agenda set forth by critical theorists like Freire.

Yet while Ana challenges her access to literacy education as unfair and inequitable, she does not question the value of learning to read and write (as encoding and decoding texts, whether in Braille or English), or what reading and writing actually mean, or even the ways in which reading and writing in Braille may differ from reading and writing in codes used by sighted people or

what may be meaningful or even problematic and unfair about these differences. Instead she challenges her lack of access to these inherent goods. She
questions the notion of free, independent agents, but she does not accept the
fact that these goods are ultimately only valuable in the ways society scripts
them to be and that this value is often unequal and unfair.

At the end of the term in his final essay for the class, Gerrell also continues to define literacy in seemingly emancipatory but ultimately oppressive
terms. From his fourth grade teacher, Gerrell says, "I was able to learn many
things, but she also showed me that I have a voice and without literacy I don't
have a voice. . . . Now I realize that literacy is a special gift, a gift to live or live
a new life. Compare to my ancestors who were slaves, I have a freedom they did
not have. A freedom to be literate and be happy" (WA5, 2–3). I meant for the
film *Central Station* and the novel *1984* to help them see the ways in which literacy may not always and necessarily be an "inherent good." Instead, many saw
literacy as a privilege they have and one that must not be squandered. As Jerron explains in his fourth writing assignment, *1984* reminds us

> how we as a nation take literacy for granted. We see young teens drop out
> of school at early ages, even through it is free and it will give us ample
> opportunity for success in the future. We also see our students cheating or
> sleeping in class, missing out on an important knowledge that is needed to
> advance us in the competitive society we live in. Compared to the charac-
> ters in the book and under their living conditions we have a good life with
> amazing opportunity that we must act on. (6)

Shaquala also celebrates this perspective:

> I always thought literacy was all about reading and writing. Now that I know
> about literacy, I feel privileged that I have the basic knowledge, so now
> when I have to do a paper, I'm grateful because I know there are a lot of peo-
> ple without literacy. . . .
>
> Literacy is a big part of our everyday life. Literacy can be a violent
> process and can be sponsored in negative ways, although there are some
> people in the world that have no choice but to be controlled and withheld
> from literacy. Literacy is the ability to read and write. There are two skills
> needed to survive in the world if you don't want to be controlled. Remem-
> ber, although literacy can be violent, as well as helpful and useful Literacy
> should be obtained. (WA4, 3, 5)

I am very uncomfortable with programs that imply students must be
awakened from their current state of "false consciousness." Like Patricia
Bizzell, I am equally uncertain "that teaching academic discourse [can actu-
ally] *cause* critical consciousness in students." As she explains in her introduction to her collection of previously published essays *Academic Discourse
and Critical Consciousness* (1992),

> I was hoping that if we were able to analyze academic discourse conventions
> in such a way as to demystify them for students, we would be contributing,
> if not to political revolution, at least to the groundwork for major social
> change through preparing previously marginalized students to speak with
> powerful voices against the mainstream. (9)

But language-use is always already shaping and shaped by the ideologies and
economics of the dominant communities of practice—those who, as Freire
explains in *Reading the World*, "have power can generalize and decree their
group characteristics as representative of the national culture. With this
decree, the dominant group necessarily depreciates all characteristics belonging to subordinated groups, characteristics that deviate from decreed patterns" (52). Why? According Freire, "The dominant class . . . has the power
to define, profile, and describe" (53). As Bizzell explains in the introduction
to the recent collection *AltDis* (2002), "language-use conventions shape participants' way of looking at the world—their worldview—including notions
of what's real, normal, natural, good, and true" (1). For this reason, if we are
going to see "academic discourse" as reproducing the dominant social order
(as Giroux, Graff, Freire, and other critical theorists do), teaching it without
making clear the ideological and political ramifications of doing so will not
empower anyone.

Even when we do, however, educators working from this critical perspective may encounter resistance. In his study *Collision Course: Conflict,
Negotiation, and Learning in College Composition*, Russell Durst offers a fascinating ethnographic account of what he calls a "critical literacy approach
that locates students in a larger cultural and historical context," asserting
from the very beginning, however, that his "goal as a teacher and a program
director is not to turn first-year students into critical intellectuals and political activists" (6).[6] Still, he encountered resistance—not just among students,
many of whom felt "they [were] being force-fed 'a liberal ideology'" (128), but
also among the first-year teachers for whom "helping [students] evolve as
socially just citizens seemed overwhelming. . . . In between conferences and
classes, [the first-year teaching assistants] sat around the office together, pon-
dering the ongoing confusion of their work. *Was the goal to teach them better
values or better writing or both?*" (128, emphasis mine).

In a sense, then, critical pedagogy seems rather ironic: Challenge all
authority and all "givens" other than the instructor's authority and the
"given" that all "givens" are suspect. No wonder students often resist this
approach in first-year composition and basic writing. The problems with
some versions of critical pedagogy became very clear to me just moments after
I (a liberal, openly feminist teacher interested in exploring social issues in the
composition classroom) began working with conservative students in north-
east Texas. Right away I wondered whether my "marginalized" or otherwise

"oppressed" students were in a better position to succeed in classes like mine than more mainstream, perhaps openly conservative students. I imagine I will always be concerned that I may be imposing (or trying to impose) my liberal agenda on my conservative students. Maybe indoctrination is the most likely outcome of critical pedagogy when the instructor is no longer concerned about (or aware of) her own power to indoctrinate (or "force-feed 'a liberal ideology'").

Most of all, I applaud Durst's efforts to meld the practical with the critical, and I agree (for the most part) with his argument that many critical literacy theorists/educators treat reflection/dialogue/transformation (173) and "instrumentalism" (Spellmeyer) as mutually exclusive goals. I certainly agree that many versions of critical pedagogy celebrate the liberal (left-wing) position and dismiss all others. However, I did find problematic many of the choices Durst made as an administrator, trainer, curriculum designer, and researcher.

Rhetorically, he seems to treat that dichotomy (the practical and the critical) as though it were much more widely accepted among critical theorists than it really is. Many advocates of a critical approach to composition instruction see practical value in what they do; thus, Durst's version of critical literacy is much more elitist than I think is accurate and his characterization of critical literacy as absolutely anti-instrumentalism seems rather wrongheaded in most cases, despite his use of Kurt Spellmeyer's *Common Ground* to the contrary.[7]

Another problem with Durst's study, as I understand it, is that though he is working with and critiquing a critical approach that celebrates self-reflection and rigorous critique of the master narrative, he doesn't really investigate the powerful master narrative shaping the American (public) understanding of what literacy education should be. He credits de Toqueville's *Democracy in America* (1835) as kicking off the "long tradition of American pragmatism" that urges students to desire/value "a form of literacy that will both make their lives easier and help them become more successful in their careers" (3). That's a start, but I find it quite problematic that he didn't deal much with the fact that this version of American pragmatism (and "success" stories in more general terms) shapes our master narratives, too. Since so much of his argument rests on student's perceptions of their own needs, I am surprised that he didn't spend more time with this particular master narrative as it informs his research project. I must.

Critical literacy forces writers (and readers) to investigate the values/ideologies they have always accepted as unproblematic "truths" Why should we challenge anything we already accept as proven (a "given," a "done deal")? The master narrative is problematic precisely *because* it is seductive and because it is seductive it organizes our world without our really thinking about it (a powerful rhetorical/ideological/cultural force). It's very difficult to penetrate the master narrative, and since Durst is so savvy about critical theory I find it surprising that he made some of the rhetorical, theoretical, and pedagogical choices he made. I'll speak about the pedagogical choices he made in a minute, but I must first explore a broader representation of the practical implications of critical pedagogy.

Teachers of critical literacy, at least the ones with whom I am most sympathetic, do not intend to force a particular political agenda. That's certainly not the goal, though I think Durst is right to point out that it may often be the end result. The goal of such courses is to force students to look at (rather than *through*) the social/political/ideological/cultural forces that shape our daily lives so that we can all make informed decisions that work against (or consciously work with) the master narrative. Still, Durst's critical examination of critical literacy is powerful precisely because he does not dismiss it. The irony is that critical pedagogy is often critical of all worldviews save the liberal one that seems to work directly against the conservative worldview.

The fact that Durst advocates a version of critical literacy that takes pragmatism into account is very appealing to me. "Read" our students as texts, too. "Read" them sympathetically—even our conservative students. Don't dismiss them and their needs. They are valid. Durst does not push for a return to the purely pragmatic in the composition classroom, and I really thought he would. That expectation led to some resistance on my part because, as I have argued, I think it is inappropriate for literacy educators to treat literacy as a neutral, autonomous simple tool that will make our students' lives easier and yield successful careers. In this case and for most people, the master narrative is simply wrong. Otherwise highly literate, hardworking people like my cousin wouldn't be scrambling from temp job to retail sales and back again more than four years after earning a BA with a 3.7 GPA.

The problem, according to Durst, is this: "first-year students typically enter composition with an idea of writing and understanding of what they need to learn about writing that are dramatically at odds with the views and approaches of the teacher" (3) and this disconnect causes conflicts in the classroom. His solution: "A reflective instrumentalist framework in first-year composition." According to Durst, this framework "takes advantage of the motivation students bring to their areas of specialization, provides students with useful knowledge, and engages students in critical scrutiny of schooling and society" (179). In this way, "this pedagogy seeks to establish a truly *common ground* between student and teacher by welcoming, incorporating, and then building upon students' primary reasons for coming to college and studying composition." An example sequence utilizing what he calls "reflective instrumentalism" is *higher education*. Durst says that this "course provides an opportunity for students to better understand what college can offer them and to take greater responsibility for their own learning" (178).

I like this idea, but it also raises several concerns. First Durst's situation at the University of Cincinnati is a little different from ours here in Commerce and from many basic writing programs across the country. Whereas most students "enter [UC] with a major, curriculum, and sometimes even an idea about where they might like to co-op already picked out" (12), our students rarely have any idea about what they'd like as a major. It seems that many (most?) of our first-year students are "undeclared" or only marginally committed to some major. For these students, "higher education" seems no less arbitrary a "theme" than any other social issue. In a situation like ours, how is a course theme like "higher education" any less likely to develop into the "collision course" Durst warns us about?

For the short time I was a high school teacher, I required my tenth grade students to explore a career option for their major research paper. The librarian collected a number of excellent resources for us so the students had much with which to work. I was pleased. It seemed like a very relevant way to make composition matter for/to them. Maybe it did. At least for some. But the students who seemed to enjoy this project the most were those middle-class, white students who had white-collar career plans that mimicked the career paths their mothers, fathers, sisters, brothers, or other close relatives had taken. This was an at-risk South Texas school with a large number of students from lower-income households, so a number of my students felt no such connection to this career project. I don't mean that no one did, I just mean that it was often different for those students whose parents/guardians were just "getting by" on the monies they were able to bring home from back-breaking labor like cleaning middle-class toilets, making tamales, and building fences. These students were often living with multiple generations of family members who worked very hard to live but certainly did not live to work.

Teenage mothers and fathers, in a school where these young parents proudly shared baby pictures and even sonograms of their children, often and quite openly resisted this project. I'm reminded of the sweet, soft-spoken, articulate fifteen year old who was so pregnant she could hardly fit into her desk. She was committed, and she wrote beautifully. After class one day, I tried to speak with her about her college and career plans as we geared up for this research project. Her response: "Are you kidding?" I was a white, liberal middle-class twenty-two year old. I didn't understand. She was bright and committed. Why wasn't she planning for college? I guess I thought she could easily work out daycare plans. Maybe her mother could look after her child while she finished up high school and drove to Corpus or Beeville for college classes (gas? a car?). I could not understand the complexity of her situation—a situation I unconsciously judged via my middle-class value-set. Monica lived with her grandmother, her mother (who may have been a teenage parent herself), several younger siblings, and—if I recall correctly—an elderly uncle. Everyone who could work outside of the home did and always had, leaving Monica to care for her younger brothers and sisters and tend to the household chores and fit homework and sleep in where and when she could. College, even when we located the financial aid, was unlikely and may have been seen as a betrayal of her family.

As I look back at this assignment, I'm kind of ashamed. Did this required career research project mock Monica and others? Did they feel it did?

Granted, Durst is talking about college students, not high school ones, and college students come to college for a career. At least most of them do. My experiences growing up in South Texas taught me something a little different, however. At least in Corpus Christi, at least among the members of my large, Catholic family, ambition of this kind is not considered an asset. My grandfather was a hardworking plumber with seven children. The female members of my extended family were encouraged to go to college, but they were expected not to leave Corpus to do so or to become too invested in their college educations. College allowed them to be teachers if they must, but the only real reason for college was to make sure they had something to fall back on if their husbands leave them (or die)—perhaps to make certain that they were, as my Uncle Frank often puts it, "on the same intellectual level" as their husbands. Among the male members of my family, lots of ambition is considered selfish. Though many of my dad's six sisters and brothers left Corpus for a short time, they returned as soon as they could and they expect their children and now their grandchildren to stick around.

Like most white, middle-class (if lower) families, no one in my extended family ever says this about ambition or higher education. These tacit expectations are simply the result of the Carter narrative of issues like "family" and "home." In fact, the majority of my aunts and uncles did get bachelor's degrees of some sort, and most do work nondescript middle-class, white-collar jobs. My dad even ended up with a MS (in math). Many members of my extended family spent their young adult years somewhere other than Corpus, but they all came back. The Carter family and home narrative demanded it.

In other words, Durst's course (and the notion of an "enriched major" on which it is based) would cause no less conflict for my cousins, aunts, uncles (etc.) who grew up in Corpus than would a course on the American family or gender roles. If we accept this, then Durst's focus on higher education as a course theme may be no more responsible or ethical a course theme than any other, but neither would it be any less responsible or ethical. So while I agree that my goals and my student's goals may be dissimilar, I do not think Durst offers an adequate solution.

I also think a number of the conflicts Sherry—the teaching assistant whose classroom interactions are the focus of the majority of Durst's study—experienced were actually built into the curriculum itself. Russell Durst designed the curriculum for the first-year sequence that moves students from the first semester into the second with a concern for the personal before "advancing" to the critical, though the first semester is spent working through a more genre-based approach that includes narrative and the like. I have several concerns with this approach, most significantly the obvious split between the personal and the political/cultural.

I understand they are working from a very well-informed (Moffett) progression from the personal to the world beyond the personal, but I think this progression is inappropriate for a course focusing on critical literacy. The move from the personal to the political and theoretical forces an artificial separation between the home/personal and school/everything else. The us/them tension Sherry experienced in the classroom is built right into the curricula to which she was bound. The writers see no personal relevance to the topics they cover in English 102 and, as Sherry and Durst point out, none of them thoughtfully or critically interrogates their own subject positions. I think this is largely because the course sequence is not set up in a way that forces them to (and guides them through doing so). If they want to get at critical literacy in English 102, it may have been a good idea to start working from a critical perspective in English 101. As Durst explains,

> Throughout the 102 course, students strongly resisted the textbook's questioning and critical attitude toward US culture. They defended and affirmed the existence of the traditional family; expressed faith in the idea that, with hard work and good attitude, anybody with talent and desire can become successful; and voted with their feet by avoiding the potentially controversial topics of racial difference and prejudice. (157)

Not only do I think the first-semester, first-year assignment sequence had something to do with this, but I also think that the lack of time they were able to spend critiquing any one master narrative is to blame. In the second semester after spending several months in a genre (not theme-based) approach, they moved quickly from topics as complex as "family" to "racial difference" to "affirmative action," spending no more than a handful of days on any one topic (each deeply complicated by master narratives like the American Dream). Even more problematic is that the text (and the instructor) offered no sympathetic readings of the master narrative and the conservative viewpoint at all—further perpetuating the us/them split.

My solution: It would seem, then, that the most appropriate solution would not be to discuss the idea of higher education with respect to their majors but to discuss the idea of academic *discourse* within the context of the various literacies life demands. A "theme" like this would help make the implicit explicit, as Durst tells us we must, without denying the goals of critical literacy. A theme like this could make critical literacy practical by examining the ideological, sociological, rhetorical, and cultural "givens" shaping literacies. We could examine the multiplicities of literacies required in an incredible variety of contexts. In doing so, we could help students develop *rhetorical dexterity* by learning how to effectively examine and negotiate the tacit expectations of different literacies (literacies required of police officers or history professors or computer programmers, perhaps). In the following chapter, I will discuss in much detail the possibilities embedded in this solution. Before I do, however, I think it important to continue our discussion of what Patricia Bizzell has called "the theoretical impasse."

THE "THEORETICAL IMPASSE"

Those of us who—like me, like Russell Durst, like William Thelin—have experienced this disconnect between the "liberation" promised by critical literacy and our own attempts to avoid imposing our politics on our students, "find ourselves at a theoretical impasse. "On the one hand, we wish to serve politically left-oriented or liberatory goals in our teaching, while on the other, we do not see how we can do so without committing the theoretically totalizing and pedagogically oppressive sins we have inveighed against in the systems we want to resist" (Bizzell 54).

In "Critical Pedagogy's 'Other': Constructions of Whiteness in Education for Social Change" (2002), Jennifer Seibel Trainor challenges those critical theorists and teachers who dismiss student resistance—particularly *white* student resistance—to the critical agenda, an agenda many of them see as "shoving dogma down our thoughts" (Rokow 11) or being "force-fed a 'liberal ideology' that does not speak to their desires for a middle class life" (Durst 128). She offers this jarring statement written by Amber, a freshman composition student: "We need the schools to sustain and oppress the lower-class children. Otherwise, who would work in the low wage jobs that nobody else wants?" Trainor urges us to understand such statements not "as an indication of a political shortcoming in the student or as the manifestation of a structural flaw in the political order," but rather an illustration of the "ethical exclusion" that is inevitable "when ["composition teachers"] define as 'other' those whose values and views do not support the quest for social justice at the heart of critical projects" (636).

It is much easier to understand Amber's statement as in direct conflict with the critical agenda than it is to see a student's insistence that literacy is an inherent good, portable, equally available to all, and necessary for survival. However, such a model does promote inequities, as scholars like Harvey Graff and Henry Giroux have revealed time and again. Thus, I am morally, ethically, and politically obligated to work against this model. The problem is that in doing so, I necessarily exclude those who can't be convinced to embrace a more ideological model of literacy. As Trainor explains, "we can't include within our borders those who advocate that to which we are morally and politically opposed. Making such distinctions are central to ethical agency. As a rhetorical move, it is crucial to how we know who we are, part of the rhetoric of our being" (636). Quoting Linda Kintz (*Between Jesus and the Market: The Emotions that Matter in Right Wing America*), Trainor argues that "by dismissing or misreading" student arguments like the one offered by Amber, we "overlook the very 'places where politics come to matter most at the deepest levels of unconscious, in our bodies, through faith, and in relation to the emotions. Belief and politics are rational, and they are not'" (639).

Still, we persist in our objective: critical consciousness. In "Standards and Access," Tom Fox implies that while we should be skeptical of "standards" as established from a *cultural* perspective (as a content-set all literate users know) and a *functional* perspective (as a skill-set all literate users possess), we should not abandon standards altogether. One "standard" he argues is compatible with the critical agenda is this: "We should expect . . . writing that interrogates cultural/political commonplaces, that refuses to repeat clichéd explanations for poverty, racism, sexism, homophobia, and all the other diseases of our society" (43), including—one could easily argue—illiteracy. Given this, can I assume Ana (or Gerrell or Jerron or Shaquala) met the requirements for passing English 100 as shaped by critical theory?[8]

Despite her own concerns with the agenda of critical literacy, Patricia Bizzell claims that the problem here lies not in the critical theorist's agenda but in a problematic understanding of power "as a unitary force within uniform effects" She attempts to address this concern by categorizing power in the classroom into three kinds—*coercion* (which is the sort of obvious control when A tells B exactly what to do and B does it), *persuasion* (when A convinces B that her position is "right" and "true" and thus persuades B to change his or her mind), and *authority*—the concept of power she contends that can reconcile the impasse so many critical educators have felt when they find themselves in positions like mine.

Bizzell offers this example to help illustrate how authority might work in line with the major goals of critical pedagogy:

> suppose I am unable to convince the class that this student's paper we are reading makes a weak argument when it rejects feminism on grounds that women are biologically determined for sole occupations of wife and mother. If I reject a return to coercion such that I require students to adopt a feminist perspective and penalize them with bad grades if they do not, what recourse do I have in such a situation? (57)

In this, then, she "imagin[es] authority as being exercised through a two-stage process. The beginning of the exercise in authority lies in persuasion: A must persuade B that if B grants A authority over B, B's best interests will be served." Thus, B becomes willing to argue from an alternative point of view he doesn't accept and/or perform other activities that are somehow meant to help him see the error of his ways and, therefore, begin to accept and develop "writing that seeks to reduce the deafening violence of inequality" (44) Fox says we must consider accepting as a "standard" for writers in a course shaped by critical pedagogy.

My concern here is that regardless of how we go about convincing students that their perspective is "oppressive," we are still working from a deficit-model of teaching—we become the enlightened ones; they then await this enlightenment. This seems very much something other than "liberation." It seems like oppression from the left, which should be no more acceptable to us than any other sort of oppression.

LITERACY MATTERS

> When dealing with this subject [of literacy] I have often been told that the more literate one is, the more successful one will be, but my teachers did not tell me about the violence of literacy I encounter every day that affects my literacy. When learning about literacy when I was younger, I was often told by my sponsors about the many opportunities the world has for me to succeed in life. But they did not prepare me for and rarely talked about the violences I may encounter that will try to keep me from my pursuit of literacy. (Jerron, WA3, 6)

Ana's experiences with literacy education further clarify the inequities Deborah Brandt locates and articulates in *Literacy in American Lives*. Without access to the necessary resources for literacy learning, students like Ana end up making greater and greater sacrifices for lesser and lesser reward. Brandt argues that schools should, therefore, compensate for the ways in which the capitalist market (and history) often fails those literacy learners like Ana, making it clear that we need to offer flexible education for multiple literacies because (1) we cannot presume to know where these learners want to take their lives, and (2) we cannot know what literacies will be most valuable in the future. Given the fact that literacy is both context-dependent and changes over time, we cannot predict the ways in which literacy will function in the lives of our students once they leave our classrooms or our writing centers, or how it has functioned in their lives during the many years before they came through our doors.

Studies like Brandt's *Literacy in American Lives*, James Paul Gee's *What Video Games Have to Teach Us About Learning and Literacy* (2003) and *Situated Language and Learning: A Critique of Traditional Schooling* (2004), Brian V. Street's *Social Literacies* (1995), and Henry Giroux's *The Literacy Myth* (1979)—among many others—prove that literacy as it functions in the lives of real people is much more complex and sophisticated than standardized measurements guided by autonomous model can capture. And while I am drawn to the possibilities shaping more people-oriented perspectives of literacy, I worry that many people-oriented metaphorical constructs of literate practice run the risk of projecting solid, static, stable rhetorical and political forces with consistent and equal membership rather than the fluid, dynamic, volatile rhetorical space with inequitable membership and regular conflict that we understand it to be. *Critical* perspectives still very much guide the *pedagogy of rhetorical dexterity* in its commitment to social justice, but I am also leery of any project that imposes my personal, liberal political agenda onto my students—doing so seems no less oppressive than the oppressive forces I am attempting to overturn in such a move.

Instead, I propose a program based on a much more *situated* perspective of literacy as it functions in the real lives of our students. It is my intention that this social, situated perspective of literacy will, as Brandt put it, "provide educators with the conceptual tools for bridging between the resources students bring to school and the different literacy practices they must learn to control" (8). In doing so, it is important to emphasize the dominant status of academic literacies (those associated with school) and the subsequent subordinate status of most other literacies; as we discussed in the previous chapter, I do not accept that academic literacies are inherently superior to vernacular ones. However, neither do I think we can ignore the fact that society as a whole places greater currency in the literacies demonstrated in certain publications (like the *New York Times*, *New Yorker* magazine, and the *Washington Post*), traded in certain spaces (workplace documents—like "White Papers"—in white-collar industries—like Microsoft; school-related documents), and measured according to certain, often commercial standards (SAT, ACT, and other high-stakes tests).

It is also important to note the ways in which such a situated perspective, at least as it is embraced by our program, extends beyond print-based contexts. As you may recall from the first chapter, David Barton and Mary Hamilton define "discourse communities" as "groups of people held together by their characteristic ways of talking, acting, valuing, interpreting, and using written language." In the remaining pages of this study, I expand what "literate ability" means to include those "characteristic ways" beyond the written word—that is, any manner of behaving, speaking, valuing (etc.) that marks a person as a member of the target community of practice. Examples include those workplace literacies and school-based literacies described above, but also the video game, Anime, acting, and other similar activities. The following chapter articulates the complexities in doing so.

FOUR

The Way Literacy Stratifies

Educational standardization harms teaching and learning and, over the long term, restratifies education by race and class. (McNeill 2000, xxvii)

ACCORDING TO MARY SOLIDAY, the primary function of basic writing in the institution is now and always has been to serve the needs of the *institution* as much as it is to serve the needs of the students. As she explains, "[s]tratification is a strategic management tool that institutions use to response to crisis in growth" (115) like that experienced right after World War II and, again, as many colleges and universities began instituting open admissions policies in the late 1960s. The State of Texas has been experiencing its own upsurge in enrollment as the number of first-generation college students increases, and, in this context, literacy education and assessment have continued to serve as gatekeeping mechanisms that separate those who may enroll without penalty from those who will be marked "underprepared" or barred from admission altogether—often those who, as study after study has proven, belong to marginalized identity groups (poor, minority). As Hunter R. Boylan, then Director of the National Center for Developmental Education, reports in his 1996 evaluation of the Texas Academic Skills Program,

> Institutions faced with substantial enrollments of underprepared students are confronted with three choices. They can *maintain standards and provide no remediation*. In this case, they will be maintaining a revolving door through which many students will enter and drop out after a semester or two because they cannot meet standards of institutional quality.
>
> Institutions can also *lower standards and provide no remediation*. In this case, they will reduce the revolving door effect and maintain student enrollments but grant degrees representing standards of questionable quality.

> Finally, institutions can ~~maintain standards and provide remediation.~~ In this
> case, they provide both opportunity and quality. (Boylan 58, emphasis mine)

Texas has been praised for choosing the "final" option, and Boylan's report, by
implication, challenges other states to commit themselves to similar programs.

Inasmuch as Ana articulated the violence of her literacy education and
spoke back to it, I would argue that she has likely developed the levels of critical literacy necessary to, as Paulo Freire puts it in *Pedagogy of the City* (1993),
"fight for the transformation of an unjust and cruel society where the subordinate groups are rejected, insulted, and humiliated" (135). But will she? Ana
is deeply aware of the institutionalized oppression at work in both Mexico
and America, especially as her blindness and the Mexican government and
her teachers' responses to it made literacy education largely inaccessible to
her (and, later, my insistence on using a film she could not access further
challenged this accessibility). Still, if we accept the tenets of NLS that an
ideological model of literacy is much more relevant and less oppressive than
the autonomous model, her conception of literacy at the end would continue
to cause her difficulties. Her experiences in our program further validated the
commonplace assumption that a "Great Divide" exists between orality and
literacy, between the "literate" and those who are not. In other words, Ana
continued to assert that while her experiences leading to her acquisition of
literacy were often oppressive and unfair, the various tiers separating "the" literate from everyone else remained unchallenged.

In writing the previous chapter, I asked of myself the same question
Robert Yagelski asks in the opening chapter of *Literacy Matters*: "How
much of what I do actually empowers students in ways that Freire and
other theorists describe? How much of what I do actually works *against*
such empowerment?" (emphasis mine). Ana completed our basic writing
program with a rather sophisticated understanding of the political complexities embedded in school-based literacy education, but the functions of
literacy in life beyond school, as the well as the disconnect between formal literacy education and way literacies function beyond school,
remained largely unexamined. In other words, Ana continued to treat "literacy as a set of 'basic' reading and writing skills possessed by individuals."
Yagelski continues:

> These beliefs about literacy and literacy education . . . are not only out-
> moded but, in a complex and increasingly technological society, often
> counter-productive. To continue to understand literacy primarily as basic
> skills that reflect individual cognitive abilities . . . ["can lead to a superficial
> kind of literacy that leaves them without the critical abilities they will need
> to negotiate their worlds"]. What's more, these simplistic beliefs about liter-
> acy can be downright destructive. Because they ignore the complex and
> ambiguous nature of literacy and its social and political uses, they can result

in the very kind of oppression—of economic and political "violence"—that Stuckey so compellingly describes. . . .

Literacy . . . is at heart an effort to construct a self within ever shifting discourses in order to participate in those discourses; that effort is always "local" in the sense that any construction of a self within discourse, though inherently social, is mediated by a variety of factors unique to a specific act of reading and writing within a specific situation. (emphasis mine)

It is within this context that I argue rhetorical dexterity may have been of greater practical and political value to Ana than critical literacy proved to be. Rhetorical dexterity asks writers to develop a meta-awareness of the ways in which literacy functions in a familiar community of practice as a first step in reading and negotiating an unfamiliar one. In this chapter, I will further articulate the theoretical framework of rhetorical dexterity by applying it to two communities of practice as they manifest themselves within the life-worlds my brother inhabits. I will end with a brief discussion of the ways in which a person's social, cultural, and economic background largely determines her access to new literacies and the value society will place on the kinds of literacies available to her.

THE RIGOR OF OUT-OF-SCHOOL LITERACIES

The limitations of academic literacy models lead teachers to think about "where students are" in terms of where they are vis-à-vis course goals or competencies. But views of "where students are" must also include an awareness of the independent literacies students experience. The reading and writing that students do outside of school is a potentially powerful force in a revitalized approach to basic writing. We must be careful to work from the ways that students describe literacy and not the way we think they define it. (Adler-Kassner and Harrington 49)

Mike, a basic writer in our program, says that as a golfer and owner of an unreliable vehicle, he "read[s] all the time." "I read two or three golf magazines a week cover to cover because they help my game. They've made me who I am as a golfer. I used to have a 1975, broken-down truck. I had to read all to the time to keep it running. I like reading stuff I can use." Through "reading" Mike has developed high levels of literacy as a golfer. He knows how to play golf, and he likely knows what sort of golfing equipment is considered most valuable for the kinds of games he likes to play; he has learned what matters to other golfers and he knows why that's significant. However, Mike has had neither a mentor nor "a golf lesson in [his] life." According to him, the sole responsibility for his development as "a pretty excellent golfer" belongs to reading. But since this sort of reading is not often acknowledged as relevant in school, he doesn't see the relevance in other sorts of more traditionally valued texts (literature, perhaps).

In *Reading Don't Fix No Chevys: Literacy in the Lives of Young Men* (2002), Michael W. Smith and Jeffrey D. Wilhelm attempt to make sense of the significant gender gap reported in the studies like those conducted by Willingham and Cole (1997). Through their close examination of several teenage boys' responses to activities in which they engage both in and out of school, the authors seek to understand a startling incongruity of literate ability that reminds me very much of incongruities my brother exhibited at the same ages: "The passion evidenced by these four young men regarding many aspects of their literate lives beyond school and many of their out-of-school activities lay in stark contrast to the much less passionate way they engaged in school in general and school-sanctioned literacy in particular" (27). Smith and Wilhelm argue that "if we understand why [our students] like what they like, we can work to create the conditions that will make students more inclined to engage in learning what they need to know. These conditions are those of 'flow' experiences: a sense of control and competence, an appropriate challenge, clear goals and feedback, and a focus on the immediate" (53). It seems appropriate to me for us to ask the students themselves to examine "what they like" to determine what elements available to them in one context (those "'flow' experiences") might be available in another (relevant academic communities of practice). Studies like Ellen Skilton-Sylvester's "Literate at Home but Not at School: A Cambodian Girl's Journey from Playwright to Struggling Writer" and Juan C. Guerra and Marcia Farr's "Writing on the Margins: The Spiritual and Autobiographical Discourse of Two *Mexicanas* in Chicago" in Glenda Hull and Katherine Schultz's collection *School's Out!: Bridging Out-of-School Literacies with Classroom Practices* (2002) and the contributions included in Jabari Mahiri's *What They Don't Learn in School: Literacy in the Lives of Urban Youth* (2004), as well as M. Knobel's *Everyday Literacies: Students, Discourse, and Social Practice* (1999) and Ellen Cushman's *The Struggle and the Tools: Oral and Literate Strategies in an Inner City Community* (1998) offer similar perspectives on the ways in which literacy education in school ignores the complex literacies that exist in students' lives beyond school.

Few studies of the out-of-school literacy practices of adult basic writers exist, but those that do offer convincing evidence that, despite their rich, complex backgrounds, "students whose cultural values and routines differ from the . . . norms may find their practices unacceptable in a particular writing classroom" (Sternglass 13). Adler-Kassner and Harrington's survey of basic writer's out-of-school literacies found that complex reading and writing experiences were plentiful in their lives beyond school, but their in-school exposure to literacies was quite the opposite. As they explain, "The literacy activities that students reported remind us that the limited appearance of their preparation for college writing may say as much about what we are looking for, and at, as it does about students' abilities" (57). In an earlier study,

Carol Severino found much the same. In her article, Severino challenges our tendency to emphasize the "gap" between our student's home literacies and those they will encounter at the academy. Instead of focusing on our differences, she argues basic writing teachers should emphasize the "common ground" that is inevitable between academic literacies and our student's own, living histories. Her survey of forty-five basic writing students and their previous reading and writing experiences, at home and school, reveals that most basic writers, contrary to popular assumptions, reported "generally positive attitudes toward reading and writing." Most also grew up in homes that subscribed to one or more magazines and the majority read these periodicals or novels quite regularly—for pleasure.

> Of course, one may reply that browsing through popular magazines and breezing through teen-age novels do not a scholar make, but these journalistic and leisure activities are undeniably common ground [that] can be expanded and cultivated by increasing students rhetorical, linguistic, and cognitive repertoires of purposes and ideas, genres, and composing processes, by helping students comprehend other's arguments, criticize them, and incorporate them into their own. (Severino 13)

As Marilyn Marina points out in a study I will discuss more in chapter 5, "learners bring a wealth of learning and knowledge to academic encounters, but the knowledge is not only undervalued by the academy, it hasn't even been named by the learners themselves" (5).

Severino takes seriously the broad-based literacy practices our students have had before they enter our classrooms—not only acknowledging them but giving students the space to "name" and articulate them. As she reveals, many of these students read magazines and other print-based materials for pleasure. If she were to conduct this study again today—almost fifteen years later—we would undoubtedly gather much data on student, text-based activities associated with the Internet. However, it seems important to explore whether identifying an activity that occurs both in the classrooms and in the homes of our students will help them develop new, productive literacies. I think it is a very important first step, but perhaps we need to force our students to take it even further.

As Kathleen McCormick makes clear in *The Culture of Reading and the Teaching of English*, the strategies one uses to read a book for pleasure differ in some rather profound ways from those used to read it in order to memorize key passages for a test, which differ still further when reading it to incorporate key issues it raises into a current research project, and all of this relies on different ideological frameworks. I think we need to validate that common ground—like reading and writing—between the academy and the home, but I think we need to be careful to avoid implying that the "autonomous model" of literacy is a productive one upon which to base the learning of new literacies. I am afraid that's the model Severino's findings may perpetuate, but only if we merely identify them and stop short of critique.

In their ethnographic study *Life at the Margins*, referred to in chapters one and two, the authors recommend that teachers help students identify the learning strategies they have used to "cope" with limited literacy skills and find ways to apply them in new contexts to learn new things. These strategies include "other oriented learning strategies" like "visual strategies (demonstration, observation), oral strategies (listening to explorations), and cooperative learning" and "self-reliance learning strategies [such as] repetition and practice, selective use of text, trail and error, and a systematic step-by-step approach to learning" (203). Again, I think this identification is an important step. One problem with this approach from a critical perspective, however, is that such a strategy does not encourage them to question what they are being asked to learn, only the methods by which they learn it. Rhetorical dexterity asks them to do both, but to focus on the social function of language rather than individual learning strategies as they do so. As the authors suggest, "Teachers should help students to identify and describe the everyday learning strategies they already employ, legitimize the strategies for use in school and work contexts, and plan how to apply them in new, tangible ways" (207). I suggest we recast this recommendation in more *situated* terms, as the original approach, while important, may promote a more skills-based, autonomous perspective of literacy learning—treating these learning strategies like "study skills" rather than actions deeply dependent on context. Rhetorical dexterity emphasizes the ideological, political, rhetorical, and socioeconomic framing that limits and shapes any community of practice and, therefore, dictates the boundaries of recognizably "literate" behavior. While I applaud efforts to help students locate relevancy in their possessed learning practices, I am worried that, without further exploration, students will be left with the impression that learning is a "portable skill set." Memorization works in some circumstances, but a box of study skills without an understanding of how "problem setting is a process in which, interactively, we *name* the things to which we will attend and *frame* the context in which we will attend to them" does not make learning new literacies more accessible or productive (Schoen 40, emphasis mine).

Teaching basic writers to investigate and use more familiar literacies in negotiating academic ones requires us to work against—consciously and actively—the dominant models of intelligence and (relevant?) content. In *The Mind at Work: Valuing the Intelligence of the American Worker*, Mike Rose asserts that "people kn[ow] things through work. And they use what they learn" (xvii), offering several case studies of men and women at work that help him articulate the cognitive dimension of what we rarely consider "mind work." Accordingly, Rose challenges what he calls our "biases about intelligence" when it comes to manual labor (like plumbing and carpentry) and service work (like waiting tables and styling hair). As he explains, when we dismiss the intelligence necessary to install a new toilet in an older home, color hair without drying it out, or effectively serve a restaurant full of hungry customers, we "develop limited educational programs and fail to make fresh and meaningful connections among disparate kinds of skill and knowledge" (216). In other words, negotiating any complex community of practice—from video games to electrical work, from the air force to the basic writing composition classroom—demands a deep awareness of the internal structure and connections among the social network that makes up the target activity systems within that community.

Like James Paul Gee, Rose argues that intelligence is deeply dependent on our ability to adapt to new situations requiring different forms of literate behavior (and, in most cases, defining what constitutes literate behavior differently). According to Rose, "intelligence . . . is the ability to learn and act on the environment, to apply knowledge to new situations, to reason, plan, and solve problems" (Rose xiii). Deborah Brandt's study of "literacy in American lives," Cynthia Selfe and Gail Hawisher's exploration of "literate lives in the information age," and—by extension—Gee's detailed account of video games as a "new literacy" make clear a very "rapid proliferation and diversification of literacy" which, as Brandt explains in an earlier publication for *College English*, placed greater pressure on Americans, "not to meet higher literacy *standards* as has been so frequently argued elsewhere but rather to develop a *flexibility and awareness*" (651, emphasis mine). Thus, what I am calling ."rhetorical dexterity," something that can only be developed through, in Gee's terms, "active and critical learning" (learning that is situated and real, much like that learning Rose portrays in his study of manual and service work), can be understood to be of practical value in a world in which "success" as a literate individual means more than knowing how to encode and decode print in English. In the very near future, in many places, perhaps even today, "success" as a literate individual will not be judged according to some arbitrary standard, as have so many school-based literacies for so long, but by, as Brandt explains, a "capacity to amalgamate new reading and writing practices in response to rapid social change" (651).

Treating activities not commonly associated with the academy as intellectually rigorous and rhetorically sophisticated may seem counterintuitive to our students, a concern to which I will return later. However, not only are these vernacular literacies relevant to academic ones, some critics argue that these out-of-school literacies (like those required of video game players[2] or basketball players[3]) require of users a level of competence that extends well beyond what literacy education in the schools often requires of students. In fact, these leisure-time activities may actually be getting more complex and requiring more of participants than ever before. In his recent book *Everything Bad Is Good for You: How Today's Popular Culture Is Actually Making Us*

Smarter, Steven Johnson argues that situation comedies, dramas, and video games have gotten increasingly sophisticated over the last thirty years. Like Gee (though published a couple years later), Johnson urges us to accept that

> [p]laying video games [or watching certain television shows] may not actually be a *complete* waste of time. . . .
>
> The first and last thing that should be said about the experience of playing today's video games, the thing you almost never hear in the mainstream coverage, is that games are fiendishly, sometimes maddeningly, *hard*. (24, 25, emphasis in original)

Similarly, in the 2004 Harvard Business School study *Got Game: How the Gamer Generation Is Reshaping Business Forever*, researchers assert that those who game are, in effect, better workers in the corporate sector (Beck and Wade).

My brother's experiences with traditional literacy education were painful for him, but his out-of-school literacies in video games, in electronic music, and in computers shaped his approaches to work and play in ways that made him extremely successful anyway. Of course, stories of one individual developing new literacies in video games and other, related communities of practice may not teach us exactly how other individuals learn different sorts of literacies (how to write a paper for first-year composition, for example)—at least not necessarily or automatically; they can, however, teach us quite a bit about how literacy functions as a "situated," "contextualized" phenomenon. As Gee explains in *Situated Learning: A Critique of Traditional Schooling* (2004): "How any one of us learns throws light, both by comparison and contrast, on how others learn. Learning is not infinitely variable and there are patterns and principles to be discovered—patterns and principles that ultimately constitute a theory of learning" (59). Thus, the stories of learning I have shared thus far and will continue to share will, I hope, illustrate "the patterns and principles of learning" from which a *pedagogy of rhetorical dexterity* may emerge as an appropriately situated and critical theory of learning and, therefore, teaching.

ARTIFICIAL LITERACIES VERSUS LIVING LITERACIES

My brother was always a basic writer; my brother was never a basic writer. Actually, his first experiences with school literacies almost thirty years ago were rather satisfying, and he was, by all accounts, a pretty good student. He was especially found of story time, during which he would lie on his back under a table, eyes closed as though he were taking a nap. Mrs. Arachi,[4] his Montessori school teacher in Riverside, California, encouraged him to do so. She learned rather quickly that Eric could not adequately experience the story any other way; he needed to close out all stimuli in order to focus on the narrative. When she questioned the children after reading the story, Eric was always the first to answer and always with responses that revealed a close and rigorous attention to detail and surprising insight for a child of his age.

By three years old, he'd learned how to write his name. Mrs. Arachi's tutoring session with Eric began with her showing him what his name looked like. Once he saw the complete picture, he "experienced" it tactile-kineti-cally, letter-by-letter; with his finger he traced the sandpaper "E" several times before doing the same with an "R," and then his entire name, "E" then "R" then "I" then "C." Next he drew it using a stencil and a large crayon. Only when he felt ready did he write his entire name without guidance, and once he had, he wrote it everywhere, proudly identifying every one of his accomplishments as his own. The symbols representing literacy in this experience were largely artificial, in a sense, but Mrs. Arachi's treatment of them bridged that gap between the mind and the body so often (artificially) imposed and regulated in literacy education.

In fact, unlike most Western classrooms, I don't recall that artificiality being a regular part of our Montessori experiences. The autonomous literacy model did not make itself known by decorating the walls of our learning spaces there. I recall no silhouettes of train cars carrying the alphabet lining the classroom walls, though every one of my elementary classrooms to follow would be decorated in this way. According to Street and Street's ethno-graphic study of a first-grade classroom, this "labeling" is a function of what they call the "pedagogization of literacy."[5] Through this, they reveal the ubiq-uity of "labeling" and how it becomes the sign system representing literacy from our earliest exposure to such "school-based" literacies. As Street and Street explain,

> The main building of the school . . . is large and square and breathes public importance. It is part of a whole genre of public architecture representing the state. . . . Inside the school, space is designated by authority and author-ity is expressed in signs: rooms are numbered and labeled, they have desig-nated functions that are likewise labeled. . . . When one enters the building, one is situating oneself physically inside a particular universe of signs. Within a classroom, the pictures and notices on the walls continue this process of situating the individual within a sign system. This is particularly evident in the first-grade classroom. *The children sit at the centre of a system of codes through which their experience is to be transformed.* It is as though the walls themselves were a filtering screen through which the world outside the school is transformed and translated into various discrete sets of analytic concepts: lists of numbers, the letters of the alphabet, shapes and colours, lists of measurements—*all the devices by which the experience of the senses can be filtered and then transformed into discrete social and analytic concepts, tabu-lated and measured.* The five senses themselves dangle on separate little

labels from a mobile. Time is filtered through a grid of days of the week, seasons, birthday charts and clock faces. The birthday chart situates the child herself within this catalogue of time, just as she is situated within space. The classroom's four walls are labeled "south," "east," "north," and "west," right and left hang on the wall—*the room is framed as a signifying space with the child at the centre, making sense of things.* These spatial categories only make sense when oriented to the child at the center of the classroom, and *they indicate in a very powerful way the contract between the individual and the institution that underpins the ideology of language within the school.* This process of writing down and labeling experiences *incorporates them into a visual system that is external to the child.* The organization of the visual environment itself helps to construct and provide a model of the child's relationship to language and to the written word. The walls of the classroom become walls of the world. The maps of the USA and the world on the wall at the front of the classroom *indicate the system of signs through which that world may be obtained.* (Street and Street 120–122, emphasis mine)

Thus, learning becomes a completely disembodied experience, abstracted from the individual experiences the learners have had on the other side of the classroom's carefully labeled walls. Literacy then becomes for us just one of the many systems of signs we use to analyze this world, and we are taught that we can only do so abstractly and generically in ways organized by authorities we may never meet and executed by our teachers, who are likewise shaped by these abstract, code-heavy forces that "represent" the world for us before we can read it ourselves.

In 1977, Eric and I entered the Texas public school system where this system of signs was much more prevalent. Eric was then four years old, and our "reading" of literate behavior in school was reinforced by our reading of literate behavior at home, a congruity Street and Street found exhibited again and again in their own study. As they explain, "it has been assumed in much of educational literature that middle-class homes are closely aligned with school practice and ideas about literacy" (104) while other groups remain at a disadvantage because their experiences at home differ from those valued in many of the schools (Gee 1989; Heath 1983). However, few studies have been conducted on this population, so we are basing such an assumption largely on speculation. A "gap" between home and schooled literacies has been shown to exist when the "home" is not "middle class"; however, no such gap was apparent in the context of Street and Street's study, which focuses on the middle-class home. The authors speculate that the degree of congruence between home and school identified here may be less a result of "school influencing home as of general middle-class values . . . affecting both contexts."

In our home—as in my mother's home growing up—we were exposed to similar signs that carry with them the middle-class value-sets we see in the classroom. My mother was a voracious reader, and reading was always—as it is in many homes—coded as an individual, isolated, private activity and an inherent good.

Still, Eric's dyslexia and his general disinterest in the artificially coded, school-based world made it difficult for him. The year after Mrs. Arachi taught Eric to write his name, we moved to Texas and Eric was enrolled in pre-K. The standards-based systems shaping Texas public schools at the time quickly taught Eric what he could not do, even when he actually could. Early in the year, his teacher, clearly guided by an autonomous model of literacy, had already expressed concern about the way Eric held his crayons and the fact that, like his mother, he favored neither hand when performing any assigned activity. Given the clumsy way he held his crayons, his very young age, and the standards-based systems stipulating what a child of his age should (and should not) be able to do, his teacher had trouble believing him when he told her he was going to sign his name to the picture he'd just drawn. That's when Eric learned he couldn't. He clearly remembered having written his name competently and legibly many times before, but he trusted his teacher; she said he didn't know how, so he no longer did. In fact he didn't "learn" again until the standards-based systems to which his teacher was bound told him he was ready to. Sadly, Mrs. Arachi's Montessori methods almost thirty years ago yielded Eric's last good experience with classroom learning. Despite—or perhaps because of—his high IQ and creativity, the Texas public school system left him scarred and jaded.[6]

The good news is that his unfortunate experiences with traditional literacy education did not preclude success elsewhere in his life; Eric, now in his thirties, has done quite well for himself. Traditional education may have failed him, but he was still able to develop high levels of computer literacy that spilled over into multiple areas of his life seemingly unrelated to the computer world. Actually, the literate practices sanctioned and endorsed by the various communities of practice shaping his daily life—work, play, home—are not compromised in any obvious way by his altogether unsatisfactory experiences with his school-based education. Today he enjoys a highly lucrative career in the computer industry as part of the research and development team at a well-established company with a national reputation for innovation and quality.

However, the traditional classroom did not support, encourage, or in any way facilitate (or even *acknowledge*) his developing computer literacies. Born in 1973, Eric grew up at a time when computers were writing themselves into every corner of our daily lives. Work, play, and everything else all centered around computers—as did our family. My father (John) earned his BS in mathematics in 1970 at the University of Texas in Austin, the very town my brother now calls home. Soon after, John became a computer programmer, a career path he would follow for the rest of his working life. Unlike me (his older sister), Eric showed an aptitude and interest in computers early on. In the years before we moved from California to Texas (when he was four years old), he tells me he can recall visiting my dad's office with my mother to play simulation games with her like *Lunar Lander* and text-based adventure games like *Wumpus* when I only remember the large, blue-and-white lined printer paper my father used to bring home for me to draw on (I was six).

In 1978, our parents purchased a "kit" with all the parts necessary (save a monitor and a soldering iron) to build our very own home computer, an Altair Z80. I found most interesting the shiny globs of metal the soldering iron yielded. Eric focused on the circuitry—how it "worked." My father designed and coded a video game for us—featuring a cowboy (with a white block hat, a hand that disappeared into a square gun that fired square bullets—very, very slowly). I wanted the graphics to be more realistic. Eric wanted to be involved in helping our dad make yet another game.

In 1980, our parents purchased an Osborne and joined a user group. The Osborne, for those unfamiliar with it, is an early "laptop"—a "portable" computer about the size, shape, and weight of a 1970s-era sewing machine, complete with a four-inch monitor. It was a machine they would lug to meeting halls in order to share, trade, and create software with other users. At that point we also began visiting the computer stores that were popping up all over at the time—regularly and for what seemed to me for hours. I focused on the older soda machine in one of the shops that released glass bottles as if through a maze. Eric listened to our parents talk "shop" with the other users, hackers, and the like—though, like his performances during reading time at the Montessori school, it didn't look much like listening to me; he'd roll around in desk chairs and spin around in circles, all the while punching buttons on every piece of equipment he could find. After we left, the clerks were likely to find every single computer with BASIC loaded on it blinking a scrolling text message that read, "Help! Let me out of here! I'm trapped in a computer!"—no easy feat, given the user-unfriendly interface mechanisms of computers at the time and the fact he'd have to make it happen without anyone noticing he had anything to do with it.

About the time we acquired the Osborne, we ended up with a modem, which my parents used to log onto bulletin boards and to play games. My father had hoped to be able to log in to data services (the precursor to online databases and libraries), but very few were available at the time. Eric joined right in, logging onto bulletin boards with my parents. He also began to develop an increasingly independent use of technology: hacking, "just for the challenge of it."

And then our parents brought in our very first console video game system—Intellivision (1982). We were among the first in our area to own a gaming system, and Eric and his friends were hooked right away. I struggled to get the army tank to turn at all, let along turn anywhere I wanted it to. Eric maneuvered this game, and all others, with ease. I never developed much interest in them; Eric's interest only increased as time passed and the video games became more complex and challenging to him.

And then it became Eric's world. Video games brought him in and kept him there. Learning new video games came easily to him, even as they became more and more complex and sophisticated. Today he tells me that he learns best by example, but some of the multiplayer games (like *Everquest* and *Ultima Online*) function within incredibly complicated, multilayered worlds involving intricate plots, lots of back story, and characters that develop and advance only by interacting with that world in ways consistent with the character's limitations and abilities and the "physical," social, and cultural "rules" of the world itself. Just watching a player may not always be enough. It is at those times that Eric consults a site like GameFAQs (GameFAQs.com: Video Game FAQs, Cheats, Codes, Reviews, and Message Boards). Those FAQs ("Frequently Asked Questions") on which he relies so heavily are written by other gamers as they advance through the game. According to Eric, "other gamers are the best resource—people who have actually played the game. They usually buy the game the first day [it is out on the market] and document what they did to get to each area. [They] keep updating the FAQs as they play." Several people trying to accomplish the same goal, for example, often submit the different strategies they used to do so. "Anyone can submit an FAQ, [and] everyone has a different strategy for doing the same thing," he explains.

These FAQs are particularly useful when one encounters a poorly designed video game. According to Eric, these are games that offer what he calls "a few minutes of stupidity," "where it's convoluted and frustrating." He cites the older PC adventure game *Leisure Suit Larry*, a particularly silly game in which the "adventure" and the narrative and gaming choices that support it are built around the primary objective to "get this loser laid."

> *Leisure Suit Larry* had a design flaw. You had to pick up a couple items really early in the game—a toupee and something called a "Grotesque Gulp" [a size or so larger than 7–11's "Big Gulp," one must assume], which you've gotta pick up at the convenience store. There was no error check, so you had no way of knowing that you are missing anything you really need until it is far too late to do anything about it. A series of challenges lead you to a boat. If, when you get there, you are without the toupee, your head will ignite from the bright sun and you will die. If you are somehow able to get out of frying from the sun, you may die of thirst because you don't have enough to drink [thus the need for the "Grotesque Gulp"]. There's no way you can know about needing those things unless you just happen to stumble across them.

The game offers none of the signs accepted by literate users in this community of practice as meaning, "Pick that up. You will need it later."

James Paul Gee defines "internal design grammars" as "the principles and patterns in terms of which one can recognize what is and is not acceptable or typical content in a semiotic domain" (*What Video Games* 30). Eric has a deep and multilayered understanding of the "internal design grammar" of adventure games. He knows not only what gamers find frustrating about poorly designed games like this, but also several innovative strategies that could fix the problem. The first is to rely on those FAQs, "Walkthroughs" (a description successful gamers write as they work—or "walk"—their way through the game), or "Cheats" (a series of commands that help players get through particularly problematic portions of the game). Through these communication points, gamers who have encountered this problem before will tell other gamers what they need to know to avoid problems later in the game ("Get that toupee in the first room because you will need it much later in the game," for instance). The game itself does not offer this information very readily, but the other gamers (peers) do.

The second solution Eric offers is even more complex, displaying a meta-knowledge of the gamer's needs from the creator's standpoint. According to Eric, the toupee problem could have been solved by some sort of "error check," and this error check must not interrupt the fantasy in which the gamer is immersed. "There should be some sort of barrier," he argues, "but the barrier itself should be seamless. You aren't aware you are hitting this wall, but you can't get past it until you get this piece that is necessary to solve the puzzle in the next place." His advice: "Always make sure they [the players] have the tools they need to not die. If the player doesn't even know what they need, they are going to get frustrated and stop playing." It is for this reason that Eric argues "a good game developer has to be a good gamer. They can't just be a good programmer; they have to be a player." Only other players know.

Gamers have certain expectations, Eric explains. They will not, for example, accept what he calls a "'Me too!' Game," a game that tries to capitalize on the successes of earlier games without really offering much new. "They can take the foundation of something familiar and build on it, [but they must also] bring something new to the table so that it's not just a 'Me too.' The gaming market is evolved enough that we won't buy that. Can't give us an old game in a new setting." It has to offer something entirely new: an innovative way to portray space (height, weight, width displayed within the confines of a two-dimentional physicality), for example; a fresh approach to the various systems of reward, perhaps. Again, Eric knows this because he is highly literate in this particular community of practice. He can not only function well as a gamer, but he can also quickly learn to play new, even quite different games and he knows the characteristics that make the difference between a good new game and a stale, dull, or frustrating one—a "'Me too!' Game" or one that has a major design flaw.

Knowing the "internal design grammar" of this community of practice as well as he does, Eric can even speculate intelligently on what makes some games work and what makes others disappear from the market moments after they first appear. Accordingly, Eric contends that "Most of the games fall into one of two categories: (1) a 'revolutionary' game and (2) a series of improvements over that." *Quake II*, for example, revolutionized the first-person-shooter games. Another very important ("revolutionary") turn in the gaming industry was the new "genre" gamers call "real-time strategy." Eric explains the difference between the "real-time strategy" genre of games and what came before this way:

> Instead of being turn-based like a board game . . . you know, I do something then you do something, then I do something again, then you do something (and so on), real-time strategy games have me doing something all the time. You have to develop your armies in real time, for example, While you are doing that (and in order for you to do that), you need a farm that will create enough food for your people. Tell your construction guy to build a farm. . . . You have to think of your long-term goals (the overall objective) at the same time make use of your overall strategy of being as efficient as you possibly can.

"Real-time strategy games" rely on what Eric calls the "twitch factor." That is, such games require you to juggle your long-term goals with your short-term goals and do it in "real time" (no time available to players to think through the next move, as you have in chess), and this mandate means that you have to learn to think and move as fast as you can and as efficiently as possible.

"When you pick up any well-designed, real-time strategy game, there are certain characteristics you expect" (Eric Carter). One of those is "realism." Realism is one of the most valued characteristics among players in this community of practice. As Eric explains, "Many sites document the trappings that game designers often fall into," problematic choices that make it easy for the players to find the tools they need to move on to the next level (the toupee or "Grotesque Gulp" they will need when they climb into the boat in *Leisure Suit Larry*, the key they will need when they find the appropriate door in many other games) but do so in ways that, as Eric puts it, "take you out of the immersion of the game. Like crates are a stupid idea." It seems that many first-person shooter games rely on crates to offer extra ammunition when the player needs it, or additional health, or something else. According to Eric,

> It's a cheesy way to do it. It's not in the real world and it puts you out [of the game. It makes no sense to have] these big, giant crates everywhere that you shoot, they explode, and you gather the supplies you need from them. That's not realistic. It's a common way of giving players what they need, but it's an

easy out for [the designers]. Like, "Hey, you'll need some additional health or a key at this point in the game, so we'll just throw down a box that you can blow up and pull out what you need." For it to be of any worth, it must be integrated into the narrative. Things like that reminds you the world you are in is fake.

No player wants to be reminded of that. So, according to Eric, games must be (1) "realistic," (2) innovative, (3) designed in such a way that the player is given the tools they need to "not die," and, as he explains next, they must be challenging.

Using the "internal design grammar" of both genres, Eric compares the pleasures of action games (like the first-person-shooter games discussed above) with adventure games (like *Everquest*, *Leisure Suit Larry*, and *World of Warcraft*). With action games, it's "more button mashing, and that can be fun. [But with] adventure obstacles, you are not only searching for stuff, but you are being given obstacles to overcome and you are given the tools to overcome them. Every genre provides a different gratification. It's like the difference between a good Western novel and science fiction, I guess. It all depends on what you like." Eric's pleasure in video games extends to many genres.

For Eric, *Ico* is one recent game that offers all four of the characteristics of a good game Eric described above: it's realistic, innovative, challenging, and it is intuitive enough to lead the user (though not too conspicuously) to the tools she needs to take on the upcoming challenges successfully.

> *Ico* was the first game that really gave you such an incredible sense of height and depth. Also sort of like a platform game . . . a lot of eye-hand coordination, like you have to have different jumps, grab onto a ledge, shimmy up, and so forth. All these puzzles and obstacles you have to overcome are based on one of these subsequent moves. And then there is the challenge of the game itself . . . the puzzles, obstacles, and the rest. It's also graphically engrossing. It's an environment you want to explore. You find it interesting.

Other characteristics of a good video game emerge here: "First and foremost, games should be fun. . . . It's a balance of complexity and fun. If it's too arduous, then where's the fun in that?" A good video game also "requires interaction. Some 'button mashers' out there where the objective never changes" don't require any real interaction. *Pac Man*, for instance, didn't require much interaction. The objective and the methods you use to reach that objective remain the same, regardless of level: eat the dots, run from the ghosts, eat a blinking dot that will allow you to eat the ghosts for a preset amount of time. Games have gotten so much more complex and gamers so much more demanding that "We don't settle for that anymore. We don't like one-dimensional games." Such games won't survive the market.

The latest *Half Life* (*Half Life II*) is an adventure game that pushes the envelope to incorporate as much realism as possible, and it is one quite popular and valuable within this community of practice because of the designer's attention to such details. According to Eric, "*Half-Life* has a very detailed physics engine" that makes things *feel* real. In the gaming industry, Eric tells me, the "physics engine" refers to "the way things interact with the environment. . . . It gives everything a sense of weight. . . . The ground has a pull" that creates more realistic effects. Especially "cool" is what is calls a "rag-doll effect." That is, if a body falls from a roof, for example, it twists and turns with the "wind" so it actually appears as though it is falling rather than flying, as has been the case with "falling bodies" in previous games. In *Half Life II*, "almost any object you can interact with. You can pick up a fridge and put it at the door . . . so your enemies can't come in. They . . . try to open it, but things have weight in the game so they can only open the door a little bit." They will likely get frustrated and try to enter the room another way—through the window, perhaps. A very realistic scenario. "You can take a grenade and throw it in a Biffi Bin at a construction yard and when it explodes, the physics of the explosion will dump the bin over so the contents rain down on the enemies" and the weight of the materials inside the bin thus trap the enemy so you can then escape. The "realism" of the experience is of incredible value in this community of practice.

When I asked Eric where the term "physics engine" came from, he made clear the ways in which he was instinctively reading what Gee calls the "external design grammar" of video games: "the principles and patterns in terms of which one can recognize what is and what is not an acceptable or typical social practice and identity in regard to the affinity group associated with that semiotic domain" (*What Video Games* 30). As Eric explains, "PC gamers are usually pretty tech savvy." They have to be, more so than even those gamers who play console games. Because new PC games often require new drivers and, many times, new hardware, gamers are constantly updating their systems out of necessity. Gamers who play console games like Sega and the X-Box are necessarily tech savvy to a lesser degree because, as Eric explains, the console is a "sealed-box system—you just pick up the game and go." And because the console is a "sealed-box system," game designers for this equipment must rely on hardware that becomes obsolete rather quickly—designing games for a system with a life of four years or more when technology advances so quickly that the system becomes relatively obsolete within months after the player purchases it. Console gamers, therefore, are not offered the latest and the best games very often because the life of the system precludes it. PC gamers, on the other hand, are "not just savvy about gaming itself [but also] the hardware as well as the software aspects of it." And because PC gamers are required to be more tech savvy than other players, "PC games are constantly evolving . . . games get more complex, cooler looking . . . and then you gotta get new hardware to play it, so the games evolve further still because the designers have better, smarter hardware to design to. It's a circular process."

These highly complex literacies associated with his gaming fed easily into his developing literacies as a composer and a musician. From early on, Eric displayed a talent as a musician—first, as a drummer, then on the guitar, then on a viola in his middle school orchestra. Through high school until he dropped out, he was always a member of several garage bands, playing everything from keyboards to bass guitar to lead guitar. His increasingly complex literacies as a musician fed into his increasingly sophisticated grasp of more and more obscure musical groups.

And then he discovered electronic music.

By example, Trent Reznor and his popular band *Nine Inch Nails* taught Eric quite a lot about how an artist can use technology (especially computers) to develop the kinds of music he most admires. According to *Iskur's Guide to Electronic Music*, "Unlike conventional music, electronic music isn't played, per se. It is PROGRAMMED. . . . More than any other music medium, electronic music thrives on technology to make it what it is." In other words, electronic music is most often composed and played almost entirely through computers. *Iskur* contends that the birth of electronic music can be traced most immediately to 1982,[7] with the invention of MIDI or "Musical Instrument Digital Interface." As Iskur explains, MIDI

> is both a language and an operating system, a protocol and a standard all in one. . . . It is like sheet music. For computers. It tells computers how to play music. . . .
>
> MIDI ushered in an age of uber compatibility across the board. Everything, from samplers, sequencers, software, synths, and effects processors could simply be hooked up to one another via two simple-to-attach cables (one to send data, one to receive it), and work together flawlessly, with little to no hassle, turning the electronic musician into an orchestra. . . . And it all started in 1982, with the creation of MIDI that allowed electronic instruments to hook up with one another, and finally free themselves from the bonds of you filthy humans.

With this, then, Eric's love of computers became one with his love of music; he could now compose, record, and play music—all on his own PC, the same one on which he had begun to play those increasingly complex video games.

Just as his developing literacies as a tech-savvy gamer led him to print-based and text-based literacies (research online via FAQs, etc.), his increasing electronic music literacy did the same. All of a sudden, he was required to research groups whose music may never be associated with any major music label, joining user groups to trade unfinished music with other musicians, to share praise and offer complex (always written) constructive feedback to peers whose work he often truly admired and aspired to emulate, and to collaborate with other musicians in other countries over the Internet.

He began reading music theory—heavy stuff—in magazines and on the screen of his computer monitor (rarely in books; more on that later). He took a class at a local community college to learn to read music and write it in the more traditional code associated with sheet music. He relied on user manuals and user reports to choose and purchase the right software, hardware, and other equipment necessary to develop his music and to push the limits of all the functions the software and hardware offer, just as he tells me PC gamers must to get and use increasingly complex video games.

All this, despite the unfortunate fact that school literacies failed to nurture Eric's literacy learning. By his junior year in high school, Eric had been so broken by the forced standards of his educational experience that he dropped out, earned his GED, and took some classes at the local community college, where he again experienced the same frustration and for the same reasons.

Traditional literacy education failed Eric. Though he has developed very complex literacies in several communities of practice, he never developed or had the confidence required to make effective use of the print-based literacies most valued in more traditional literacy education. He can read scores of complex music theory or heavily technical, jargon-filled user manuals on the computer screen or in a magazine, but he has a very hard time reading the same sorts of things in those "page-bound texts" (Johnson) so coveted in traditional school settings. Though he can (and does) write many complex and provocative reviews of a latest musical creation, a "Me too!" video game, or his own music lyrics, he can hardly pick up a pen to write out a birthday greeting without second- (and third-) guessing himself.

But what if things had gone differently? What if instead of telling Eric he was too young to know how to write his name (judging what he can't do), his pre-K teacher allowed herself to wait to see what he could do? What if instead of requiring Eric to answer multiple-choice questions to determine the main idea of a short passage about Walt Disney, he had been asked to examine his music (or computer or video games) and develop a meta-cognitive understanding of the strategies he's using to negotiate them, critique them, or innovate beyond them? For instance, what if a tutor were to ask him to talk about what he enjoys doing most (music, video games)? What if the tutor then asked him to talk about what he likes about video games (or music)? What if he were to list those things I shared above: a good video game is (1) realistic, (2) fun, (3) creative/innovative, (4) challenging, and (5) do-able. Perhaps the tutor could then ask him to talk about this kind of thing in terms more recognizably valuable in the academy. For instance, what makes for a good book? Maybe the tutor could articulate several points of contact between why she enjoys books and what he says he enjoys about video games so he can then apply these same principles at school. Even if traditional education does not—or cannot—change, even if standardized tests are here to stay, for example, what points of contact could Eric draw between his video game literacies and those required to take and pass the reading portion of a standardized test?

The ultimate goal of rhetorical dexterity is to develop the ability to effectively read, understand, manipulate, and negotiate the cultural and linguistic codes of a new community of practice based on a relatively accurate assessment of another, more familiar one. Eric knows electronic music, video games, and computer hardware. He knows how to "read, understand, manipulate, and negotiate the cultural and linguistic codes" of the communities of practice associated with electronic music, for example. Fans of electronic music can identify "good" music, often even when hearing it for the first time. Not every fan will agree on what's "good," of course, but every "real" fan can identify ("read") and articulate ("write") the characteristics that make for good electronic music, at least in terms other members of this community of practice can understand, value, and take seriously—even when they disagree. Once he is able to identify the "cultural and linguistic codes" that determine membership in this community of practice, Eric can more easily and deliberately learn the "cultural and linguistic codes" of a new one, especially inasmuch as he can identify the points of similarity between these two communities of practice, something we call here "points of contact."

But traditional education did not help him make these connections. In fact, if judged by his ability to respond appropriately to questions designed to "test" literacy, especially as determined according to state-mandated "standards" like those on TASP, my brother would likely be labeled "illiterate." He would most certainly be labeled a "basic writer" according to many traditional literacy assessment measures. In his case, the very fact that he earned not a high school diploma but a general equivalency diploma (or GED) earned him a seat in "Remedial English" during his first (and last) year of college.

Ironically, as I hope I've made clear in the previous pages, Eric is far from illiterate. As we've already seen, he has developed increasingly complex rhetorical strategies for using the texts he encounters and creates on the Internet (blogs, e-forums, chatspaces, video game "walkthroughs" and "FAQS," web design). Even if literacy "skills" could be accurately measured by standards-based tools, I hope it is abundantly clear that any failure to meet those narrowly defined standards has by no means predicted failure in any other aspect of his life, at least not those that traditionally measure success in America: material assets, professional status in a white-collar position, high salary, valuable skills (his computer literacy). That is, he may not express his increasingly complex literacies in terms more traditional assessments of literate ability can recognize, but he is nonetheless *highly* literate.

Yet Eric's story may also offer further evidence of the ways in which *literacy education is not, in fact, equally available to all who want it*. Like the many literacy histories Deborah Brandt gathered and analyzed in her award-winning study *Literacy in American Lives* (2001), Eric's story shows us literacy learning is not equally available to everyone, even in countries like ours with compulsory systems of education—"a tangible reminder that literacy learning throughout history has always required permission, sanction, assistance, coercion, or, at minimum, contact with existing trade routes" (19). His increasingly complex literacies were dependent on a rich network of what Brandt calls "sponsors": "agents, local or distant, concrete or abstract, who enable, support, teach, and model, as well as recruit, regulate, suppress or withhold literacy—and gain advantage by it in some way" (19). The various political and social forces ("agents") shaping Eric's formal literacy instruction in school ("school writing") functioned as "sponsors" in that they "regulat[ed], suppress[ed]," and largely "with[held]" literacy learning from him. In "Writing on the Bias," Linda Brodkey speculates that this failure of literacy education is rooted in the emphasis in writing "rules" ("writing as a ritualized performance") rather than writing as an event with social, political, and material purpose. As she explains,

> Over the years schools have probably quelled a desire to write in a good many children by subjecting them to ritual performances of penmanship, spelling, grammar, punctuation, organization. . . . Every generation mixes its own nostrums and passes them off as writing. The fetishes may change but not the substitution of some formal ritual performance for writing. (34)

Whereas the schools he attended can take little credit for "enabl[ing], support[ing]," or "model[ing]" his literacy learning, the material and sociohistorical circumstances of his life most certainly can. Eric grew up white, male, and middle class. His parents sponsored his computer literacies by acting as "models" in this capacity: his father made his living designing computer software, and both his parents regularly and enthusiastically exposed Eric to the complex yet playful world computers had to offer. They had enough disposable income to purchase equipment like video games, modems, and home computers long before it was cost-effective to do so. We lived in a suburban area with easy access to multiple computer stores filled with cutting-edge equipment and personnel who were no less excited about technology than our parents.

In other words, Eric's particular circumstances sponsored his literacy learning, however informal that learning was. Had Eric grown up in a different place (perhaps far from those computer stores) in a different socioeconomic bracket (perhaps without the disposable income to purchase the technology he enjoyed), he may have been unable to succeed as he has. No doubt Eric is naturally bright and curious, so he should get much credit for his hard work, too. But hard work and intelligence in and of themselves are not enough to develop new literacies: learners need sponsors, and sponsorship is not a neutral condition for learning. As Brandt explains,

Sponsors . . . embody the resource management systems of literacy, particularly avenues to access and reward. Sponsors also introduce the instability in the worth of people's literacy. As various sponsors of economic and political competition, so go the prospects of those they sponsor, both in terms of opportunity and the worth of particular literacy skills. (26–27)

Even those literacies, once obtained, may not have equal value to others obtained through no less rigorous means. In other words, an autonomous model of literacy that implies a certain fluidity of movement among very different communities of practice is available to those who work hard enough for it. Deborah Brandt's ethnographic study *Literacy in American Lives* complicates things further by revealing the ways in which the ability to acquire more and more complex literacies—in fact, even the *value* of those literacies once acquired—is deeply dependent on layers of material and historical circumstances that demand our attention. In fact, the ability to learn new literacies depends, to a great extent, on what she calls "literacy opportunities." As Brandt uses the term, "literacy opportunity refers to people's relationships to social and economic structures that condition chances for learning and development" (*Literacy in American Lives* 7). Even more important, perhaps, "opportunities for literacy are not merely the *occasions* on which people learn to read and write or not; from a biographical perspective, they can be the *internalized structures* that organize and define individual skill" (Brandt 71, emphasis mine). Such "literacy opportunities" are not equally accessible to everyone who works for them. The resources are not equal. Access isn't equal. The value of these literacies once attained isn't even equal.

Raymond Branch and Dora Lopez, for example, were both born the same year (1969) and raised in the same place (a university town in Wisconsin). Access to the "literacy opportunities" they desired, however, was far from "the same." As Brandt explains, "Although both young people were pursuing projects of self-initiated learning, Branch in computer programming and Lopez in written Spanish, [Lopez] had to reach much farther afield for the material and communicative systems needed to support her learning" (175). At the time of the interview (1995), Branch had a bachelor's degree and a highly lucrative career as a freelance computer programmer. Lopez, on the other hand, was a single mother still pursuing an associate's degree at a local community college, barely scraping by financially "by cleaning office buildings in the city's downtown" (172).

So what happened? Should we assume Branch is simply a harder worker than Lopez? Perhaps he's just smarter. Brandt's study suggests otherwise, revealing the ways in which "literacy clusters with material and political privilege. It favors the richer over the poorer, the freer over the jailed, the well connected over the newly arrived or left out" (169). Branch grew up white in a largely middle-class (or upper middle) neighborhood, the child of a university professor with a doctoral degree from an Ivy League university and a real estate executive mother; Lopez grew up Latina, the child of former migrant farm workers and, later, lower-level employees at the same state university in which Branch's father worked and in a neighborhood populated with, predictably enough, others in similar circumstances. Lopez's father had a two-year community college degree in accounting and worked as a shipping-and-receiving clerk in the university mail room; her mother worked part-time in a bookstore.

In this environment, Lopez taught herself to read and write in Spanish. As she explains,

> I learned by reading first. I read phonetically. The way I spoke is the way I figured it was said, and later on, I asked either my mother or someone who knew Spanish if I was right. Then, writing. I tried to write phonetically, the way you hear it. . . . I practiced for a longtime, and then I would write letters to my cousins in Mexico [and a friend in] Columbia. (174)

Access to Spanish-language texts was not easy to come by in her community, however. Although the Latino population was increasing rapidly at the end of the 1990s (the time of the interview and subsequent publication of Brandt's book), throughout the 1970s and 1980s, the population held a pretty steady minority at about 1 percent of the total. When she worked at the bookstore, Lopez's mother purchased some Spanish-language children's books. However, early access to additional, mass-produced tools was limited to her family's regular 70–mile journeys to the "big city to find . . . suitable groceries" and Spanish-language magazines and newspapers (173). Neither her brother nor her cousins born in the United States could read or write in Spanish. Her parents could, but they used written Spanish very rarely, as there was no cause to at work and little time to at home. Lopez had no access to formal schooling in written Spanish until high school, and then only as a "foreign language."

But whereas for Lopez access to the tools necessary to develop Spanish literacy was hard to come by, Branch's literacy opportunities were plentiful. Branch was immersed in computers from a very early age. His father's position at the university granted him access to top-notch equipment in his father's science lab, where he was able to work side-by-side "in the company of," as Branch puts it, "real users" (173). His first-grade classroom was hooked up to the mainframe at an area "elite" university (near Silicon Valley). In a summer enrichment program following sixth grade (in 1980), he took a course in BASIC (a computer programming language).[8] During this same period, he wrote his first computer program, an "adventure game" that he then rewrote on the new Apple II he received for Christmas a few months after returning from camp; he was twelve years old. The next Christmas, he received a modem. As Branch explains, "[a]t the time the only people who had Apples were people who were programmers, too. At the time, [personal] computers weren't made to be used for much. You had to learn a little about the language to get anything done" (177).

For Branch, learning to program meant taking advantage of the multiple resources at his disposal: "the books that came with" the Apple II that were "fairly good about teaching you Basic and so forth"; the "published work" of other programmers, especially games, which he would then "pick apart [to] find out how the person did what they did, and then duplicate that"; "utility software" that helped new programmers develop new software themselves; the "pirated material" he received from friends who had "cracked" programs, especially games and that "usually included a little note about how they cracked it"; the "user groups" that brought together hackers and other computer enthusiasts—first face-to-face, often informally at the multiple computer stores cropping up within biking distance of his home, and, later, through his new modem, which allowed him to "transfer software to people in Minnesota or Washington or whatever" and "sped things up considerably" (177).

Lopez's experiences in this very same town differed from Branch's in some rather profound ways. Whereas for Branch, "a university town in the 1970s provided an information-rich, resource-rich learning environment in which to pursue his version of second-language learning . . . for Lopez, a female member of a culturally unsubsidized ethnic minority, the same town at the same time was information- and resource-poor" (174). Both Lopez and Branch are obviously passionate, driven, hard-working individuals, so neither can really be seen as more (or less) responsible for their success (or failure) than the other. Neither can we blame a lack of parental support, as so many have elsewhere. At home, Lopez's increasing Spanish literacy was considered very valuable, and her parents did what they could to support their daughter's development in this area. It was the public sector that lacked support for her Spanish-language learning, as we've explained.

Branch's parents were also very supportive of his literacy development, including purchasing a computer that, as Branch put it, wasn't "really made to be used for much" (177). But "it is not the lack of family support for [Lopez's] literacy learning—but the fact that family was the only source of support—that distinguishes the experiences of Lopez so sharply from that of Branch" (180). Once acquired, this Spanish literacy had much less market value than did Branch's computer literacy. In his mid-twenties, Branch was doing quite well as a writer of computer software and software documentation, putting his new literacies to work in society and reaping grand rewards for it. Lopez, on the other hand, found her Spanish literacies held little value in society, save the fact that "in her janitorial job," she was able to "communicat[e] on her supervisor's behalf with the largely Latina cleaning staff." Brandt articulates the reasons for this discrepancy this way:

> In these accounts, we can see how the development and eventual economic worth of Branch's literacy skills were underwritten by late twentieth-century transformations in communication technology that created a boomtown need for software and software documentation. Lopez's biliterate abilities paid off much further down the economic ladder, in government-sponsored summer programs [where she worked as a teacher's aid for children of migrant farm workers when she was fourteen years old] and commercial enterprises that, in the 1990s, were absorbing surplus migrant workers into a low-wage, urban service economy. (175)

In other words, "the outlets for [Lopez's] biliteracy were shaped by the low status given to Spanish and its native speakers. Part of the general economic devaluation that put Latinas as a group in one of the lowest rungs of the economic reward ladder" (180).

So can we assume Lopez would be better off had she chosen to develop literacies in something else—perhaps computers—rather than Spanish? Actually, no. The concept "literacy sponsorship" helps us see why. As noted previously, Brandt uses the term "sponsor" to describe a very specific phenomenon: "Sponsors are delivery systems for the economies of literacy, the means by which these forces present themselves to—and through—individual learners. They also represent the causes into which people's literacy usually gets recruited" (20). Branch's sponsors, then, were his parents, whose job and status in the community (and location of residence) allowed their son access to people (the researchers, the hackers), places (the university science lab, the computer stores), and things (the new computer for Christmas, a summer enrichment program that included formal instruction in BASIC) that Lopez's family simply could not provide. Her parents did not have access to the same university resources available to Branch and his father, even though her father worked there, too. Unlike Branch, Lopez's first introduction to computers was not in a vibrant, university environment with "real users" but in a remedial reading program for the children of migrant farm workers, where she worked as a teacher's aid resetting the programs that ran multiple-choice question sets. Unfortunately discrepancies like these are not uncommon. In the 1995 study "Information Technology and Low-Income Inner City Communities," researcher Krieg found that "children in wealthy neighborhoods tend to use technology for complex, problem-solving activities, while children in poorer communities are more often expected to use computers for drill and practice" (131–132).

Unlike Branch, Lopez did not receive her first computer at twelve. When she graduated from high school and began her studies at a local community college to become a bilingual social worker, her father purchased her first "computer"—a secondhand "word processor that had been advertised for sale by a university student" (Brandt 175). They "sponsored" her computer

literacy inasmuch as was possible for and visible to them. The kind of computer literacy Lopez was able to attain did not have the same value (to her or
society at large) as the kind Branch was able to attain. As Brandt puts it, "Just
as, it seems, the rich get richer, the literate get more literate" (169).

"What happens," Brandt asks, "when literacy itself is capitalized as a productive force? And what impact does such an investment have on individual
literacy learning?" The fact is, Branch's computer literacy (the programs he
writes, the code he is able to "crack") has market value that far exceeds any
Lopez is able to obtain. According to Brandt, "Literacy takes on unusual status in an information economy. It is a form of labor power, to be sure, a
human skill, an input. Yet it is also an output, a product of varying value in
use and exchange, a means of production, and a kind of raw material (or an
element . . . in production)." Lopez's literacy in Spanish may only be sold as
"labor power," not necessary as "product output," "an instrument in production," or "raw material." Branch's computer literacy, on the other hand, can
be sold as "labor power," "product output," "a means of production," *and* "a
kind of raw material." How? As Brandt explains,

> If this economy buys and sells written and spoken words, graphs, charts,
> images, software, and other symbolic products, these products themselves
> are formulated out of rawer but still symbolic materials. Budgets are made of
> numbers, forecasts out of trends, insurance policies out of actuarial tables,
> texts, in general, out of other texts. (171)

Though we are discussing Spanish and technology—two literacies we
don't automatically associate with the "ability to read and write in the dominant language" standard that is so often associated with public debates about
the value of literacy—Brandt's study shows us how the same ecological constraints apply with respect to more traditional, print-based literacies. Dwayne
Lowery, for example, is a union worker whose life has changed significantly
over the years as a direct result of the changing value of the kinds of literacies he has already acquired and to which he has access.

Because his father was a committed and active member of the United
Rubber Workers, Dwayne Lowery, born in 1938, was exposed to much
"union-based literacy" from a very early age, though he didn't become
involved in it himself until he joined a newly developed public employees
union some thirty years later. In the early 1970s, he earned a union-sponsored
grant that sent him to Washington, DC, for four months to learn about, in
his words, "regulations, systems, laws. We did a lot of work on organizing, you
know, learning how to negotiate contracts, contractual language, how to
write it. Gross National Product, how that affected the Consumer Price
Index. It was pretty much a crash course" (53).

When he returned, he took a full-time job as a field staff representative
for the union and, for years, this "crash course" served him well. Most of the

negotiations centered around "talking" with "part-time people" lacking even the four months of training for such work that Lowery received. The problem was that as the union gained strength, the employers became increasingly leery of such negotiations, sending in not "part-time people" but lawyers. At this point, according to Brandt, "all activity became rendered in writing: the exhibit, the brief, the transcript, the appeal" and most of the negotiations took place behind closed doors, "after solitary deliberation over complex sets of documents" (54–55).

Basic writing student Jerrron speaks directly to the specific ways in which inequitable access affected (and continues to affect) the ways in which he experiences literacy education. In the first place, he had to rely on the access to "better skills" he was able to gain by putting down an address of a relative or a friend rather than his own: "We stayed in communities that would have forced me to go to schools that were not as academically advanced as others. My parents used addresses of friends and relatives that put me in better school districts, which allowed me to go to better schools." While his parents were able to make this change for him, the material conditions of his particular educational opportunities continued to place him at a disadvantage:

> Even though [my parents] did put me on the right track and are continuing to pay for my education, they could have held me back from some key ways of improving my education. They could have been more involved in my education and helped me out when I had difficulty understanding certain subjects. My parents always told me to make good grades and every now and then helped me with my homework. But because they worked so hard when they came home they did not want to do homework. They wanted to relax. . . . Since the world is constantly improving and changing some of the classes we have now they did not have back when my parents went to school so my parents did not have the same education I did. Now that I am in college I will be taking more advanced classes that my parents cannot help me with. Some students' parents got degrees and already took college courses so if they need help they can ask their parents for advice, but I do not have that same privilege because my dad did not go to college and even though my mom went she did not get a degree. (WA3)

From her examination of "literacy in American lives," Brandt not only found that "literacy changes" but that the value of certain literacies fades as new ones emerge. Thus, Lowery's skills as a "consummate debater and deal maker"—a good talker—lost value as "face-to-face meetings became occasions mostly for a ritualistic exchange of texts" rather than deal making. In *Literate Lives in the Information Age*, Cynthia Selfe and Gail Hawisher's exploration of digital literacies revealed much the same thing. In their case studies of twenty Americans born between 1955 and 1986, they focused on their experiences with the "literacies of technology [over] the last 25 years or so" in order to "begin tracing technological literacy as it has emerged over the last few decades within the United States" (3). As they put it in their concluding chapter, "new forms of literacy don't simply accumulate. Rather, they have life spans: they emerge; they overlap and compete with pre-existing forms; they accumulate, significantly, perhaps, in periods of transition, but they also eventually fade away" (213).

Such "changing literacies," Selfe and Hawisher predict, mean that "parents, educators, and policy makers" must begin to "understand literacy as it has changed and continues to change, in the digital age, to formulate new insights about what it means to read, compose, and exchange text in electronic environments" (184)—changes not only to our print-based literacies in response to this new information economy but changes in the very modes of literate expression: webpage development, text messaging, blogging, and the rest.

Danielle DeVoss, for example, born in 1973, was introduced to computers very early—she was only ten—and very quickly developed a passion for them that shaped how she approached other new literacies. From the beginning, she "used the computer as a social space" through online gaming, bulletin boards, and chat rooms—a practice that continued on through and well beyond her teenage years. Her passion for and competency in increasingly complex digital literacies bled into other, more conventional literate practices. In these spaces, Danielle "became increasingly adept at reading and interpreting imaginary scenarios and composing the exchanges between characters of various types and abilities . . . learning to read and predict rule-based movements of characters in time and space, visualizing, mapping and navigating her own way through the multidimentional compositional space of games" (185).

However, while Danielle was and still is, by all accounts, a very strong reader and writer in more conventional contexts (at the time of this study, she is an assistant professor of English at Michigan State University), such contexts rarely felt as satisfying to her as digital ones did. In fact, as Selfe and Hawisher explain, "Few, if any of Danielle's teachers were likely to consider the games and chat rooms in which she participated to be an appropriate context for the instruction of literacy," despite the fact that such experiences had much to do with the new, expanding literacies so increasingly prevalent in this information age.

Literacy changes and our schools are not keeping up. In fact, our schools may actually be retarding the complex literacies many adolescents and young adults develop just by virtue of their "real-world" interactions with these changing literacies. "Teachers," as Selfe and Hawisher explain, should "pay increased attention to the new-media literacies students bring to the classroom, comparing these literacies to more conventional literacies and seeking to learn from this comparison more about the worlds that students inhabit and believe they will be facing in the coming years" (210).

Danielle DeVoss was born around the same time as Dora Lopez and Raymond Branch from Brandt's study (and the same year as my brother, Eric); therefore, she grew up in the same digital age that Branch prospered within and, sadly, Lopez experienced only peripherally. When our students arrive with such rich backgrounds in a variety of very complex communities, it seems unreasonable to ignore them. We must rely on them to help them learn new literacies, the transference of which may depend on their ability to develop *rhetorical dexterity*. Danielle DeVoss's extensive experience with online gaming, for example, gave her much fodder for the development of web texts. As Hawisher and Selfe explain, "Danielle enjoyed composing webtexts, in part, because these activities resonated with earlier literacies she practiced in gaming environments" (185). Unlike the conventional literacies demanded of her at school, which were "increasingly limited to the alphabetic and to the two-dimensional representational space of the page," composing web texts "allowed her to combine alphabetic and visual elements," as did her gaming (186). "Both kinds of composition allowed her to . . . organize texts along temporal and spatial axis" as well, something that in online gaming she called "creating mental maps":

> Trying to create mental maps of the text-only games I played taught me a
> lot about mapping out textual spaces and trying to think in terms of "real"
> space. . . . I remember when I first started playing games in these realms and
> being lost, I'd wander in circles and wasn't able to return to particular areas
> within the game. It was frustrating, so I became much more adept at creat-
> ing mental maps of where I was and where I wanted to go. I started by pay-
> ing attention to short distances, mapping how I was moving during one stint
> of playing. As I did this, I was able to create larger maps and form a stronger
> sense of the realm in which I was playing. (185–186)

As a child, Stephen Foote (born in 1969) created similar mental maps of these early, text-based games, even developing—collaboratively, with his older brother Michael—a physical "map" that enabled them both to more easily and effectively negotiate the text-only adventure game *Raaka-tu*. Recently, Michael ran across this very map, scanned it, and sent it to Stephen, who then shared it with me and I now share with you (Figure 1).[9]

As you can see, this "map" includes strategies as well, allowing the young players to, as Selfe and Hawisher describe it, "explore the structure of large bodies of complicated material"—a composing skill Danielle also found particularly useful in developing her web texts (186).

Charles Jackson, born in 1985, developed an early interest in games and game design. His experiences taught him not only to "read and predict rule-based movements of characters in time and space" as Danielle learned to do in her role-playing games (185) but, in fact, to "*read the texts of the*

FIGURE 1
Map created by Michael Foote and his younger brother (Stephen)
to negotiate the text-only adventure game, *Raaka-Tu* (circa 1981).
Additional information about *Raaka-Tu* is available at http://www.figmentfly.com.

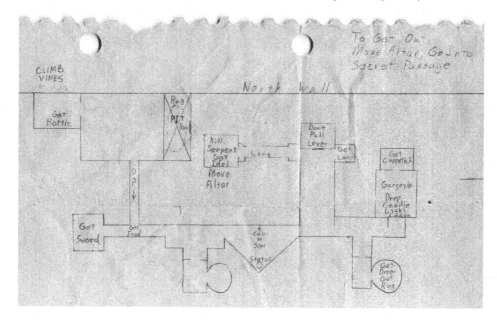

games themselves—figuring out the grammars or rule-sets that shaped his interaction with these dynamic environments and acquiring the kinesthetic, intercultural, and problem-solving skills that the games demanded" (200, emphasis mine).

Again, one of the primary objectives of a pedagogy of rhetorical dexterity is to help students identify and articulate what I call points of contact between new literacies and more familiar ones. We can, of course, find many points of contact between Charles's gaming experiences and his experiences with more conventional literacies. He actually identifies several himself: "Games have different genres just like books do. So when you pick up a game of a certain genre [action, for example] you kind of expect how to know how to play that game," just as you would expect to know how to approach that book based, to a certain extent, on the genre. He continues:

> playing games has taught me about writing because a lot of games are like problem solving . . . when you are making a computer game, you have to think about everything and what can go wrong, what you are forgetting. And this has helped me in writing because *it's the same thing when I am com-*

posing a paper for a teacher. I have to think of everything that I am writing
and everything that I can do to make it better and everything I have done
that might make it wrong. Might make it not work or flow correctly. (Selfe
and Hawisher 200–201, emphasis mine)

The fact is, as Selfe and Hawisher contend, "[t]eachers and schools today . . .
must be prepared not only to work with students and their new literacies in
productive ways, but also to modify current curricula to account for students
who spend as much time reading the texts of coded simulations or visual arguments as they do the pages of novels" (183). Our students have much to teach
us, if only we treat what they know and who they are more seriously: video
games, golf, blogs, Anime, and other passions should be understood as communities of practice with their own, very specific rules for literate behavior.
Learning new literacies, therefore, extends beyond learning to read and write
for school-based audiences. Learning new literacies can, in fact, include
learning to blog in a new environment, appreciate and/or create graphics-dri-
ven texts (Anime, comics), or even play a video game. As James Paul Gee
argues, many video games are rigorous, intellectually challenging "semiotic
domains" that require of players what educators should require of their students: "video games build into their designs and encourage . . . good principles of learning, principles that are better than many of our skill-and-drill,
back-to basics, test-them-until-they-drop schools" (205). In fact, "when people learn to play video games, *they are learning a new literacy*" (Gee 13, emphasis mine).

What we want from our students is not simply *accessible* literacy, indicat-
ing an ability to *access* a particular community of practice at some "basic"
level (whatever that means), but rather *productive* literacy, giving students
not only the ability to function within a chosen community of practice but
to actually gain some level of control over it—perhaps even effect change
within it, if the student so desires. Learning productive literacy, as we understand it, demands many of the same components that Gee asserts are required
for critical and active learning to occur in any "semiotic domain"—a term he
uses to get readers to think of literacy in new ways; a "semiotic domain [is]
any set of practices that recruits one or more modalities (e.g., oral or written
language, images, equations, symbols, sounds, gestures, graphs, artifacts, etc.)
to communicate distinct types of meanings" (17, 18). Therefore,

For learning to be critical as well as active . . . she needs to learn not only
how to understand and produce meanings in a particular semiotic domain
that are recognizable to those affiliated with the domain, but, in addition,
how to think about the domain at a "meta" level as a complex system of
interrelated parts. The learner also needs to learn how to innovate in the
domain—how to produce meanings that, while recognizable, are seen as
somehow novel or unpredictable. (23)

Adrian, a fifteen-year-old, highly literate player of the role-playing game *Everquest* spends much "more time trying to crack the game open" than he does actually playing it (qtd. in Gee, *What Video Games* 174). For him, doing so allows him to go beyond mere "understand[ing] and produc[ing] meanings" within the game as it is currently configured—though he is, by all accounts, a very adept player—in order to "think about the domain at a 'meta' level as a complex system of interrelated parts." As he explains it, he uses "hex editors" "to crack the game open [in order] to see what makes it work."

> What a hex editor does is it basically breaks up computer code into pretty much binary code, and on the left side it gives you a bunch of zeros and ones and, then, on the right side it tells you what the code actually does. And, so, if you go and look on the right side, you can actually edit it. You don't learn this stuff by taking a class on it. It's just like here and there you pick stuff up. (174–175)

Danielle, as we may recall, develops this meta-awareness of the games she plays by creating what she calls "mental maps"—maps that allow her to "explore the structure of large bodies of complicated material" (Selfe and Hawisher 186). Charles reaches these levels, too, by learning to "read the texts of the games themselves—figuring out the grammars or rule sets that shaped his interaction with these dynamic environments" (200). In Brandt's study, we see that in the semiotic domain of early computer technology, Branch quickly develops this same understanding of "the system of complex, interrelated parts" that make up the computers he was growing to know. As he explains, "[t]he way you really learned . . . was probably the same way you really learn to write. And that's by picking apart other people's published work. Find out how the person did what they did" (Brandt 177). Like Danielle, Charles, and Adrian, Raymond Branch developed an ability to "innovate in the domain—how to produce meanings that, while recognizable, are seen as somehow novel or unpredictable" (Gee, *What Video Games* 23). Branch was able to develop them into quite a lucrative career; he saw innovation in computer technology all around him, so he simply built on these models of literate practice.

Lopez, on the other hand, was not given the necessary "literacy opportunities," in Brandt's sense of the term, to develop a meta-awareness within this semiotic domain. As we recall, her early experiences with computers did not allow her to use them actively or productively but rather passively, in a "remedial," skill-and-drill format.

Later, she was able to develop accessible literacy in a sense—at least at the level of word processing on the secondhand unit her parents were able to procure for her. We don't have the information necessary to determine whether she was able to develop productive literary in Spanish. We know she located several "literacy opportunities"—writing her family in Mexico, reading the Spanish language newspaper—but we do not know the extent to which such experiences offered her opportunities to "innovate," "to produce meanings that . . . are seen as somehow novel or unpredictable."

Dwayne Lowery, the union worker in Brandt's study, was also unable to develop the meta-awareness necessary to "innovate," and later even survive, as a union negotiator because the necessary literacies changed. Even his opponents changed; gone were the former factory workers who would negotiate with, as Lowery puts it, "talk and a handshake"—replaced by young, hotshot corporate lawyers with no direct experience in the kind of blue-collar work Lowery's union represents. When he could no longer rely on his ethos and experience as a former factory worker, he felt he had to, like the basic writers discussed in chapter 2, "start from scratch."

The meta-awareness we value, the levels of understanding that make innovation possible, are available to our students who develop rhetorical dexterity. Had Lowery been offered "literacy opportunities" like those offered via a pedagogy of rhetorical dexterity, he may have been able to continue to be as effective a negotiator as he had been, even in the face of changing opponents. Doing so would require him to identify those "points of contact/dissonance" between his familiar literacies and the new ones required of him, carrying over those strategies from his familiar literacies that seem most appropriate, abandoning others, and, where necessary, developing new strategies altogether.

Thus far I have described the ways in which people who are successfully literate in a variety of activity systems associated with multiple, often overlapping communities of practice have developed the flexibility and awareness necessary to develop multiple literacies. In the following chapter, I will further outline the ways in which we might make deliberate use of this pedagogy of rhetorical dexterity in training students called basic writers.

FIVE

The Way Literacy (Re)produces

From a contextual perspective, literate abilities originate in social postures and social knowledge that begin well before and extend well beyond words on a page. Serious programs of literacy instruction, many argue, must teach toward these contextual and contextualizing dimensions of literacy if they are to be successful and just. (Brandt, *Literacy in American Lives* 4)

HENRY GIROUX TELLS US that literacy is "a political phenomenon . . . [that] represents an embattled epistemological terrain on which different sociological groups struggle over how reality is to be signified, reproduced, and resisted" (*Theory and Resistance* 237). For this reason, "literacy can be neither neutral nor objective, and . . . for the most part . . . is inscribed in the ideology and practice of domination" (225). A pedagogy of rhetorical dexterity makes use of this assumption and attempts to develop critical consciousness with practical, rhetorical, and even political applications. Working from the assumption that the autonomous model of literacy is both ubiquitous and harmful to those attempting to gain access to dominant communities of practice like the ones associated with the academy, rhetorical dexterity attempts to redefine literacy as a socially sanctioned and situated, politically relevant, and local "people-centered" (Royster). To do so means that we can separate neither content nor functionality from the communities of practice that define themselves through these activity systems. Thus, the current chapter will begin by articulating the ways in which *content* may function in a given community of practice. Next, I will examine the ways in which *skill* is contextually bound, socially sanctioned behavior, especially as it applies to political and pedagogical attempts to reify literacy as a set of generalizable, testable skills. Once we establish the philosophical framework on which a pedagogy of rhetorical dexterity is based, I will share with you a curriculum employed to make use of this pedagogy, as well as student responses to the relevant readings and assignments.

LITERACY AS CONTENT

The autonomous model of literacy informs public policy and the vast majority of arguments presented in the public media that "Johnny" (or "Jenny") can't read/write. As we discussed at some length in chapter 2, this model is shaped in part by a perception of literacy as a "bundle of skills" (Resnick); however, it is also quite common for this model to be informed by a cultural perspective: "literacy" as determined by knowledge of particular "content" rather than an ability to perform specific "skills." A key force shaping this perspective is E. D. Hirsch. In his best-selling books (including, most significantly, *Cultural Literacy: What Every American Needs to Know* and a series of books for children at every grade level, like *What Every First Grader Needs to Know, What Every Second Grader Needs to Know*, etc.), Hirsch argues that "literacy is far more than a skill and . . . it requires large amounts of specific information" (*Cultural Literacy* 2). He sees this information as a static "network of information that all competent readers possess . . . background information . . . that enables them to take up a newspaper and read with an adequate level of comprehension, getting the point, grasping the implications, relating what they read to the unstated context which alone gives meaning to what they read."

In his presentation at the first Shaughnessy Memorial Conference in April 1980,[1] Hirsch tells the audience of writing teachers:

> we have stressed the process and product of writing at the expense of the huge domain of tacit knowledge which is never written down but which, though quite invisible, is just as operative as the visual written word. A writing task could be compared to an iceberg whose visible tip is arrangement, syntax, rhetoric, spelling, coherence, and so on, but whose bigger, invisible base is tacit, cultural knowledge—not just linguistic knowledge and knowledge about the topic, but also, and most important, knowledge of what others also know and expect about the topic, about the form, about the writer, and about the world. In short, *the cultural dimension is that whole system of unspoken, tacit knowledge that is shared between writer and reader.* (28–29)

To clarify his point, Hirsch speaks of a then recent experiment conducted on the streets of Boston by a "clever Harvard undergraduate." Through this experiment, the researcher reveals the differing ways in which adults respond to his request for directions ("How do you get to Central Square?"). He discovered that the responses he received depended on the way he asked it, what he was wearing when he asked it, how "native" his outfit, demeanor, speech patterns, word choices, and other codes made him seem (or how "nonnative" these same codes made him appear to locals).

In the first series of experiments, he made his request "as a native. He is carrying a copy of the *Boston Globe*, and he affects a strong Boston accent. Invariably he gets a very brief reply to his question" ("How d'ya get to Central Square?" "First stop on the subway") (33–34). In this instance, Hirsch argues, the strangers, whom we presume to be natives of Boston themselves, "had to assume the questioner . . . knew: where the subway is, which direction you go on the subway to get to Central Square, and also the convention that Bostonians do not use elaborate forms of courtesy when addressing unknown fellow Bostonians—and this is to mention just the most obvious assumptions about the knowledge the other person is assumed to have" (35).

In the "next phase of the experiment," the researcher emphasizes his "out-of-townness," first by "prefac[ing] his question with the statement 'I'm from out of town,' [then simply] by adopting a rural Missouri accent which is exotic enough in Cambridge to indicate 'I'm from out of town.'" When he requested directions as a nonnative of Boston, strangers relied on a very different set of assumptions about his knowledge base, and thus they offered a more elaborate series of directions. In response to his question ("I'm from out of town. Can you tell me how to get to Central Square?"), the stranger "typically" responded with something like this: "Yes. You go down these stairs into the Subway . . . and take the train headed for Quincy, but you get off very soon, the first stop is Central Square, and. . . . Be sure you get off there. You'll know it because there's a big sign on the wall, it says Central Square and . . ." (35).

For Hirsch, this experiment[2] exposes what he calls the "invisible cultural dimension of writing—a knowledge of the reader's knowledge—a range of knowledge tacitly shared" (33). Thus, the goal of literacy instruction becomes making certain we all share as much content knowledge as possible; Hirsch assures us he doesn't mean that we should all have the exact same education, but it really seems he means just that. He says we need to have if not the same content knowledge, at least the same *types* of content knowledge—perhaps we don't all need to read the same Shakespearean tragedy, but he argues we should all read at least one. Maybe we don't all need to watch every episode of *MASH*, but we should all know at least one. According to Hirsch,

> Back-to-the Basics needs to be supplemented with Back-to-the Classics; back to content, shared knowledge, cultural literacy. Cultural literacy implies shared knowledge about ourselves, our history, and our work, our laws, our political, economic, and social arrangements, our classical texts from a great many domains including TV, the movies, and literature. (45)

In "Arguing Literacy" (1988), Patricia Bizzell calls attention to his "concessions to popular and minority cultures such as . . . Fredrick Douglas [and] . . .

Pinocchio. By and large, however . . . the core of this list is the core of western high culture" (146). As Paulo Freire explains in *Literacy: Reading the World and the Word*,

> In general, dominant segments of any society talk about their particular interests, their tastes, their styles of living, which they regard as concrete expressions of nationality. Thus the subordinated groups, who have their own tastes and styles of living, cannot talk about their tastes and styles as national expressions. They lack the political and economic power to do so. Only those who have power can generalize and decree their group characteristics as representative of the national culture. With this decree, the dominant group necessarily depreciates all characteristics belonging to subordinated groups, characteristics that deviate from decreed patterns. (52)

"The dominant class . . . has the power to define, profile, and describe the world" (53). Within this context, Hirsch's model of "cultural literacy" is particularly oppressive and problematic even from the most practical standpoint (application) because it obscures the ways in which literacy actually functions in the real world.

James Paul Gee offers this example in his regularly cited article "What Is Literacy?," which may help us understand another major concern Hirsch's curriculum raises in a diverse, pluralistic world:

> It is a truism that a person can know perfectly the grammar of a language and not know how to use that language. It is not just what you say, but how you say it. If I enter my neighborhood bar and say to my tattooed drinking buddy, as I sit down, "May I have a match, please?," my grammar is perfect but what I have said is wrong nonetheless. It is less often remarked that a person could be able to use a language perfectly and still not make sense. It is not just how you say it, but what you are and do when you say it. If I enter my neighborhood bar and say to my drinking buddy, as I sit down, "Gimme a match, wouldya?," while placing a napkin on the bar stool to avoid getting my newly pressed designer jeans dirty, I have said the right thing, but my "saying-doing" combination is nonetheless all wrong. (525)

Through Gee's hypothetical conversation in a bar, we learn that his competency is determined not just by *what* he says ("May I have a match, please?") or *how* he says it ("Gimme a match, wouldya?") but even by what he is wearing and doing as he speaks within that context.

One of the writers in our basic writing program pointed out that *who* you ask matters as well. According to him, "It makes no sense to ask the guy with a Bible in his hand and a t-shirt with Jesus Saves on it. Why not ask the guy behind him with a beer in his hand and a cigarret [sic] in his mouth?" Even barroom literacy ("competence" as a participant in a barroom conversation) depends on the bar itself and the persons with whom I am speaking. If I am in a bar where smoking isn't allowed, for example, the very act of asking for a match at all would reveal my outsider status in that public space. In that situation, it wouldn't matter who I asked, how I asked it, or even what I wore and how I behaved as I did so; the only thing that would really matter is the simple fact that I had asked for a match at all in a place where I shouldn't have any reason to need one. And if I asked for a match at a bar in College Station near the Texas A&M campus while wearing an "Angry Orange" T-shirt and baseball cap with "University of Texas" plastered across the front, it may not matter how I ask the question or whether I say anything at all. The very fact that I am sporting the rival team's propaganda marks me as an outsider automatically. If I am from someplace else (far, far away), my unfortunate choice of attire may be uninformed rather than malicious because I may not be aware of the intense rivalry between the Texas Aggies and the UT Longhorns. If I am aware of the rivalry, however, it seems likely that I may have chosen to wear these colors specifically because I *knew* doing so would be considered an act of rebellion. In a situation like this, the fact that I don't fit in would not be a problem for me because in that case I *chose* not to fit in.

In the first case, the outsider status—the lack of belonging—may be quite undesirable. The visitor may be confused by the local reactions to her. She may wonder what she was dong wrong. In short, she will have little control over her outsider status in that social space because she is not literate in Texas college football culture. On the other hand, the rebellious wearer of UT paraphernalia is quite likely *highly* literate in Texas football culture and chooses to actively provoke the members of that community by violating the social expectations that UT will not be represented in that culture, at least not with any reverence.

Sometimes outsider status is, in fact, what students want. However, even when they wish a particular group to view them as outsiders, I suspect that most students (most of *us*) would like to be in control of the ways in which they display this lack of belonging. When a person is judged to be an outsider yet can't figure out why, we can assume this person does not possess "competent" levels of literacy in that particular rhetorical context (or "community of practice"). Literacy is less about possessing a particular "skill" or content than it is a way of acting and conversing with others who have particular expectations about how one should act or speak.

In this sense, writing is conversation because writers must consider the expectations and the concerns of the actual people living and thinking in a particular place. Communication like this depends on more than "shared knowledge," as Hirsch would have it. Writers must think about how potential readers may react to the words they place on the page. Writing is, fundamentally, a social act. Even in the world of print, multiple social concerns affect the way the people will read any text I write, from the way I ask for a match to the place in which I ask for it (i.e., the place where my text is read), from the audience I target to discuss my lighting needs to what I am "wearing" as I do so (i.e., the style and genre, etc., I choose to use as a writer). All of these things may make my readers accept me as an insider who knows what matters and who they will take seriously or reject me as an outsider who doesn't know what matters to readers and who, therefore, shouldn't be taken seriously, and these issues change from community to community (and often even from member to member to some extent, depending largely on the role and status of the participant).

Another example that helps complicate Hirsch's insistence on a "Back-to-the-Classics" movement is this: On the back cover of Hirsch's best-selling book *Cultural Literacy: What Every American Needs to Know*, the publisher asks us to "test" our "cultural literacy. Can you put the following in context?" Listed are things like "Alamo," "Billy the Kid," "El Greco," "penis envy," "tabula rasa," "Zeitgeist," and other items every "literate" American is supposed to know. According to Hirsch, "to understand what somebody is saying, we must understand" not only "the surface meaning of words" but also "the context as well." In other words, "to grasp words on a page we have to know a lot of information that isn't set down on the page" (2). While I certainly agree that context is of primary importance when attempting any literate activity, it is important to point out the futility of knowing all the "background information" necessary to comprehend any text a reader may encounter. The words the publisher lists on the back of Hirsch's book certainly require knowledge of Western canonical information like Freudian psychology, Renaissance art, major thinkers of the Enlightenment period, and the like. However, who determines which background information is necessary to attain appropriate levels of "cultural literacy"? Whose standards are used?

"Literacy" as a reader of *DC Comics* (which includes superheroes like Wonder Woman, Superman, the Flash, and Batman) depends on a very different network of information,[3] though it may also draw on the network of information included in Hirsch's list. To test our "cultural literacy" in what these readers call the "DC Universe" (as opposed to the "Marvel Universe," which includes Spiderman, the Incredible Hulk, X-Men, and the Fantastic Four), we could ask whether a reader can put the following in context: "the Golden-Age Flash," "the Silver-Age Flash," "Crisis on Infinite Earths," "Jay Garrick," "Barry Allen," "Wally West." To do so would depend on a deep knowledge of more than sixty years of storytelling. Knowing that readers are unlikely to be familiar with all of the complex and multilayered back stories that feed into any single issue, writers fold pertinent "cultural" information right into the current story—mostly seamlessly but always obviously.

The "Golden-Age Flash," I am told, refers to the Flash with the secret identity "Jay Garrick" who existed around World War II, but disappeared during the McCarthy era, along with several of the other lesser-known superheroes like Green Lantern, Hawkman, and Sandman. As the story was retold in JSA[4] (*The Justice Society of America*, February 2005), it seems that the McCarthy hearings resulted in an order that they "take off their masks," an order these heroes refused to obey and thus went into retirement. This issue (#68) begins with Stargirl (the "Platinum-Age" reincarnation of several "Golden-Age" heroes like the Star Spangled Kid and Starman) at her home in Blue Valley, Nebraska, at 5:14 A.M. "today." She says, "I'm learning how to be a hero. But I'm tired." She just arrived home from a night of crime fighting as a "member of the Justice Society of America . . . and now I've got exactly two hours before I catch the bus to Blue Valley High." But she is proud to be a member of a group with such an important and rich history. The next panel takes us to "October 13, 1951, Washington D.C.," where the McCarthy hearings are currently in session.

> and I'd like to again just reestablish the importance of what we're trying to do here. These are dangerous times for America. The enemy lives within us. It hides among us. And no longer can this great country take anything for granted. Since 1940, the Justice Society of America has been a group of heroes that every American, including myself, have been thankful for. They helped keep our beautiful land safe when we were at war. They've saved more lives than anyone can count. But recently, we've been forced to question their motives. These . . . men and women who work outside of the law with powers and technology far beyond any we've dreamed of. No longer can we rely on what we might believe. Enemies are hiding inside our society. And if you are good Americans—you will take off your masks.

Such a story line certainly expects the target audience to have some familiarity with the McCarthy era and all it represents, but it is equally dependent on other, less traditionally "canonical" information. The "Silver-Age Flash" (aka Barry Allen) took his name from the "Golden-Age Flash," who, for him, existed only as a comic book character, but the story line established via the McCarthy Hearings reveals he existed in another, "parallel Earth" yet was forced to disappear (for political reasons? moral reasons?). The Silver-Age lasted from about 1960 until the *Crisis on Infinite Earth* (in 1985), when DC Comics decided they had far too many parallel Earths with far too many conflicting story lines to keep up with. This 12–issue "maxi-series" gathered all the heroes from all the various "Earths" together and, through a series of rather complicated plot twists, collapsed them all into one, destroying all others—a move they didn't really complete until 1994, when they introduced the concept ("Zero Hour").[5] According to long-time comic book fan Stephen Foote (highly comic book literate), the effects of Zero Hour were short-lived:

> Actually, Zero Hour was supposed to finish fixing what Crisis on Infinite Earths was supposed to have done: Create one linear timeline. It turns out,

though, that multiple timelines is too good a story device to pass up. The concept of "Hypertime" was invented. Hypertime contains every time-line/continuity that has ever existed, including those that were written only as "imaginary" or "ElseWorlds" stories, such as the Cold War favorite "What if Superman had landed in the Soviet Union?" or "What if Batman had existed in 1881 London?" and so forth. Hypertime was first used in the miniseries "Kingdom," which linked mainstream continuity with the critically-acclaimed dark-future ElseWorlds miniseries "Kingdom Come."

Only those familiar with "the DC Universe" can make sense of all these twists and turns. Only those who are "literate" in this "culture" know the significance of these events. I have read only a handful of comic books in my life and those only very recently, so I can only share this complex history with you because I have a friend who was willing to walk me through some of these major points, dig through his rather extensive comic book collection, and lay them in front of me so that I can gather enough "cultural literacy" in the "DC Universe" to make this point: To identify a "basic writer" according to the network of information she is (or is not) familiar with is to make a judgment about what sort of information is important enough to know. Who has the authority to make this sort of judgment? What motives are identified in making judgments in this way?

LITERACY AS "SKILL"

Communities of practice are reproduced by the members themselves via content generated by and consumed among them, and this content cannot be effectively separated from the activity system of which it is a part because, as David Russell explains, it is also "historically situated, mediated by tools, dialectically structured, analyzed as the relations of participants and tools, and changed through zones of proximal development" ("Activity Theory and Writing Instruction" 54). To demonstrate the futility of teaching students "to write" or "to improve their writing" in any general way, Russell "draw[s] an analogy between games that require a particular kind of tool—a ball—and activity systems (disciplines, professions, businesses, etc.) that require a particular kind of tool—the marks we call writing" (57). Teaching a player to use a ball or "to improve their use of a ball" in any general way is no less absurd than teaching a writer to improve their "writing," as he explains:

> Some people are very adept at some games and therefore at using some kinds of balls, whereas they may be completely lost using a ball in another game because they have never participated in it. (I play Ping-Pong pretty well, but my 9-year-old daughter laughs at my fumbling attempts to play another game with a ball of a similar size—jacks.) However, ways of using a ball (ball handling, if you will) are "generalizable" to the extent that in two or more

games the tool (ball) is used in similar ways and for similar object(ive)s. A good croquet player might easily learn to putt, or a good tennis player might learn squash. However, *there is no autonomous, generalizable skill called ball using or ball handling that can be learned and then applied to all ball games.* (Russell 57, emphasis mine)

The activity "ball handling" exists as a recognizable practice only within the particular communities of practice using the ball—the game for which the ball is intended. The tool (ball) varies from game to game ("large, small, hard, soft, leather, round, oblong") in response to the objective of the game itself, the history of the game as it relates to the overall objective and key strategies players typically use to reach that objective, and so on. A Ping-Pong ball makes little sense as a tool in a football game as the objective of the game (to reach the opponent's goal with ball in hand) and the material conditions of the playing field (very large) demands that the ball chosen be able to travel vast distances. An oblong shape is, therefore, most appropriate, and uses of this oblong-shaped ball within a given activity system (football) must achieve the objective of reaching the opponent's goal in ways that do not violate the rules and values established and maintained within the community of practice of which football is a part.

Literacy cannot be reduced to an autonomous skill-set, but neither can it be reduced to a particular content. The content thus becomes shared knowledge among members of a given community of practice, and these members both produce and maintain the "content" most appropriate for them and their key objectives. The knowledge football players/viewers/coaches/fans share is multifaceted, dynamic, and historically situated. Football and its rules are historically situated, and they are not even consistent throughout the relevant communities of practice, as college football differs from high school football, which differs still further from professional football. The rules, tools, and objectives for fans within this community of practice also differ from the objectives of the players, which differ (slightly) from the coaches and those officiating this sport.

Thus, literacy, and, therefore, literacy education, must be treated as entirely dependent on context. For Russell, this means that literacy may be most profitably taught in the disciplines because, as he explains, "[a] discipline uses writing as a tool for pursuing some object. Writing is not the object(ive) of its activity" (70). A WAC program offers students a "real" context in which to develop new literacies because such programs "are focused on students and teachers pursing object(ive)s in specific activity systems using the tool of writing" (71). By writing in the disciplines, students learn to treat writing as a tool for learning some discipline-specific content or discipline-specific way of knowing or behaving. Students learn to write and read like a historian or a journalist or a biologist rather than as a generic "writer." Each discipline functions as an activity system in that it values particular content and strategies over others, and students can learn to "become" historians or journalists or biologists by writing their way into these academic communities of practice (see, particularly, James Paul Gee's *Situated Learning*).

Several years ago I was presented with a case seemingly far removed from the problems our basic writing students confront yet nonetheless relevant, as we shall see. A well-meaning education professor on our campus decided to require each of his students to visit the writing center within the first weeks of his doctoral-level class to assess their "general" writing ability. These students were clearly writing in a discipline (education) for a specific purpose (to create new knowledge in the discipline of education). If writing is an activity system rather than a generalizable skill, we were, of course, no more fit to judge their writing ability than a tennis player with little experience playing basketball is an appropriate judge of a basketball player's "general" ballplaying ability. However, we may assume that such writers developing familiarity with education as a scholarly field of inquiry would be able to generate prose that looked strong to a reader less familiar with that field. As I said, the instructor had good intentions, and he hoped to use our "expertise" to identify those with "problems" (early on) so that he could develop an appropriate plan to address those "deficiencies." He did not explain to me why he was sending his students over, only that he would. I was brand new at that point, so I am certain I didn't ask the right questions.

Another issue complicating this "assessment" activity is the fact that this course was taught in the evening to a group of students with schedules that made it difficult for them to visit our brick-and-mortar writing center; most were teachers and public school administrators, and at the time our writing center was only open a few evenings a week. Those students chose to use our then brand-new "Online Writing Lab" (OWL), submitting writing "samples" like the following for us to assess and then judge:

> I am a doctoral student in the XX program and my professor has asked that we all come down to the writing center to have you assess our general writing abilities. I work full time an hour from here and therefore will be unable to come to the writing center to be assessed.
>
> Will you please look at the above message and tell me if you see any problems with my skills as a writer?

Obviously I cannot assess this doctoral student's "skills as a writer" anymore than a "ball user" can assess the ball-using ability of a basketball player by examining/witnessing a "ball-using" sample unrelated to the real-life context in which he will be using the ball (on the basketball court with other basketball players mediated by the rules of a basketball game, etc.).

My solution was to request that this professor ask his students to visit us with a sample of "authentic" writing created in a course not unlike the one in which they were currently enrolled. Though all of the graduate students working in our writing center at the time were majoring in English studies rather than education, most could recognize the vaguely defined borders of "effective" academic discourse in education research as they overlap with English studies. Does the writer seem to display the rhetorical "skills" typically valued among writers in academic contexts (well organized, good use of sources, clear, focused)? "Skill" can only vaguely be judged by outsiders to this discipline and only because they are insiders in a somewhat-related community of practice. However, no authentic measure of a writer's ability can occur without judging the writer's grasp of the content valued among members of this community of practice and nonmembers cannot make this judgment with any degree of accuracy.

In the same volume in which Russell's piece "Activity Theory and Writing Instruction" appears, Cheryl Geisler complicates matters further via her argument that writing cannot be successfully used by learners to create knowledge except among those marked as "experts."[6] Working against the growing number of claims by composition scholars that writing *creates* knowledge, Geisler insists that "learning already extant knowledge and making new knowledge are quite distinct activities" (101).

> Learning extant knowledge is the job of students. Making new knowledge is the job of academic professionals. These two groups, even though they inhabit the same institutions and organize their activities around interactions with texts, are generally worlds apart with respect to knowledge, separated across what I have called the Great Divide between expert and layperson (Geisler 1994). . . . [S]tudents in the academy do not use writing for the making of new knowledge in the sense already described. Instead, they use writing primarily for the "lay" purpose of learning extant knowledge made by others more "expert" than they. And, as the research reveals . . . writing is a fairly poor tool for this purpose. (102)

Geisler's argument rests on the problematic and ubiquitous practice of assigning writing merely to display knowledge generated by experts elsewhere and presented to them via teachers and the texts with which they interact. In other words, "in the academy, students do not actually do very much extended writing and the writing they do is for the purpose of demonstrating knowledge to the teacher as examiner" (108). Even "analytic writing," she argues, "is not a good way for students to acquire the kinds of information routinely tested in school" (111). The results are dramatically different, however, when the tasks for which writing is assigned "made significant departures from the standard knowledge-transmission purposes of the schools" (113). Our goal in the "violence of literacy" sequence described in chapter 3 was the latter, though I accept the fact that such literacy experiences are uncommon among college writers.

A critical theoretical framework, however, insists that educators liberate learners by refusing to participate in what Friere calls the "banking model" of education, insisting instead that we make use of "problem posing" education. In the former, "education . . . becomes an act of depositing, in which the students are the depositories and the teacher is the depositor [and] . . . the scope of action [for the student] extends only as far as receiving, filing, storing the deposits" (*Pedagogy* 72). In the latter, however, "people develop their power to perceive critically the way they exist in the world with which and in which they find themselves; they come to see the world not as a static reality but as a reality in the process of transformation" (83). In doing so, they come to "name" that world: "to exist humanly is to name the world, to change it. Once named, the world in its turn reappears to the namers as a problem and requires of them a new naming. . . . Dialogue is the encounter between men, mediated by the world, in order to name the world" (88). Geisler accepts the importance of this "problem-posing" education, but argues that writing is "at odds with learning— when learning is characterized as the acceptance of a web of cultural knowledge" (116), when "students" are treated as "depositories" of knowledge rather than creators of it (Freire 72). "We write," Geisler argues, "both to contribute to and to counter the current trajectory of our culture" (116).

Thus, "writing to learn" "extant knowledge" may be ineffective, but writing to create new knowledge is, in fact, what "motivates us to pick up the pen (or turn on the computer) in the first place" (Geisler 116). Teaching students to write (or to use a ball) in any general way is problematic from the standpoint of application because neither writing "skills" nor knowledge of writing as content separable from the context in which it is used enable writers to create knowledge; however, it is also problematic from the standpoint of *motivation*, as general skills instruction or lessons in "general" knowledge ("what every American needs to know") asks writers to accept without critique the "cultural facts and values" perpetuated in the academy. Teaching what Joseph Petraglia calls "General Writing Skills Instruction" (or GWSI) is, therefore, oppressive because it necessarily and consistently validates the "content" shared by scholars in our various disciplines and invalidates the content shared among members of communities of practice not directly associated with the school. As Geisler explains, "the move to professionalize can, in fact, be defined as a move to remove knowledge from the public sphere" (116). We should instead make use of what Antonio Gramsci calls "organic intellectuals." As Gramsci explains, "there is no human activity from which every form of intellectual participation can be excluded" and everyone "carries on some form of intellectual activity . . . participates in a particular conception of the world, has a conscious line of moral conduct, and therefore contributes to sustain a conception of the world or to modify it, that is, to bring into being new modes of thought." Thus, "organic intellectuals" can be agents of change in ways "traditional intellectuals" cannot.

Not Foucault.

It is primarily for this reason that, while I have been heavily influenced by David Russell's work, I think that his solution (teaching writing within the disciplines) is incomplete since it perpetuates the notion that the only content worth knowing and activities worth emulating are those generated within and shared by members of academic communities of practice.[7] By applying both Russell's assertion that "improving the uses of the tool of writing means using certain genres to choose, enter, become a full participant in, and, eventually, change for the better one's chosen activity system" (69) and Geisler's argument that "experts" generate knowledge the students are typically asked to "consume," I am forced to rethink my original interpretation of my education colleague's decision to use the writing center as a center for diagnosing writing problems.

First and foremost, I should ask, is this doctoral student an "expert"? What is the function of writing for him in this context? Is he expected to generate knowledge in his profession or merely consume it? It certainly seems he's expected to do a little of both. That is, he is currently a member of the education profession (a principal of a local high school); he is also a student of the academic discipline that is education, perhaps even a specialization within that larger discipline. His experiences as a school-based teacher and administrator enable him to understand the real-world applications of education as a social practice, but do they enable him to make use of the genres produced and sustained by the facets of this community of practice that treat education not strictly in terms of its potential and practical applications but as a site of intellectual inquiry? I would say no. The genres with which he has experience (teacher evaluations, student disciplinary reports, etc.) may have little direct relevance in this academic community of practice where the vaguely defined genre of "academic argument" reigns supreme. The evidence, value-sets, special terminology, ideological framework, and other aspects of his daily life as a principal might actually conflict with the activities produced and validated within the academy. The tool called "writing" as an educator functions quite differently in public school contexts, which means the genres themselves will function quite differently as well. He is an "expert" because he has been working within the field for several years, but he will be considered a "novice" throughout much of his time as a student (even as a doctoral student) in this new community of practice.

However, while the genres themselves might not be immediately transferable from the discipline of education to the profession for which they are supposedly being trained, they are not entirely unrelated or isolated from one another. My concern with Russell's model is that it seems to leave little room for comparing the new communities of practice with the ones the writer already knows quite well. In a general sense, both the academics of the discipline and the practitioners "in the field" belong to the activity system that is "education" and, as Russell explains, that system is "historically situated, mediated by tools, dialectically structured, analyzed as the relations of participants and tools, and changed through zones of proximal development." The history of education-the-discipline is informed by the history of education-the-profession and vice versa, but the activities of the doctoral student within this system differ from those expected of the principal, which differ still further from those required of the professor. In this system, however, the "expert" is not assumed to be the practitioner "in the field" but the academic "in the ivory tower" separated *from* the field.

The disconnect between what the learner already knows and what she is expected to know is all the more significant among basic writing students because they are most often understood to have no experiences relevant to the general academic communities of practice in which they are attempting to gain membership. Can basic writing students profitably treat literacy as a community of practice that reproduces itself through the activities performed by members of that community? To do this, Geisler asserts by implication, would require that we "reinvent education . . . not for lay consumption or expert production, but . . . for lay production." As she explains, "[t]his alternative . . . encourages us to work for a new relationship between experts and the general public, to find ways in which dialogue can be fostered and mutual dependency acknowledged" (119). It seems more likely that members of education-the-discipline might "foster . . . dialogue . . . and mutual dependency" with members of education-the-profession than it does that basic writing teachers might develop relationships like these with the writers they teach. Thus, a pure writing-in-the-disciplines approach to literacy education seems unlikely to disrupt that "Great Divide between expert and layperson" (Geisler) because the teacher maintains the role of "expert" in the genres that function as the writing tools of a given discipline and the learner maintains the role of layperson who must gain fluency within these specialized genres. However, as Russell points out, "the writing of genres is generalizable to the extent that written text is handled in similar ways for similar object(ive)s" (59). Thus, it seems possible that the "expert" in the genres of education-the-discipline might wish to learn more about the genres of education-the-profession, genres with which our principal is the likely expert. Education-the-discipline and education-the-profession rely on one another in ways that inform both, and while many assert that this is the case among basic writing students and their teachers, few programs make use of this mutual dependency.

The basic writing program at the University of Pittsburgh as described in David Bartholomae and Anthony Petrosky's *Facts, Artifacts, and Counterfacts* treats the basic writing classroom like a graduate seminar, and this model is one we have mimicked in our own basic writing program as it certainly seems to honor the basic writer's ability to construct "really useful knowledge" (Gramsci). In a later article (discussed at some length in chapter 3), David

Bartholomae represents the problem basic writing students confront as "invent[ing] the university . . . or a branch of it." In other words, these students are asked to successfully maneuver the tacit expectations of a community of practice with which they have had little or no experience. As Bartholomae explains,

> Every time a student sits down to write for us, he has to invent the university for the occasion—invent the university, that is, or a branch of it, like History or Anthropology or Economics or English. He has to learn to speak our language, to speak as we do, to try on the particular ways of knowing, selecting, evaluating, reporting, concluding, or arguing that define the discourse in our community. (4).

In her important and regularly cited article "Revising Writer-Based Prose" (1981), Linda Flower argues that basic writers are "trapped" in a private language ("writer-based") and need to learn to revise in ways "expert writers" do, thus generating much more public, "reader-based" prose. David Bartholomae contends that such a representation is inadequate: "Students . . . are not so much trapped in a private language as they are shut out from one of the privileged languages of public life, a language they are aware of but cannot control" (9). He argues that in order for students to "appropriate (or be appropriated by)" the specialized discourses associated with the academic community, they must "invent the university by assembling and mimicking its language, finding some compromise between idiosyncrasy, a personal history, and the requirements of convention, the history of a discipline" (5). In doing so, the student must "take on the role . . . of an authority whose authority is rooted in scholarship, analysis, or research" and this is a very complicated task for one who is wholly unfamiliar with the communities of practice in which this authority is rooted.

In the first example ("'The Clay Model' paper" from a placement examination), Bartholomae points to the various ways in which the writer is able to "take on" this "role" successfully, by "speak[ing] to us as a companion, a fellow researcher." However, not unlike most basic writing students, as he explains, this student "slip[s] . . . into the more immediately available and realizable voice of authority, the voice of the teacher giving a lesson or the voice of a parent lecturing at the dinner table" (6). Early in the semester in our program, we regularly observe basic writing students using the pronoun "you" to, in Bartholomae's terms, "invent" the authority they see necessary for the writer to embody—treating the reader as a student, a child, or a member of a church congregation, and often following such positioning with moral imperatives about what the reader should or should not do. "To speak to us as a person of status or privilege," Bartholomae explains, "the writer can either speak to us on our terms—in the privileged language of university discourse—or, in default (or in defiance), he can speak to us as though we were children, offering us the wisdom of experience" (8). It is not, then, a problem of "immaturity" that the basic writing student exhibits in her prose but rather a problem rooted in "context." In further representing the particular issues facing the student whose placement essay "The Clay Model" marked him "basic writer," Bartholomae makes this argument:

> I think it is possible to say that the language of the "Clay Model" paper has come *through* the writer and not from the writer. The writer has located himself (he has located the self that is represented by the *I* on the page) in a context that is, finally, beyond him, not his own and not available to his immediate procedures for inventing and arranging text. . . . It is . . . the record of a writer who has lost himself in the discourse of his readers. There is a context beyond the reader that is not the world but a way of talking about the world, a way of talking that determines the use of examples, the possible conclusions, the acceptable commonplaces, and the key words of an essay on the construction of a clay model of the earth. (8)

The solution Bartholomae offers is this: the basic writing program should help the writer more appropriately read that context by more completely situating himself within it via a curriculum designed to help the basic writer "invent" the university "for the occasion," experiencing how (and why) one might "take on the role . . . of an authority whose authority is rooted in scholarship, analysis, or research" (5, 7). As he explains, "I think that all writers, in order to write, must imagine for themselves the privilege of being 'insiders'—that is, of being both inside an established and powerful discourse, and of being granted a special right to speak" (10). In the program he designed with Anthony Petrosky at the University of Pittsburgh,[8] students take on an academic issue like "adolescence and growth" in many of the ways scholars might in the various communities of practice associated with their work. Doing so makes much clearer the social and procedural dimensions by which the "scholarship, analysis, [and] research" on which academic authority is based comes about, "allow[ing] them [basic writing students] to act as through they were colleagues in an academic enterprise" (7, 11). Basic writing thus becomes restructured as a way for students to "join the conversation" in a particular community of practice, a conversation that is already in progress—what is often called the "Burkean parlor":

> Imagine that you enter a parlor. You come late. When you arrive, others have long preceded you, and they are engaged in a heated discussion, a discussion too heated for them to pause and tell you exactly what it is about. In fact, the discussion had already begun long before any of them got there, so that no one present is qualified to retrace for you all the steps that had gone before. You listen for a while, until you decide that you have caught the tenor of the argument; then you put in your oar. Someone answers; you

answer him; another comes to your defense; another aligns himself against you, to either the embarrassment or gratification of your opponent, depending upon the quality of your ally's assistance. However, the discussion is interminable. The hour grows late, you must depart. And you do depart, with the discussion still vigorously in progress. (Burke 110–111)

As I have suggested, expanding the definition of literacy to domains beyond print seems necessary because encoding and decoding print is an activity embedded in a larger social network. "What our beginning students need," according to Bartholomae, "is to extend themselves into the commonplaces, set phrases, rituals, gestures, habits of mind, tricks of persuasion, obligatory conclusions, and necessary connections that determine 'what might be said' and constitute knowledge within the various branches of our academic community" ("Inventing" 11). Certainly the model he articulates treats academic discourse as a "social" construct, yet the critical perspective demands that basic writing students be taught to read and "approximate" more than the intellectual and ideological dimensions of academic literacy. They should also come to understand the function of conflict[9] in approximating this discourse (see Min-Zhan Lu and Bruce Horner[10])—a conflict between "home" and "school" that is often understood to be much more profound for basic writing students than those not marked "basic" and one to which I return again.

Another concern with the curriculum Bartholomae and Petrosky advocate is that it appears to privilege an area in which they will likely continue to be, as Geisler puts it, "laypersons," though they can certainly mimic the moves made by writers in highly specialized disciplines. Bartholomae and Petrosky's curriculum offers writers the opportunity to use their own experiences as evidence for their arguments, naming their place in the world as they read and write within the contexts created via the conversations captured in their readings of texts generated by the field's "experts." However, it does not treat the communities of practice with which the basic writing students are most likely to be "experts" themselves as intellectually viable spaces that are relevant (or can be *made* relevant) to academic communities of practice.

A few years ago as I was attempting to work through what would become *rhetorical dexterity* and a curriculum for our basic writing program, I asked students in a graduate-level course ("Teaching Writing to Diverse Populations") to compare academic literacies with out-of-school ones.[11] Jake Pichnarcik, an English major with several years experience as a tutor in our program and, before that, as a tutor in a Texas state jail, began the semester articulating the points of contact between academic literacies and those associated with "Trekkies":

Consider the people who call themselves "Trekkies" (students/fans of the Star Trek television series . . .). I never quite saw the reasoning behind many of the things Trekkies actually do—for example dressing like a Klingon and

going to a convention to get William Shatner to pose for a photo with you—
but that community is certainly an academic discourse community. Many
Trekkies can not only identify virtually every character from the show, but
some know the chronology of fictional events over thousands of fictional
years (historians) [and many debate the trajectory of this history over several
new *Star Trek* series that may have been filmed in a different order than they
are supposed to represent in the "real" "Star Trek time continuum"], some
can discuss the actual, extant quantum theories behind the technology presented (scientists), some can speak the Klingon language, and even have
added words to the vocabulary (linguists), and the list goes on.

He explains that "other than Trekkies, the list of academic discourse communities could easily include other groups with less esoteric taste," such as
"amateur astronomers" or "baseball fans."

They ask the same big questions. The baseball fan asks how a certain
player added to a team will affect the dynamic of the club, how his past
performance might be an addition or a subtraction from the team as a
whole when projected into the future. The Trekkie discovers a new application of phonemes in the Klingon language that can be used to describe
a color between indigo and royal blue. These are philosophical questions
capable of demanding as much intellectual horsepower as the questions we
ask ourselves—some with considerable practical value such as when we
consider what techniques we use when we teach, some with less value (as
when we debate the merits of the rhythm of speech Shakespeare chose to
use in his plays), and some that seem to have no practical value whatso-
ever—like when we discuss evidence of latent homosexuality in a particular author's work.[12]

According to Pichnarcik, the *points of contact* between these various communities (Trekkies, academics, baseball fans) include the following:

• The most important commonality, I think, is that *members of the community*, to be honest members of the community, *must have a driving desire to
  seek knowledge for the sake of knowledge*. . . . True academic discourse should
  be made with the aim of expanding the knowledge base and encouraging
  interest by providing multiple viewpoints and new, potentially practical
  solutions to old problems.
• Notice I said "potentially practical solutions." That's my next point. It
  seems to me that *academic discourse, with some exceptions of course, is an
  exercise that most often has no immediate practical value*. As individuals we
  have to labor away, thoughts confined to our braincases, while we consider
  and theorize and project. The first person who rubbed two sticks together
  and made fire (not academic discourse) never imagined that fire would

someday forge steel (a result of centuries of academic discourse about fire and metal and probably other stuff, too). So we need to find a reason to continue this discourse knowing that any possible practical use is, most likely, not going to happen for quite some time. Ah, *dedication*. *Another requirement for inclusion in the community.*

In much the same way, basic writing students are already experts in a given community of practice (*Star Trek?* baseball?). I argue that in focusing on their familiar literacies and what they might have to offer academic ones, rhetorical dexterity forces them to think of writing and reading in more flexible and contextually driven ways. While difficult, transferability from activity system to activity system is not impossible, as Russell explains:

> As one becomes adept at more and more activities that require writing and hence at writing more genres, it is more likely (but by no means certain) that one will be able to master a new genre more quickly, because it is more likely that there will be some features of the new genre or activity that resemble features in a genre or activity one already knows. (59)

However, I argue that when the activities with which a participant is already "adept" appear irrelevant to the current academic contexts, transferability is unlikely to be automatic. In his midterm reflections, for instance, one basic writing student expresses his surprise at finding that his out-of-school experiences may be of any use to him in school. As he explains, in this class "I was able to compare NHL 2006 (a Play Station 2 game) to writing which was weird. It's weird because I have never thought of writing in this way, such as the tools of writing, the terminology, of writing, and the knowledge involved in writing and then comparing it with something I do quite frequently" (Michael). An autonomous model that separates skills from content, content from context, and even, as I will argue, orality from literacy also limits among basic writing students their ability to draw from the great variety of communities of practice in which they are already considered "experts." When a "layperson" developing "expertise" in a community of practice like education-the-discipline can rely on previous experiences in communities of practice that hold similarly dominant status in society, that "layperson" is more likely to transfer relevant strategies and content into these new contexts. Experts make use of this artificial system in ways that make the system itself largely irrelevant; those from marginalized groups may find transference much more difficult as the artificial system continues to separate them from "real" writing and reading experiences, making the artificial system very relevant indeed.

Russell continues: "It may also be true that a person may have "learned how to learn" new genres. That is, one may have learned to be alert to the role language plays in an activity system, to take instruction from and adept in the genres one is trying to learn, to notice the differences in writing processes of various activity systems, and so on" (59).

When teaching basic writing students, we should make explicit the ways in which they have learned to negotiate familiar communities of practice may help them in developing new academic literacies. When the literacies with which they are most familiar and feel most confident are those associated with video games or service work, for example, few learners are likely to find such literacies relevant, at least not without encouragement. Rhetorical dexterity asks literacy learners to examine the similarities and the differences among a variety of communities of practice, making explicit comparisons among the behaviors that mark one as literate in communities of practice beyond school and those more traditionally associated with the academy.

LEARNING VERNACULAR LITERACIES

We have thus far been speaking of the ways in which one learns new literacies when the new literacy is a dominant one (like academic discourse) and the possessed one is a "vernacular" one (like *Star Trek* discourse). What we have not yet considered is the important question of transference from dominant literacies to the vernacular. In other words, what happens when a learner relies on dominant literacies to learn more vernacular ones (like video games)?

A pedagogy of rhetorical dexterity demands that the learner identify contexts in which she is already highly literate, mapping similarities between the two spaces and developing an understanding of and (at some level) acceptance of those systems of logic incongruous with the systems of logic that shape other contexts in which she finds relevance, agency, and competency. Thus, it seems useful to examine the ways in which the points of dissonance one experiences may shape one's ability to obtain new literacies, even when the new literacy is not a dominant one (like academic discourse) but a vernacular one and the learner is basing acquisition of this new vernacular literacy on familiarly with dominant ones. How might one quite competent in one dominant community of practice experience literacy learning in one considered less valuable? I ask this because, like James Paul Gee, "I am always struck by how many people, even some of the liberal advocates of multiculturalism, readily decry and seek to override people's cultures when these cultures are popular, peer-based ones centered around things like video games" (*What Video Games* 10). In the exploration that follows, a successful writer (possessing high levels of literacy in standard written English—an obviously "dominant" discourse) tries to learn (and find value in) a popular video game (a vernacular and, in this context at least, "marginalized" literacy).

In his quirky and irreverent study of American popular culture from a bitter, Generation X perspective, critic Chuck Klosterman takes on *The*

Sims—a video game with a premise that seems far too "enchanting (and just too weird) to ignore" (Klosterman 12). When I first learned of its existence a few years ago, I, too, found the concept quite compelling. For someone who grew up in rhetorical spaces (time and place) saturated with video games but who has only been able to feign interest in them herself, *The Sims* promised to be my way into communities I recognized but could not yet communicate within. Certainly our students are often highly literate members of communities of practice distinctly informed by what James Paul Gee calls "the semiotic domains" of video games. Yet I could not read the "written language" embedded in these vernacular literacies, and in order to teach these students I needed to learn. As the case studies in "The Future of Literacy" illustrate,

> [t]he U.S. educational system and its teachers must be ready to meet the needs of students who compose meaning not only with words, but also with digitized bits of video, sound, photographs, still images, words, and animations and to support communications across linguistic, cultural, and geo-political borders. (DeVoss, Hawisher, Jackson, Johansen, Moraski, and Selfe 261)

For readers not "Sims literate," here's how it works: "You create a human character, and it exists. . . . Your character . . . reads the newspaper . . . takes naps, plays pinball, and empties the garbage. [He] invites friends over to his house, and they have discussions about money and sailboats. You buy oak bookcases and you get pizza from Dominoes" (Klosterman 13). No one chases you. No guns are involved. No spaceships or aliens threaten your planet. In fact, you never even leave your house except to go to work at a place the real you will never see and knows only as "work." Your lone enemy is your own ineptitude. You must train your character to get out of bed when he wakes up and take himself immediately to the bathroom (early in "life" Sims characters have a tendency to wet themselves). You have to watch him closely as he cooks breakfast because he doesn't automatically know how to use the stove and he's apt to burn down his virtual house instead of making his eggs (though once he reads a manual, even just enough to accumulate one single point, he becomes quite the little virtual cook). In a sense, you must teach him strategies used by those literate in everyday life at the same time you develop your new literacies in a video game *simu*lating your everyday life. The goal? "[K]eep yourself from becoming depressed" (Klosterman 14). A lack of fun resulting from a lack of social opportunities makes your often socially inept SimSelf sad, and this sadness worsens when tired or hungry. In this virtual world depression kills, as your Sims character can, in fact, starve to death.

Chuck Klosterman explores this postmodern reality game by creating himself ("SimChuck"), and he finds himself utterly fascinating, at least to the extent that SimChuck performs according to RealityChuck's current worldview (a standards-based system against which the value of all others is measured). Katie, his six-year-old niece, serves as RealityChuck's "apprentice"—to use James Paul Gee's terminology—because she herself is highly Sims literate (Gee, "What Is Literacy?" 527).

Like members of any community of practice, however, those who are Sims literate have a "characteristic ways of talking, acting, interacting, thinking, believing . . . valuing," interpreting and using written language (Gee, *The Social Mind* 20), and Katie's impatience with her uncle's questions reveals a profound incongruity of values—one that has important implications for teaching and tutoring, as I will explain. Not unlike many teachers and tutors of what seems "obvious," she isn't terribly patient with Klosterman's questions because to her (and likely others literate in this virtual world) his concerns are ridiculous and irrelevant: "Who put all that food in my fridge? Elves, perhaps? Can I trust them? Why don't I need a car? Where did I go to college? Don't I have any old friends I could call on for moral support?" "That's the way it is," she tells him. "Nobody knows. You're just here. . . . Be quiet!" (Klosterman 16).

Klosterman finds Katie's unwillingness to help him create some sort of recognizable context puzzling. As he explains, "when playing with real-world toys . . . there's no limit to the back story Katie will create." The conclusion he draws from this disconnect: "Clearly, video technology cages the imagination. It offers interesting information to use, but it implies that all peripheral information is irrelevant and off limits" (16).

I disagree with his hypothesis, though I share it here because it is one I have often heard those highly literate members of dominant communities of practice (like teachers) say of television, video games, and popular music. Instead, I argue that what he perceives as Katie's unwillingness to "color outside the lines of perception" in the Sims world when she enthusiastically does so in other game-like contexts is not her own deficiency but a problem with Klosterman's limited tolerance of contexts differing from those with which he is most familiar. I say this as a fan of Klosterman-the-music/cultural critic (especially *Fargo Rock City*), but it is Klosterman who is actually the one unwilling to "color outside the lines of perception"—"caged" as he is by a singular worldview that guides what he does, sees, says, and values in all other contexts. The technology does not imply, as Klosterman insists, that "all other information is off limits"; that limitation of vision is embedded in the user, not the tool. As Gee explains, "we can learn a lot from those young people who play games, if only we take them and their games seriously" (*What Video Games* 10). Klosterman took neither *The Sims* nor his "apprentice" Katie very seriously. In fact, he insists that what he has to learn from SimChuck is only what can be reconciled with his current worldview—and he couldn't find much to reconcile.

Ultimately, however, the most severe disconnect thwarting his ability to develop Sim literacies is this: his decision to validate one vernacular literacy system based entirely on a dominant one may actually serve standards-based perspectives that make transference from one community of practice to the

next a moot point because any literacy worth having is the one already possessed. Actually, the questions for users developing video game literacy
should not begin with how the game complies with the reality it "simulates"
but rather how to make the character do what he should do to meet the
game's objectives—in this case, eschew the blues.

THE DISTANCE BETWEEN HOME AND SCHOOL

> We will find it hard to assess the difficulty of acquiring the academic world
> view until we know how different it is from basic writers' home world views.
> Even though we cannot now say how great the difference might be, since
> we do not know enough about basic writers' original world views, basic writers
> "outlandishness" in college strongly suggests that the difference is great and
> that for them, to a much greater degree than for other students, acquiring
> the academic world view means becoming bicultural. (Bizzell, "What
> Happens" 18)

Klosterman's attempts to develop new vernacular literacies based on his experiences with more "educated" ones were ineffective for a number of reasons,
not the least of which was his assumption that the same perspectives and
value-sets that served him well as a professional writer (popular culture and
music critic) were equally relevant to his developing Sims literacies. Thus, as
we understand it, not all literacies are equally valuable in all contexts. Of
course, perceived inequities among literacies cause problems for all learners
of new literacies, but such problems are all the more profound among those
for whom the new literacy being learned ("school" literacies) is one of much
greater value than the ones already familiar to them (those more closely associated with "home").
    Understanding the complexities of rhetorical dexterity requires that we
first try to make sense of, as Patricia Bizzell puts it in "What Happens When
Basic Writers Come to College?" (1986), the distance basic writing students
must travel to acquire these new, academic literacies. As she explains,

> basic writers, upon entering the academic community, are being asked to
> learn a new dialect and new discourse conventions, but the outcome of such
> learning is acquisition of a whole new world view. Their difficulties, then, are
> best understood as stemming from the initial distance between their world-
> views and the academic world view, and perhaps also from the resistance to
> changing their own world-views that is caused by this very distance. (18)

In her analysis of then-current scholarship in the field, that "distance
between home" and the academy is marked by a clash between these two
social spaces with respect to three factors: the writers' home dialects versus
"standard English, the preferred dialect in school";[13] the "discourse forms"

associated with the writer's home and those reproduced among the communities of practice most closely associated with school;[14] and the ways of thinking and knowing perpetuated in out-of-school contexts and those required of academic discourse[15] (15, 16). Taking into account the validity of all three of these approaches and recasting them in more socially situated terms, Bizzell "want[s] to find an approach to the difficulties of basic writers entering college that can take into account these differences in dialects, discourse conventions, and ways of thinking" (16). Before she can, however, she must "ask three questions: what world views do basic writers bring to college? What is the new world view demanded in college? And do basic writers have to give up the world views they bring to college in order to learn the new worldview?" (18).

In the years since Bizzell published this provocative analysis of "what happens when basic writers come to college," a number of studies have emerged that attempt to make sense of the ways in which basic writers negotiate (are required to negotiate) that gap between home and the academy, including Anne Dipardo's *A Kind of Passport* (1993), Deborah Mutnick's *Writing in an Alien World* (1995), and Marilyn Sternglass's *Time to Know Them* (1997). Such projects offer detailed case studies of students enrolled in a variety of equal educational opportunity programs and the complexities involved in negotiating that gap—from the perspective of the basic writing students themselves, their teachers, and administrators responsible for the programs. In every case, we learn there are no easy answers. As Min-Zhan Lu contends, this disconnect between home and school causes basic writing students both "conflict and struggle." Lu insists we should not attempt to overcome these conflicts and struggles but actually embrace them since they offer writers the opportunity to productively engage with this gap between home and school instead of quietly submitting to the assimilation required of school literacies.

In addition to the research conducted to make sense of that distance between home and school that the basic writing students may be required to traverse—and the theoretical (Lu, Horner, etc.) and programmatic (Fox, McNenny) solutions offered—several scholars have developed persuasive *curricular* solutions to the problem. I will devote the next several pages to those solutions most relevant to the current study as I am attempting here to offer a curricular solution as well.

CURRICULAR SOLUTIONS TO THE HOME–SCHOOL SPLIT

In their ten-year, collaborative study *The Discovery of Competence* (1993), Eleanor Kutz, Suzy Q. Groden, and Vivian Zamel articulate, design, and share a curriculum that seems entirely responsive to the problems basic writing students face as they "travel" that metaphoric distance between home literacies and those most relevant to school. As they explain, "[T]hroughout this book we . . . describe our concern with building frameworks that can provide coherent underpinnings for our students' work of discovery and from which they can argue, construct new understandings, make sense of the positions of others, and offer interpretations of their own" (164). In other words, they concern themselves with what students already know—already care about— and they build from there. In the preface, they make the distinction between those programs that focus on what students can't do or don't know and those who learn from what the students already do and know well:

> Typically, faculty complain that students are unable to write complete sentences or coherent paragraphs, or to spell or punctuate correctly. We have tried, instead, to focus on the underlying competence in learning and in using language that our students bring to their work as writers, to find ways to see and understand that competence, to help students build on it, systematically, in the classroom, and to create a pedagogy through which students may discover their own competence. (x)

My brother was never asked to do this. Using the research findings in second-language acquisition, Kutz, Groden, and Zamel offer a very persuasive lens through which to view and help students make use of their own competencies. Had Eric been guided in "discover[ing] [his] own competence," it seems his school-based experiences would have been much more positive for him. Even so, however, I am not certain that in defining literacy in largely print-based terms, even their program would have reached Eric. For someone like my brother, the best avenue appears to be technology: video games, music, computer hardware.

In other words, not only should we concern ourselves with "the underlying competence in learning and in using language that our students bring to their work as writers," but also those things less typically understood in terms of "language" and "literacy" learning but still very much possessing the characteristics of academic literacy as a social construct. As Linda Brodkey explains in *Academic Writing as Social Practice* (1987), "All writers use the language of a community, and all must write in ways deemed appropriate to and by a community" (3). If it truly is the case that our students "can't think" or "can't write," it seems important that we ask them to teach us some of the extremely complex activities we can't do that they can, locating what Kurt Spellmeyer has called "a common ground" between home and school. Kutz, Groden, and Zamel's program calls this "common ground" "interlanguage" and focuses quite extensively on the ways in which these ESL student experiences in second-language acquisition might serve as a productive source from which to develop new competencies in academic discourse. While extremely useful on a number of levels, especially with ESL students, however, I worry that such a curriculum focusing on language acquisition may be less effective with native speakers in that it fails to make explicit the ways in which developing academic literacies requires of literacy learners the acquisition of new discourse conventions and, more often than not, a new worldview (see Bizzell, "What Happens"). It seems that second-language learners may be more cognizant of this fact than native speakers.

In "Toward a Consciousness of Language: A Language Pedagogy for Multi-Cultural Classrooms" (1997),[16] Mary Soliday outlines a curriculum that focuses on "student's language use in social contexts," specifically "the relationship between their own and the dominant languages" and the student's "critique" of this relationship, which Soliday argues cannot happen for many students until they develop a "consciousness of language's potential to shape, not just to convey, information about social experience" (63). In doing so, she hoped to better enable her students to "situat[e] their own stories within a broader cultural context" (65).

Soliday's students in one class concluded, among other things, that "different language groups develop code languages in order to survive within mainstream culture." She continues:

> One student studied the profanity used by women in a homeless shelter and concluded that their harsh speech was "the language of a mask," or a defense against difficult circumstances. Another student studied "the language of necessity" in a restaurant, concluding that servers developed a code that helped them to cope with stressful, unrewarding jobs. (69)

In drawing her students' attention to the ways in which oral language is no more "natural" than written and in asking them to examine the ways in which the language they use in their everyday lives is no more (nor any less) likely to mean exactly what it appears to say, Soliday was able to develop in her students more critical literacies. As she explains, "the awareness that language can say more than is literally said may be a precondition for achieving literacy" (65).

Language "is not just a functional instrument." Such a perspective, Soliday reminds us, "is common among students from white, middle-class homes." However, for her "students reflecting upon the nature of language involves a more complex reflection upon self and relationships to different groups or communities." She continues: "It is vital that this sort of reflection occur, partly because, to succeed within the academy students have to contend with the fact that language is not literal or self-sufficient" (72).

I agree that such reflection is, indeed, "vital," and I am excited about the many interesting ways Soliday's curricular choices led her students to talk about language. However, I worry that developing in our basic writing students an understanding that "language is not literal or self-sufficient" may not be enough in and of itself to clarify the academic literacy experience for them—at least not in ways that are likely to give them lots of control over it. The social dimensions of language are available to the students through this project, but I believe the *contextualized* dimensions (as peopled, but also as located in a particular place and time, for particular purposes) would be more obvious to students were they to examine discourse use rather than language use. For Gee, "Discourses are ways in which people coordinate and are coordinated by language, other people, objects, times, and places in order to take on socially recognizable identities" (360). Furthermore, "[o]perating within a Discourse we align ourselves with and get aligned by words, deeds, values, thoughts, beliefs, things, places, and times so as to recognize and get recognized as a person of a certain type" (360). And while many of the writers in our basic writing program are likely be all over the idea of "critiq[uing] mainstream language" as was Soliday's goal, I worry about the practical benefit doing so would be to those students who do not wish to accept that "mainstream language" is, as Adrienne Rich puts it, "the oppressor's language"— exploited by what bell hooks calls, "white supremacist capitalist patriarchy."

Contradiction

A *pedagogy of rhetorical dexterity*, on the other hand, leaves room for those willing to challenge what may be institutionalized oppression, yet it also enables those who would rather not challenge mainstream discourse systems, instead recasting their perceptions of literacy so that they can more profitably adopt to the ever-changing literacies that make up their future, regardless of their politics.

In "Reinventing the University," Jane E. Hindman (1993) challenges the popular curriculum David Bartholomae and Anthony Petrosky articulate in *Facts, Artifacts, and Counterfacts* for not going far enough. As Hindman explains, her "curriculum acknowledges that for basic writers, the problem of writing in the university is a problem of appropriating power and authority through a particular way of writing." While she celebrates this aspect, she contends that in order to enable students to be "the agents of their own marginalization, basic writers need to be able to recognize their position at the center of a system that—in part at least—gains its authority by de-authorizing them."

Like Soliday, Hindman argues that critical consciousness can be stimulated and guided by a curriculum "whose content is language-centered, rather than focused on the topics of adolescence or of work," as was the case with Barthomae and Petrosky's sequences presented in *Facts* (62). Their semester-long, seminar project considers such questions as the following: "Who is authorized to speak in the discourse of any particular group? How is such authority recognized and practiced? What privileges does the authority provide? How do the dominants of the group protect privilege?" (64). Like the curriculum I will outline in the following chapter, Hindman's project asks students to investigate and compare language practices of "those familiar groups" with those of the academy. Unlike the curriculum I advocate, however, these studies focus on "language-use" not "discourse systems," "authentic," verifiable research methods not "reading the world."

In observing the language practices of the academy, these students actually examine "audio tapes of holistic training sessions [in which teaching assistants notions of unsatisfactory, "average," and "sophisticated college writing are aligned"], a large sampling of student exams with the scores they earned, interviews with graders." Such "a pedagogy" she explains, enables "students [to] develop the critical consciousness necessary to being the authors of their own movement *from* a dependent, uninformed, 'marginalized' position at the center of an obscure, enigmatic system *to* an autonomous position on the 'margins,' that place where successful writers 'aggressively poise themselves in a hesitant and tenuous relationship to the language and methods of the university'" (63).

Though I am excited about the possibility of critiquing the value-sets shaping the academic communities of practice most relevant to our basic writing students—those responsible for their placement in basic writing—I wonder about the practicality of such an endeavor. Because Hindman did not include any discussion of her students' responses to the curriculum she outlines, I cannot be certain she has been able to share it with them. I am particularly interested in hearing whether or not she ran into any difficulties getting permission for the students to observe the creation of such traditionally private and "institutionalized" artifacts. In light of the goals of critical pedagogy, the very restricted nature of such artifacts would have been an incredibly interesting discussion to me as well. Even if a basic writing instructor were able to use the artifacts of placement in these ways, however, I worry about the insistence on mainstream ethnographic research procedures used to get the basic writing students to read this unfamiliar community of practice. I will discuss this concern in much greater detail later; in short, I do not wish to imply that students must go to such lengths to learn new literacies. I want basic writing students to understand that developing new literacies does not depend on an entirely accurate reading of the target community as such—simply a *critical* reading of the systems of signs valued in that space. The system of signs separating the members of the target community of practice from the "world" is largely invisible to them, and "reading" this community through an intricate set of tools is not going to put them much closer to an accurate reading of the signs than if they were to simply observe for themselves and discuss their findings with the class—other nonmembers. Perception is, in fact, all we have.

In "When Working Class Students 'Do' the Academy" (1997), Martha Marinara offers a compelling argument for the use of narrative to help working-class students "question the assumption that a college education as defined by the academy" is more valuable than the rich knowledge and "lived relations they bring with them" (5). As she explains, "When students are encouraged to narrate their own educational and work histories and then deconstruct their own stories, this not only broadens the parameters of the lives of working class students, but at the same time raises questions about academic knowledge" (9). In doing so, she challenges what Freire would call the "false consciousness" that leads so many other students to accept the oppressive, class-based ideologies and assumptions foisted on them by the academy and the dominant groups represented by the academy. Her intention is that "explor[ing] the events in their working class lives as operating within the boundaries of a socioeconomic context and . . . question[ing] their beliefs about work, especially when those beliefs come up against their or 'others' lived realities" will enable them to "understand how their selves are determined by various institutions, including those educational systems that offer the hope of economic 'rescue' [from] the lower classes" (12).

In addition to the compelling and sympathetic way she describes her students' intellectual projects, what I find so fascinating about Marinara's article is her regular references to experiences that remind me so much of my own classroom—experiences in which the objective of the curriculum seemed as out of reach as the institutionalized systems of oppression seemed doomed to perpetuate themselves, especially among those students who continued to "[b]uy into the myth of social and economic ascendancy" that "reify existing class structures." Her students tell stories that could have been excerpted from any of my students' essays. According to one student, "My grandfather didn't go to a fancy university, but he owns his own charter business. I just don't want to spend my life working outside" (8). Another tells her: "What I learned from my first job is that I should go school and get a better job" (12).

A few years ago I chose to design a sequence on "work" and the "American Dream" for similar reasons, mostly to get students to question the terms by which we define work, assign it status, and define ourselves and others by such definitions. We read Debra Ginsberg's *Waiting: The True Confessions of a Waitress* (2001), Barbara Ehrenreich's *Nickel and Dimed* (2002), and selections from *Gig: Americans Talk About Their Jobs* (2000) and we watched *The Full Monty* (1997). In including Ginsberg's *Confessions*, my intention was that their reading of it would give us some common terminology through which we could examine and discuss the complexity of the work to which Ginsberg eventually returned (that of a waitress), not only purposefully but also enthusiastically after "getting educated and acquiring other skills" (the response Marinara's student had to the notion that someone could be "a hardworking waitress for fifteen years" [12]). Ehrenreich's study—a first-person account of the impossibility of "getting ahead" on minimum wage, no matter how hard you work—both intrigued and infuriated our basic writing students. Many of them had spent large segments of their lives "living" on a minimum wage income and found Ehrenreich's inability to do so to be her own fault. Several concluded that you have to learn *how* to live on minimum wage; it is complicated, they explained, and someone unaccustomed to it can't just drop into this life and expect to "get by." Many students were particularly put off by her decision to spend $12.00 at a local Applebee's in celebration of her new job: "That's irresponsible," they complained, "Ridiculous!" in fact. "You celebrate some other way—some *cheaper* way!"

Most of the students so miffed by Ehrenreich's problematic spending choices did begin to make moves to critique her choices as a likely consequence of ideological structures that shape individual and material circumstances in different ways. However, a large number of them continued to read her circumstances as irrelevant to their own. While they were able to begin exploring "the events in their working lives as operating within the boundaries of a socio-economic context," few actually came to "question their beliefs about work"—even "when those beliefs came up against their own or others lived reality" (Marinara 12).

As noted in chapter 3, I am concerned about making critical consciousness (Freire) a primary objective in my basic writing classroom. While it will always be a major force shaping the choices I make as a teacher and an administrator, I worry about this critical perspective as it relates to evaluation. Should my students who continue to believe in self-determinism as the only force at work in their lives, in fact, *fail* basic writing? Lose points in some way? As Marilyn Cooper argues, "our central purpose in a first-year writing class is to convince students of the value of using writing to criticize and change their social world" (28). What if they don't want to change it? What if they like it the way it is and only want to change the material conditions of their current life (the American Dream)? What are the practical, real-world, right-now consequences of clinging to what I (and most scholars I have cited thus far) understand to be an oppressive worldview?

These questions make me uncomfortable and complicate further my role as guide between familiar literacies and those as-yet unfamiliar—between home and school. Rhetorical dexterity, on the other hand, seems to offer what Kay Halasek and Nels P. Highberg call in their introduction to *Landmark Essays on Basic Writing* (2001) a "post-critical pedagogy of basic writing." As they explain, "[u]nlike the critical educators of the 1980s and 1990s who promoted marxist and leftist agendas in their classrooms (e.g., Giroux), theorists and teachers who advocate 'post-critical' pedagogies encourage students to 'decide for themselves' the ends to which they'll put their educations—regardless of those ends" (xvi). It is to the practical applications of this "post-critical pedagogy" that I now turn your attention.

SIX

The Way Literacy Lives

What does the world look like outside of school? What do the people do or say or even write outside of this school community? There are many different things that shape up a community. It's not only about the rules for the system, but the people who share certain use of language, clothing, or even style. Instead it can be a group of people who are passionate about the same thing.

For me, art is everything. I started drawing ever since I learned how to hold a pencil. I'm not good at talking or expressing myself in words and sentences, so I put my feelings into figures. And no matter what happen, I will always be a part of this community, unknowingly. . . .

Artists express their feelings through lines and shapes. . . . A painting . . . with lots of curve lines express confusion. A man with his face covered represents mystery. . . . Through all the graphics and colors, we communicate in our own language. (Marian, "The Language of Figures")

RHETORICAL DEXTERITY treats learning new literacies as a situated activity; thus, in a sense, this means the basic writing classroom with rhetorical dexterity as its goal offers learners the "legitimate peripheral participation" Jean Lave and Etienne Wenger contend is a necessary prerequisite for joining any community of practice. As they explain,

Learning viewed as a situated activity has as its central defining characteristic a process that we call legitimate peripheral participation. By this we mean to draw attention to the point that learners inevitably participate in communities of practitioners and that the mastery of knowledge and skills requires newcomers to move toward full participation in the socioeconomic peripheral practices of a community. "Legitimate peripheral participation" provides a way to speak about relations between newcomers and old timers, and about activities, identities, artifacts, and communities of knowledge and practice. It concerns the process by which newcomers become part of a community of practice. (29)

A curriculum shaped by a pedagogy of rhetorical dexterity thus asks students to examine the "process by which newcomers become part of a community of practice" as they have experienced it in an out-of-school context and apply that process to the ones required of newcomers in academic communities of practice. In doing so, we ask students to consider questions like the following: What are the activities that make up a community of practice with which you are deeply familiar? How did you learn them? What identities are constructed via these activities? In other words, how is who you are shaped by your experiences within this community of practice? What artifacts are produced via the activities of this community of practice and how might those compare with the artifacts produced in academic communities of practice?

An approach like this forces participants to pay attention to the inequitable ways literacy is represented and how that representation paralyzes many already-marginalized writers, but, as I will try to make clear in the current chapter, it does not stop there. Certainly, such inequities must be acknowledged before students can gain control over the academic literacy measures shaping their student lives. As writing teachers, we represent and are most often proficient users of standard edited English; thus, it is imperative that we recognize these inequities and speak to them—with our students and *for* our students—especially given that inequities among literacies and among literate users largely determine how one learns new literacies (see chapter 3). However, as I discovered myself via different curricular choices (especially ones deeply informed by critical literacy)[1] and as I have argued elsewhere, pointing out and giving students the space to speak back to those inequities will not be enough to enable them to subvert them—or even, in many cases, to begin to represent literacy differently to and for themselves. Instead, we must give them the tools they need to *experience* literacy differently—to look again at the ways in which literacy functions in the multiple and intellectually viable lifeworlds in which they are already full-fledged members.

THE CURRICULUM

I really do not know who I am as a writer, but I know I am a bad writer. (Dominique, "Thoughts of a Troubled Writer")

In working with the writers in our program and in training new educators to do the same, we begin by working against the myths that shape commonsense understandings of what basic writers need, but in keeping with the findings of the New Literacy Studies, we do so within the context of what we know about how literacy functions in the world beyond the largely artificial "school" literacies we often celebrate (see Appendix C for sample assignments). In other words, we teach basic writing by articulating and helping our students articulate the way literacy actually lives, which, as Brandt explains in "Accumulating Literacy," places greater pressure on Americans "not to meet higher literacy *standards* as has been so frequently argued elsewhere but rather to develop a *flexibility and awareness*" (651, emphasis mine).

Like many programs, we begin by asking students to articulate the ways in which they have experienced literacy and learning thus far, especially how they understand the "rules" for writing in school and whether those rules have changed over time, from subject to subject, from classroom to classroom, from project to project. Many basic writing students tell us that such rules do change, and these changes often confuse and frustrate them. As one writer explained it recently, "I've been told one thing I did in a previous class was wrong in another. When it was said, I became very upset because I'd been doing what I was taught. Once that barrier was broken I had to *start from scratch*" (emphasis mine). As we know, when literacy is understood as a matter of "correctness," the "standards" by which "correctness" is judged can cause writers much confusion, especially those who, like this student, witness the standard mutating right before their eyes.

In the next three essays, students investigate "vernacular" or familiar literacies. We discuss the concept of "communities of practice," reading a brief essay called "What Is a Community of Practice?" (Carter) that articulates the ways in which "communities of practice" may function as an appropriate framework for investigating familiar literacies and learning new ones. They are then asked to explore the "rules" that all literate users must come to know, understand, and be able to negotiate in order to be heard, understood, and taken seriously in that particular community of practice (as a plumber, a deer hunter, or a fan fiction writer for example).

In the second writing assignment, they are asked to investigate a familiar literacy of their choice. Students have selected everything from quilting to playing dominoes to creating Anime, and these early essays are often quite general in their descriptions of "literate ability" within this target community of practice. The writers are surprised to find that someone could be as "football illiterate" or "Christian illiterate"[2] as they learn I am, as they learn other readers who are not members of that community of practice tend to be. The primary objective at this point is to learn how expertise (i.e., "literacy") functions when trying to communicate among people whose experiences, interests, and expertise may differ in some rather substantial ways.

Essays 4 and 5 require a more detailed and sophisticated analysis of two different categories of communities of practice: workplace literacies and those more closely associated with leisure. In preparation for the third essay on workplace literacies, students read and present to one another chapters from

Mike Rose's book *The Mind at Work: Valuing the Intelligence of the American Worker* (2004)—a series of case studies that articulate the cognitive abilities required of electricians, plumbers, carpenters, welders, waitresses, hair stylists, and other similar occupations.[3] In doing so, they consider the special tools, terminology, values, and body movements that might be required of users to be accepted as members of these communities of practice (the literacies associated with waiting tables, styling hair, installing a light fixture). Many students draw upon their own expertise in the fields they investigate (the daughter of a plumber, for example, a Mexican immigrant with fifteen years experience as a building inspector, among others). Reading and analyzing Rose's book in the ways we did was a new experience for many of these writers, and several found working in these ways with this text and their groups to be particularly enlightening. As one basic writing student and art major put it,

> Reading for me used to be just about finding out what happened at the end of the story. Did the bad guys die? Did the hero save the world? The storyline in the book was the thing I value most. When I read Mike Rose's *The Mind at Work* through the summer, I found that [he] has a way of putting down a lot of specific details. The writing itself was brilliant. But when we were doing the assignment in the class over the book, we did it chapter by chapter, and then different little parts like terminology, tools, and body movements. That assignment forced us to look into the text and read not only the words, but the context also. . . . I had fun breaking down the text and the meaning in it. All the stuff from the book might one day be able to help create our own social circle because it gave us the idea of how to fit into a different community of practice. It didn't just GAVE us the details and need-to-know facts about different discourse communities, but also TAUGHT us how it works for a person to learn something entirely new. (2–3, 4)

In preparation for Essay 4 (on literacies associated with "play"), we examine and discuss excerpts from Steven Johnson's *Everything Bad Is Good for You: How Today's Popular Culture Is Actually Making Us Smarter* (2005) and James Paul Gee's *What Video Games Have to Teach Us About Literacy and Learning* (2003), both of which, as we've already discussed, treat video games as intellectually rigorous spaces that demand much of players—not only those learning to play the game for the first time but also those already highly literate players.[4] Previous students have examined the "rules" for membership in communities of practice like skateboarding, photography, basketball, *Halo 2*, and cheerleading. Again, they analyze the specific strategies literate users employ to be heard, understood, and taken seriously among other literate members of this community of practice. Here, they begin to really articulate the specific events that taught them what they needed to know to become insiders in the target community. At this point, many students even begin to think of one another in terms of the familiar communities of practice with which they most identify.

Gretna describes her writing group this way: "Our [group] was made up of: Kailey the cheerleader, Markwen the rapper/construction worker, Bryson the . . . hunt[er], Sincar the gamer . . . Maria the . . . cook[er] of authentic Mexican food, Dorothy the basketball player, and me, the softball player" (Final Reflections).

The next two essays are revisions of earlier ones. In Essay 5, we return to the literacies the students associate with school, asking them to "think about all we've done in class thus far and consider what it might have to teach us about the 'rules' for writing in school and how they might be established, upheld, and perpetuated. What special terminology is embedded in these rules? How does it change from context to context? How do we learn these rules? What special knowledge do we need to have before we can embark on a new reading/writing project? Why?" In doing so, we hope they will begin to represent their experiences with school literacies in less "autonomous" and more situated terms. Most do. Essay 6 is a revision of one of the three essays that explore vernacular literacies.

The final essay asks students to compare and contrast a community of practice seemingly unrelated to school with those literacies required of writers at the college level. Ideally, students can merely combine and rework Essays 5 and 6, as Essay 5 examines in-school literacies and Essay 6 explores an out-of-school literacy. In preparation for this essay, writers develop a one-page handout comparing these two literacies, which they then present to the class.[5] The presentation itself serves as fodder for the final essay.

The genre these writers use to report their findings (WA1–WA7) is important as it forces them to develop a meta-analysis of a given community of practice in terms those illiterate in that community might need to make sense of it and perhaps even learn what they need to join it, if possible. Reporting on the findings of his 1985 study of the effects of writing on learning, Cheryl Geisler shares Copeland's "warning":

> [I]n using writing to help students learn, one should structure writing activities so that they help students incorporate in their writing those particular ideas they are expected to learn. If students write about a topic but are not asked to do so in a way that helps them focus upon the targeted information, writing may not help students achieve the learning goals set forth. (Copeland qtd. in Geisler 115)

The "targeted information" in rhetorical dexterity is the way literacy lives within a variety of communities of practice; thus, the genres themselves ask writers to consider what someone unfamiliar with that community of practice might need to know. According to Marian, the basic writer and art major quoted earlier, this meta-awareness is very useful. As she explains, in investigating familiar literacies in this way, it forced her to articulate things about them that she instinctively knew in some ways but not enough to make use of them in new contexts. Communities outside of school and those related to work

don't usually have written rules like academic communities of practice, so
we had to look beyond words to find out what the rules were. . . .

 After all the assignments we've done so far . . . I felt like I know myself
better than before. All the rules in the . . . communities we all know that
they are there, but writing them down and analyzing them sort of marks
their existence in our mind. (3, 5)

Each community of practice is made up of, among other things, behaviors
shaped by ideologies particular to that community that may seem odd to outsiders but to members of the community are merely common sense. From the
ideologies informing a particular community emerge the "rules" one should
know and apply before one will be considered "literate" by other members.
The problem is that without working consciously against those things we
instinctively assume to be plain common sense, the real "rules" will remain
largely unavailable to outsiders and unteachable by insiders; ideology, as Marilyn Cooper explains, "just sits there, making the world we think we know"
(159). The genres by which these writers are asked to communicate the invisible "rules" users must know and make use of in order to be heard, understood,
and taken seriously "marks their existence in our mind," which enables them
to analyze and make deliberate use of that knowledge base in new, largely
unfamiliar contexts.

 The curricular choices that might effectively make use of a pedagogy
of rhetorical dexterity extend well beyond the ones described earlier. What
I offer here is just one option, and we will continue to rework our own curricula as interest and student needs demand it. In the remaining pages of
this chapter, I will attempt to describe student responses to this particular
curriculum in ways that I hope will enable readers to see what they were
able to gain from this incarnation of it. I will end with a discussion of the
ways in which we will likely alter future versions of the curriculum to
enable students to develop a deeper understanding of the ways in which
literacies differ across the curriculum (see "Field Research Project,"
Appendix C).

SCHOOL LITERACIES (WA1, WA2, AND WA6)

They are outrageous with the rules. They've even gotten to the point where
they've started combining shit. Like combining a period with a comma and
calling it a semi-colon. They even use two upside down commas beside each
other known as quotations.

 I interviewed my friend Jessica. She says, "I don't like semi-colons.
Why can't they just be a damn comma[?]" (Lamanda)

Student representations of school literacies largely replicate what Adler-
Kassner and Harrington describe in *Basic Writing as a Political Act* and "Just

Writing, Basically" as a "huge gulf" between "being a writer" and "learning to write." In other words, few saw themselves as real writers, despite the fact that many write quite often in their lifeworlds beyond school. Holly, a theatre major who describes herself as an "avid reader with severe dyslexia," reads and writes pages of fan fiction each and every day. Fan fiction, as I learned from Holly, is fiction developed to extend the story lines created and reproduced in media outlets like comic books, Hollywood films, television, and even video games. Fans of particular television shows/books/video games/films extract their favorite characters and develop stories around them, stories that must be consistent with the "universe" in which this character first emerged but can take liberties that may not have occurred in the original. Holly describes the appeal of fan fiction this way: "Fan fiction has now become quite a habit for me. In high school, I'd come home as fast as I could, sit down in front of the computer, and read for hours on end, getting drawn into these stories. It takes me away from reality and I find myself becoming a character in one of the many stories." The stories themselves are generated by fans and circulated among these same fans via Internet sites devoted to the subject. Thus, as Holly is a fan of the Anime series *Techni Muyo!*, she frequents fan fiction sites devoted to that series and its key characters.

Like many students in our basic writing program, however, Holly has never found reading and writing for school at all appealing. Thus, many begin the term by describing themselves as "bad writers" who "hate" writing, a self-assessment they attribute to either a lack of familiarity with "the" rules for writing or an "obsession" with the rules. As one writer puts it, "Beginning writers often want to know what hard and fast rules are, the rules we simply must follow. Sometimes writing teachers and books of advice even provide us with the rules, which we then get obsessive [about]" (Dominique). In his second essay, another basic writing student concurs: "Sometimes when I am writing, I get frustrated by minor things. . . . For example: when I'm writing a sentence, I still have ideas or words that still go with that sentence. But I can't finish it, because then it becomes a run-on sentence. *Once again, I become a victim of the rules*" (emphasis mine).

The rules for writing, it seems, are both mysterious and confining. Many express frustration at their inability to learn "the rules" of writing, as well as the ways in which they feel that once learned, these rules continue to distance what they *want* to say from what they feel they *can* say. Ruben offers an incredibly generous portrayal of the function of the writing "rules," but finds that they often "tend to stop me from expressing everything I want to say." The disconnect between home and school felt all the more profound for Ruben because, as he explains, "I was raised in a Spanish speaking community, so you can only imagine how difficult this is for me." Another ESL student (from Korea) describes his previous writing experiences this way: "I didn't know how to learn Standard English and everything I wrote was wrong" (Wong).

In her sixth writing assignment, Emilia makes a similar argument: "If you are given certain . . . rules to follow, that limits your ability to express yourself as an individual writer, stripping you of your creative rights." In her second essay, "No Rules, No Pass," Ashley concurs, arguing that the rules, especially what she calls "the five paragraph rule . . . limits my ability to express how I feel about the writing assignment." In fact, "I think that rule sucks and should be removed from wherever the rules of writing are made. I suggest that teachers of the future should: first, open children minds that there are many different ways of writing . . . and never teach a child that their teaching of the rules is the only way we should know."

They understand, instinctively, that the rules change, but the changes seem unpredictable and largely arbitrary. Steven asserts that "the . . . rules, for some reason, seem to change according to the person grading." Others, like Emilia and Caroline, locate the source of this change in the circumstances in which school writing takes place. Writing near the end of the semester, Emilia explains that

> Before taking this class, I thought writing was pointless, boring, frustrating, confusing, and had too many rules to follow. All those feelings came from many years of being taught so many different rules and being penalized for using them. The most recent case of that happen was my sophomore year in high school when we had to take a practice test of the new standardized state test, the TAKS. Now we were not given any previous warning of how the test was to be graded or what was expected to be written. . . . [Before the test], I had been making super grades in my English class because I had mastered the art of whatever rules for writing we were expected to follow, so I thought I had that test grade in the bag. When it came down to it, I had scored a one (the lowest grade possible) out of a possible four *because I was following rules that no longer applied to the new writing styles of the present time.* . . . I began to realize the severity of how these rules were affecting my grades as well as my knowledge as a student. (emphasis mine)

In her sixth essay entitled "Stupid Rules for Stupid Writers," Caroline puts it this way: "There are so many rules, rules, rules, and more rules when it comes to writing. With so many rules to follow there are also consequences in writing. Like a bad grade, red marks all over the paper, and hearing the teacher telling the student to redo it until it's better. And than it take like forever to be revised until it's better." Another writer offers a similar reading of his experiences with writing "rules": "There are so many different ways of writing. I learn one way then have to learn another. What I mean

by this is what I write really depends on my teacher and my surrounding."
From this experience, he likely learned what Emilia describes as "the
severity of how these rules were affecting my grades as well as my knowledge as a student." For Emilia, thank goodness, the consequences of not
knowing the new rules for the latest high-stakes context would not continue to be quite as negative, at least as far as TAKS was concerned. As she
explains,

> Later on in my sophomore and beginning of my senior year of high school,
> I learned the "correct" way to write for TAKS, and went in knowing what
> was expected to know in order to pass the writing portion of the test. From
> taking this English 100 class, I know there really isn't a "correct" way to
> write and it isn't always pointless.

Like Ashley who argues that the "five paragraph rule sucks" and should
be changed, many of the writers in our program view this rule-making
dynamic as mutable, but they have difficulty locating the persons or institutions responsible for making these decisions. Shatavia asks, "Who created
these rules, the government? It's funny how these rules come up but no one
knows who created them." Among those who grew up in Texas where writing "rules" are largely upheld by high-stakes tests—preparation for the tests
and the test itself—many hypothesize that these rules were, in fact, made up
by the government itself. In his fourth essay, Ruben tells us that "the government plays a big role in the creation of the rules of writing because of all
the tests they make for us to go to college," tests, he explains, "the government was making . . . harder and harder as time was passing" (3). Desmond
reminds us how intricately connected are the "rules for writing" as enforced
via state-mandated tests like TAKS and THEA and the very courses in
which he must enroll: "As the years continue to go by, the government
seems to keep enforcing more and more rules, and laws that you must write
a certain amount of essays each year you are in school. Some college classes
and high school classes are taken due to requirements of the government
even though they might not be needed." He ends on a note that succinctly
expresses the powerlessness writers often feel in the face of further marginalization via institutionalized oppression like this: "if you were to try and
fight the government about this issue, then they would probably try to take
what ever you already have away and not even give it to anyone else." Caroline responds to this hopelessness with biting humor: "Who invented these
rules? The government? If a writer messes up, would the FBI come and arrest
them? How dumb can that be? It's like an unexplainable mystery waiting to
be solved."

It was not until we began exploring other literacies that writers like these
would began to speak of literacy in terms that seemed to free them from the
frustrations imposed on them via artificial and arbitrary writing rules.

OUT-OF-SCHOOL LITERACIES

Every now and then I am given the opportunity to write about something I am passionate about. If feel like I can express my thoughts in an orderly fashion and feel good about it. I do not think of it as a waste of time or a blow-off assignment to make a passing grade in class. It is a chance like this, which makes me feel like I am able to write and get my point across effectively. It is the only time I really enjoy writing. (Gretna, "Writing's Hold on Me")

Mike began our program, as he explains in his final reflections near the end of the term, "a very frustrated twenty-six year old man." His frustration was, in part, a natural consequence of returning to school after several years in the manufacturing sector of the workforce, but it was amplified considerably by our requirement that his first paper for us speak directly to his experiences with writing in school. As he remembers his response to the first-day writing assignment several weeks earlier, "writing in school was just a very sore subject for me at the time that paper was written." In the second week of the class, he came to the writing center for assistance with his paper about the "rules" for writing in school; he was understandably frustrated: "Look, I haven't been in school for almost ten years," he said, growing obviously and increasingly more agitated. "I never knew the rules then, and I certainly can't talk about them now."

"Okay, so talk about what you *do* know," I said. "There are no wrong answers." He remained unconvinced. I asked him to tell me what he did in his spare time. "I don't know. Why does it matter?" He finally told me he did a lot of hunting, so I asked him to talk about the "rules for hunting." How did you come to learn them? Are they written down somewhere? Can you break them? What is their purpose? After quite a bit of discussion about hunting, we returned to his experiences in school. "Tell me a story," I requested. "What's the first thing you remember about school—not necessarily the rules associated with writing but with your experiences as a student." He started to write. Later in the term, Mike would describe our exchange this way: "Dr. Carter and I went back and forth for at least an hour about why she thought I could write this paper. Finally, I gave in and began writing. I didn't stop until I had three pages. Something happened inside me [that day] and I knew I was going to love to write." But it would not be until he started to unpack the literacies associated with his workplace experiences that things would really begin to change for him as a writer.

When I started Literacies at Work, I was so excited. I had a lot of work experience to draw from for this paper . . . [b]ut after brainstorming for a while I decided that the most interesting job to write about would be injection molding. . . .

> This paper was about my employment with R____ Tool Company and
> all the processes that were involved in manufacturing carbide parts using
> injection molding equipment. I had several people read this paper and I
> revised it three times before turning it in to my teacher. When [my teacher]
> returned the paper back to me, I could tell that she was impressed with my
> work. She had probably never heard about most of the information in this
> paper because this type of work is unique and there are only three company's
> in the world that have been able to perfect making carbide using low-pres-
> sure injection molding techniques.

That paper about the literacy requirements of R____ Tool Company would
make the greatest difference for him as a writer. "After writing" the essay
about his workplace literacies, he argues, "I had pretty well figured out that
English writing class was not the only literate community on the planet" (8).

Younger writers may have had fewer workplace experiences from which to
draw, but most found the experience of investigating a familiar community of
practice associated with the workplace nonetheless useful to them in rethinking the way literacy lives in communities of practice beyond school. Many
drew from their experience with part-time jobs as a cashier at McDonald's, a
shift leader at Jack in the Box, a waitress at IHOP, or a grocery clerk at the
local supermarket. As Derek describes it, his position as a "courtesy clerk" at
Brookshire's can be summed up this way: "What I do at my job is talk to people, make them feel comfortable where they are at, and pack the hell out of
their groceries while talking to them." Steven chooses to describe his job as a
cashier at the same grocery store as decidedly more complex. At first glance,
he explains, the job of the cashier may seem simple enough: "The cashier . . .
must . . . make sure he hands back the correct change and [that] you walk out
with everything you have paid for." However, while this may seem "easy . . .
there are many things that are in a cashier's mind while checking out a customer," things like "his scan time" ("how many items he can scan per minute
is crucial. A top scan time could earn honors like Employee of the Month"),
keeping the cash drawer accurate, and "memorizing the produce codes."

As Derek describes his position, the primary value-sets in the community
of practice that is "packing groceries" are activities that make the customer
feel "comfortable" and get the groceries packed quickly. The customer's
"comfort" is important to Brookshire's management as they must compete
with the lower prices Wal-Mart offers just down the road. "Courtesy," according to employees like Steven and Derek, is "what sets us apart." An awareness of the, in Gee's words, "external design grammar" of a given community
of practice thus enables Derek and Steven to prioritize activities within their
positions: Wal-Mart offers "low prices" but not the "courtesy" available to
shoppers at Brookshire's (no one carries out a shopper's groceries at Wal-
Mart, for example). Steven knows that a quick "scan time" and an accurate

cash drawer are valuable activities in this particular community of practice, as well—a value established and reinforced within this community of practice via "honors" like "Employee of the Month" based on criteria like "scan time" and "accuracy." He is also aware of the "internal design grammar" that affects his ability to meet the objectives valued within this community; things like "memorizing produce codes" are important because looking up these produce codes would reduce his "scan time" considerably.

Speed and accuracy are valuable in Paola's work as a waitress as well, and this community of practice also requires "good social skills" a "good memory," and the capacity "to do two or more things at the same time." As she explains, "every job has its own rules, ideas, and its own way to get the job done." The activities required to "get the job done" are reproduced organically by virtue of the "tips" that work as incentive within this community of practice, but they are also reproduced more formally by the specific tools made available to them via the restaurant in which they serve and the systems by which the supervisors and the corporation of which the specific location is a part have in place. For Paola, this meant that

> when I started to work as a waitress, my boss explained to me what I should have to do, how to serve the customers, used the register machine, and write the tickets, that way the cook would not get confused with the order. I had to follow one of the waitresses with more experience to see how to serve, take people's orders, ask for drinks, and give to the customer an appetizer while they are waiting for their food.

Thus, it appears that several of the activities reproduced in this community of practice are learned by newcomers via what Lave and Wenger call "legitimate peripheral participation." While training, Paola "participated" in this community of practice by shadowing a full-fledged member to learn what she does so she can, in turn, begin performing the activities of waiting tables in many of the same ways. Again, the values guiding work as a server appear to be courtesy, accuracy, and speed. She needs a system for approaching the tables in order to keep the customers happy (drinks refilled, food ordered in a timely manner and in such a way that "the cook would not get confused," etc.). Her "legitimate peripheral participation" in this community of practice while training enabled her to develop fluency in the "internal design grammar" of this system.

Some values-sets are reproduced via more formal training materials, as is the case with the large and highly regulated company McDonald's. As Courtney explains, the activities reproduced in McDonald's are much more formalized than they seem to have been for servers at IHOP. According to Courtney,

> When working at McDonald's you must be train before [being] put in a specific area. You have to watch videos on everything a McDonald's

worker have to do. The video might take all day or make two day. You must watch video on how to cook the food from fries, to meat, breakfast item. . . . Also you must know how to clean. You can not clean a McDonald's restaurant like you clean your house. You must have cleaning item that McDonald's get from a company. Such as special Windex, sanitizer for towel and dishes as well.

Thus, the systems McDonald's employees must adhere to when completing tasks within this context are deeply dependent on the corporate structure of which their particular location is but a part. The values reproduced within this community of practice may be accuracy and speed, but of primary importance here is uniformity—in methods, in tools, in the artifacts produced. As Courtney puts it, "McDonald's is a fast food business, but that does not mean we are always fast. Sometimes we might take the wrong order, put the wrong things in the bags, or might not give the right change back." As Steven describes his work as a cashier at Brookshire's, these activities would be grounds for dismissal in the communities of practice with which he is most familiar. At McDonald's, however, at least according to Courtney, they are quite commonplace.

WHAT OUT-OF-SCHOOL LITERACIES
HAVE TO TEACH US ABOUT ACADEMIC ONES

Derek doesn't play many video games because of his visual impairment. As he explains, "I cannot see the detail that is needed to play some of them." He does play a lot of Madden 2003, however—a football simulation video game. Derek is drawn to this particular video game, he says, because he's a football player and, according to Derek, "the ethics and terminology is about the same. I have found that it is a lot easier to play a game that you will already have some kind of understanding to. It has so much to do with past experiences." In many ways, then, this game parallels for him more traditional education. As he explains, "I feel that video games are very educational, because you have to take time to learn them meaning of the game . . . the purpose of the game, and . . . the combinations of codes that will have to be used to successfully beat the game." Likewise, approaching a new writing assignment requires writers to take time to learn the internal and external design grammars limiting and shaping the relevant rhetorical spaces, the "purpose" of the assignment itself as understood by the key evaluators responsible for it, and "the combinations of codes" (language use, special terminology, rhetorical moves) that will be required of him as he negotiates this complex writing task. Thus, a familiarity with similar activities—particularly as the similarity is based on the new literacy being a simulated version of the one already well known to him—enables him to adapt quickly to this new environment.

Derek understands, however, that many times the new literacy being learned will depend on codes, conventions, and rules that are largely unfamiliar to him. While this budding awareness does worry him a bit, he tells us that he is much happier thinking of literacy as "different" everywhere rather than always the same.

In his final essay (entitled "Knuckle Grinding"), Brad argues that his learning new literacies depends not so much on familiarity—as Derek contends—but on a willingness to take risks. Accordingly, as Brad explains, "writing is a lot like playing extreme paintball: When you're on the field and you don't know the game, you're going to get shot down, and it hurts. . . . So when this happen all you can do is sit out that once and wipe the paint off and jump back in, and use the skills you learned from the last game like what to do and not to improve your skills that much more."

Likewise, a pedagogy of rhetorical dexterity requires that the learner not only redefine literacy in terms more consistent with the ideological model Street advocates, but also to develop a willingness to take risks to determine the limits and possibilities available within the new context and weigh the consequences of adherence with any desire to resist doing so. The value of risk-taking behavior in learning new literacies is often much more visible in communities of practice associated with video games than those associated with school, however. In the strange but provocative weblog *The Dancing Sausage*, a contributor makes clear that the "video game literate" are those who are "willing to die."

> The ultimate test of video game literacy is this: Are you willing to die? The video game literate generally are. . . . They'll try any button until they figure out what works. They will walk over the shimmering circle which may be a land mine, may be a warp portal; they will chase after the bouncing ball which may turn out to be a health restorative, may turn out to be a bomb. They'll try anything once. If it proves to be lethal, they'll try not to do it again.

According to her argument, literate players are willing to die for at least two reasons. First, they know "death" is the likely consequence of taking the risks necessary to learn what's possible in this new context; second, because in video games, "death" is relatively insignificant. Each player usually has multiple "lives" available to her. If her ship sustains too much battle fire to go on, she's simply issued a new one. No questions asked. If she "dies" more times than the number of "lives" allocated to a given player, she simply starts a brand new game. They risk death in order to learn from it, and they are willing to "die" because death in this context is relatively meaningless.

It is important to note, however, that to the video game literate, a willingness to "die" is not the same as finding no value in "living." Quite the contrary. Actually, death in a video game is no more (and no less) than the ultimate threat—a danger one immediately takes charge of when one is willing to die. "Death" for the literate gamer is a necessary risk; otherwise the user can never really learn what's possible within that virtual context and which activities are too deadly to ever try again. For Brad, "death" in a game of paintball offers him the same opportunity to learn, and in comparing this important prerequisite for learning in playing paintball with the need for risk-taking behavior in developing print-based texts in school, he learns to embrace risk there, too, rather than continue to, in his words, "play it safe." In order to develop enough familiarity with a new video game to eventually "beat it," literate gamers know they can't be "afraid to screw up." According to the blogger cited earlier, "[t]hey'll try any button until they figure out what works. . . . They'll try anything once. If it proves to be lethal, they'll try not to do it again." Learning new literacies thus becomes a process energized by the excitement of what may be possible in this new context rather than a chore stifled by a constant fear of "death." Thus, transference from a familiar literacy to an unfamiliar one is easiest for Derek when the new literacy is not completely unlike the old one; for Brad, this transference is possible once he learns to value and again make use of risk-taking behavior.

Gretna also chose to compare out-of-school literacies with writing as a learner, paying particular attention to the ways in which she became a "legitimate" member of more familiar communities of practice and how she planned to make use of these lessons in this new context. You may recall that one of the key issues that continued to affect Gretna's perception of herself as a writer was her concerns about the constraints of time. But in developing her presentation that compared gaming literacies to what she called "writing literacies," she began to consider the ways in which her success in the video game *Dance Dance Revolution* (DDR) also depended on her ability to think fast. As she explains, throughout the game you must think "the steps through," much like she discovered she had to when writing her timed response to the high-stakes test that placed her in basic writing. DDR is a console game that uses a floor pad on which players "dance" rather than a control unit with obvious buttons or a joystick. The player (or players) selects a song, then attempts to step where the signals on the television screen tell her to step (signals on screen are color-coded, as is the floor pad).

According to Gretna, this experience requires lots of quick thinking. Apparently, when playing DDR, players must ask themselves, "Which foot will they have to move their bodies to dance as efficiently as possible? It's the same thing with writing. The topic you are writing about requires thinking it through and finding the best way to explain something. Timing is everything [too]. Being able to pace yourself according to the time given to you and the length of a song are definitely a big part of both activities." Thus, in making these comparisons, Gretna was required to consider the ways in which she had been able to successfully negotiate time constraints in some rather complex spaces (like DDR), a revelation that helped her develop much more confidence as a writer in unfamiliar rhetorical spaces. Interestingly enough, she does point out at least one advantage "writing literacies" have over gaming literacies: "While writing, you are able to think about what you are going to write about. Unfortunately, you are not able to plan out or predict the steps you will be making while playing DDR. The screen only shows you a small amount of what you will be dancing to at a time" and you get no choice in the dance steps you are required to mimic.

Rather than examining the "in-the-moment" experiences of playing/writing in contexts like school and video games, Desmond compared the *processes* involved. In comparing training for a game of football with writing a paper for school, he focused on writing and football as processes that take place in phases and over time. As he describes it,

> A rough draft would be considered a full practice day because you are giving it all that you have to give. When a person makes a rough draft, they should write it like it is a final draft. In football when it is a full practice, the coach wants his players to play like they are going to play in the big game. So therefore when a rough draft is written, it would be written like its ready to be presented at that very moment.
> . . . The next step in writing is letting others read what you come up with. This is what we call an open practice in football, which is when you allow people to come in and watch you practice.

In a similar way, Adrian, an avid player of what he tell us is "futbol" (not "soccer," he tells me), chose to compare team "formations" to rhetorical traits of writing like "organization." As he explains,

> when you use formations in futbol you use it so that you have organization on the field in order to develop a play. . . . A formation is all about placement and it does affect all the other player[.] If one player doesn't know it doesn't work. A formation is chosen by seeing what formation an opponent is bringing on the field and then you use a formation that will hurt them. . . . Well with writing you can use formations in order to organize your paper and even develop a well organized paper.

Sports were a common choice among many writers in our program. "Danny" compares reading for school with his position on the football field as a linebacker.

> In my mind there are many ways of reading. . . . When I played as a linebacker, I would have to read plays. First I would have to tell if it was a passing or a running play. If it was a passing play, I would have to drop back into my zone and cover whoever entered it. If it was a running play, I would have

to figure out which side the play was going to, who was carrying the ball, which hole it was going to go through, and what my job was. I had to read all this all within three seconds. I found this very difficult.

Danny "read" the football field in many of the same ways Adrian and his teammates "read" (current formations) and "wrote" (new formations) in response to this reading. As players (of football, in Danny's case, of "futbol" in Adrian's case), they had to anticipate where the players were going—the logic guiding their plays so Danny/Adrian could know how he should behave. They had to do this quickly, and only the football/futbol literate know how. Danny continues: "In a way this is also how we read books. When you read a book you have to be able to tell who was telling the story, where the story was taking place, when the story was happening, and what the story was about."

In making these comparisons, then, these writers were able to redefine literacy in terms more in keeping with the way literacy lives, (re)produced within a given community of practice with a deeply situated, people-oriented set of behaviors considered "literate" and very specific consequences for not following these rules. As Marion puts it in her response to WA6 assigned late in the term, "No matter what we think of these rules, obey is the only option. Every community formed its own language. . . . If we are in school, this community of practice, then we have to follow the[ir] rules, because that's how this community works. People who can't follow the rules will be left out of the community, no matter how intelligent they are."

By the end of the term, most writers understand that these rules change as context changes. Marion offers the interesting example of the common elementary school lesson "ain't ain't a word." According to Marion, students are taught early and often that "[t]he word 'ain't' can never be seen in a formal paper." She finds this lesson highly problematic; as she explains, "[t]he word 'ain't might not need to be defined as non verbal but" instead as "a word that belongs to another community." This statement alone reveals the ways in which she is beginning to treat literacy as a social practice rather than a universal norm.

In effect, the real objective of the course is not to get the students to produce sophisticated academic discourse that is well organized, concrete, and convincing. That is certainly *an objective*, but as one reviewer for an earlier draft of an article-length version of this project (in the *Journal of Basic Writing*) pointed out, "What makes you believe that it is this particular sequence of essay/readings/coursework that helps students toward rhetorical dexterity, rather than the simple fact that they write six college-level essays, with the support of studio-type peer- and mentor-feedback"? From our analysis, it appears that the students do, indeed, learn how to produce academic discourse that may be judged effective in even the most traditional of contexts. I agree, however, that their abilities to do so are more likely the result of smart, constructive "peer- and mentor-feedback" than the curriculum alone.

What they do gain from a pedagogy of rhetorical dexterity and this particular curriculum, I argue, is a new understanding of the way literacy actually lives—a meta-cognitive ability to negotiate multiple literacies by understanding that "literacy is not literacy is not literacy" (Hull 19). The course did not, necessarily, give them "literate strategies" that they could easily translate from one community to the next, at least not automatically or without rereading the unfamiliar community of practice in similarly rigorous ways. In the end, then, making relevant the communities of practice with which they were already quite familiar (often even experts in) helped them redefine literacy for themselves in more productive ways. As one writer puts it in her final reflections for the course, "Overall, I learned that academics can be related to everything we do. . . . Some people find it as hard as I did at first to relate their [familiar] communities to academics. As I found out by doing so, everything we do or say is related to academics in some way or else how do we learn to do or say these things?" In other words, how we learn in *any* community of practice is necessarily going to help us understand how to learn new literacies in academic ones. It appears obvious, once we make it obvious.

REFLECTIONS

As previously stated, two hours each week English 100 students meet with a group of five to seven other writers led by a peer tutor—this in addition to the three hours each week they spend with their English 100 classroom instructor. In these writing groups, students workshop papers and challenge themselves and one another to think of reading and writing in new ways ("reading/writing the world") via their Dialogue Journals (as suggested by Ann Berthoff) and their Dialogue Journal Conferences (as suggested in *The Journal Book: For Teachers of At-Risk College Writers*), all of which inform their development of a reflective essay in which they articulate the ways the work they generated this term meets the following objectives:

> The student will (1) understand that literacy is context-dependent, (2) validate and investigate one or more familiar communities of practice, (3) articulate the unwritten rules participants must obey in that community of practice if they want to remain/become accepted as members, (4) investigate new literacies in order to articulate the unwritten rules participants must likewise obey (or at least acknowledge), (5) locate and articulate the *points of contact* between familiar literacies and unfamiliar ones, (6) examine and articulate the *points of dissonance* between different literacies, and (8) put *rhetorical dexterity* to use in a variety of contexts for a variety of purposes. (English 100 syllabus)

At midterm, the students submit a draft of this project (Critical Reflections), which their tutors then bring to a panel of readers made up of all the English

100 group tutors, the graduate administrator(s) of the writing center, and myself (the director). Readers assess this draft according to a rubric I've developed for just this purpose (built on the objectives outlined above), and the assessment (provided by two different readers) guides the writer in her revisions of her critical reflections (see Appendix D for a copy of both the writing assignment and the rubric we use to respond to it). The rubric helps these new educators determine the effectiveness of the current draft in meeting the above objectives via prose that meets the demands of this particular academic community (effectively organized, filled with what the community might consider "relevant" evidence, focused on the issue at hand, clear, and relatively free of surface-level concerns). Readers ask themselves questions like the following: Does the writer understand what other literacies may have to offer her as she attempts to learn new ones? Can she articulate this understanding and reveal the ways in which the work she has produced this term (her essays, her presentations, etc.) serves as evidence of this understanding and her ability to apply what she has learned here to new contexts?

The final portfolio for each English 100 student should include a revised draft of these critical reflections, as well as deeply revised drafts of the essays and presentations the student completed (as articulated above). It, too, is graded by a panel of readers. The following information is included on their English 100 syllabus: "Your Final Portfolio will be reviewed by a panel of experienced English 100 instructors. This panel will be looking for things like this: How evident is your growth as a writer? Is there evidence here that you understand the importance of deep revision? Is there evidence of your ability to effectively rework these writing assignments to meet (or exceed) specified criteria? Are you ready for the demands of English 101?" Thus, the specific educational benefits of this program are determined by the student's ability to articulate these benefits in the critical reflections and to provide evidence of the applicability of this *pedagogy of rhetorical dexterity* via the final portfolio.[6]

CHANGES

Though we have found the curriculum described above to be effective in teaching basic writing students and new educators to think of literacy in new, more productive ways, many of our students have found making comparisons to school literacies more difficult than I expected them to and, while most have begun to rethink literacy in terms much more closely approximating the ideological model Street advocates, they continue to speak of school literacies in monolithic terms. The major reason for this may be that they have had so few experiences with college-level literacy. Thus, future versions of this curriculum will include an additional group project. This project, assigned early in the semester and completed in their English 100 writing groups, would require students to explore the disciplinary differences among literacy requirements as represented in a set of journals and books collected and placed on reserve by a campus librarian.[7] That is, students would share their majors with their group tutors, then pair up with some one declaring a major unlike their own (a history major may pair up with someone interested in the health sciences, for example). Again in pairs, they would analyze the literacy requirements of each discipline as represented in one or two journals and books. The analysis should follow a set of criteria that might include use of informal language (personal pronouns, contractions, etc.), graphs, charts, surveys, polls, statistics, interviews, and special terminology. Finally, they would compare and contrast each, articulating the points of contact and points of dissonance between each discipline and, finally, presenting those findings to their writing group. My hope is that in doing so even more students will discover the number of ways in which "correctness" is context and, in fact, discipline specific (see especially Geisler and Russell). Of course many of our students have not yet declared majors. Thus we ask these "undecided" students and suggest a discipline from there.

PORTABILITY

Given public perceptions of this always new "literacy crisis," those of us hoping to "make basic writing a political act" would do well to represent literacy in more appropriate and contextualized ways. However, given that policies like "No Child Left Behind" show no signs of fading and that state-mandated "remediation" mirrors public perception of what "basic writers" need, it seems unlikely that many of us will be able to do so beyond the learning spaces for which we are responsible, at least not immediately or directly.

In the short term, I seem to be without the power to make major changes to the institutionalized oppression that regularly represents the way literacy functions and measures it in inappropriate ways. I suspect I am not alone in this. Thus, a *pedagogy of rhetorical dexterity* seems to lend itself to application in other institutions and contexts, especially as such a philosophical perspective enables us to work toward social justice by making changes within basic writing programs at the levels of curriculum, tutor training, and teacher training—in my case, all within the confines of the system my predecessors established in response to the TASP law almost twenty years ago (enacted in 1989). It is my hope that such moves will extend far beyond the classroom—into conversations with colleagues about what basic writing students need, into forums that allow us to confront reticent colleagues and administrators (perhaps even politicians and the general public) with what basic writing students can already do (abilities they had long before attending our programs), maybe even into a series of colloquia in which former "basic writers" speak with the general public about literacy in smart, flexible ways (perhaps within the presence of those who define it in much less informed ways). At an area conference in 2007, one of our former basic writing students did just this.

Overturning the institutional, political, social, and economic infrastructure invested in the autonomous model of literacy requires time, patience, and—above all—diplomacy. Taking that ideological model of literacy public through the mouths and texts of current and former basic writing students seems to me the sweetest revenge possible for the many ways in which that autonomous model has stigmatized them. Not only do I think such publicity is (eventually) possible; I think it is, in fact, inevitable.

Conclusion

Our goals should be to challenge conceptions of literacy, to provide more and better opportunities for students (and teachers) to use literacy in ways that engage their worlds. . . .

Students need to understand what kinds of judgments are made about their writing by what institutional powers, and they need to understand how to adjust their own writing in order to be successful in other institutional settings. Putting literacy definitions in the center of the curriculum is the best way to show students how literacy is politicized through assessment and curricular sequencing. . . .

To those who would argue that such an approach might be too difficult for our students-called-basic-writers, we offer these two words: It's not. (Adler-Kassnor and Harrington 103, 102)

FINALLY, WE COME to the question of evaluation: Are academic literacies, in fact, better suited for more complex intellectual activities than more vernacular ones? Literacy scholars like William Damon and basic writing scholars like Mina Shaughnessy say yes. In "Reconciling the Literacies of Generations," Damon reminds us of the complexities involved in the calculations the Brazilian candy vendors in Geoffrey Saxe's study (see chapter 2) are able to perform, despite the fact that many of them "lack certain formal literacy and numeracy skills usually learned in school [and thus] cannot read or represent large numerical values in the conventional, multidigit manner of modern arithmetic." Even so, they

> continually perform complex numerical calculations that would make our grown-up heads spin. . . . To begin with, the candy sellers must buy larger boxes . . . at wholesale prices . . . sort the candies into types, subdivide the amounts, and mark up the prices for their own retail street sales . . . all [of which] requires a working understanding of ratios and fractions.

. . . Brazil's triple-digit inflation rate [demands a "further quantitative perversity"]. Because some weeks pass between purchase and completed sales of the candy, the seller must factor the decline of the cruzeiro's purchasing power into the pricing decision. . . .

Not only do the young candy sellers master the formidable mathematical tasks, but they do so without the aid of their culture's conventional symbol system. This precetype of orthographic ignorance . . . would place these children squarely in the category of the numerically "illiterate." (36)

Even so, however, Damon concludes that their "illiteracy" in the "culture's conventional symbols system" is indeed "a real handicap . . . because facility with written symbols is essential for further progress into algebra, geometry, calculus, and other forms of higher math" (38).

Thus, he warns us against favoring unschooled literacies over schooled ones or vice versa. As he explains, "just as we should not lose site of the remarkable adaptiveness of some unschooled abilities, we must guard against expecting more from them than they can deliver" (38). That is, we must recognize that "schooling is the primary context in which children learn the most advanced forms of thinking available in a culture." This does not mean that "schooling is always strictly necessary for the attempt of useful thinking skills . . . [but] it . . . is close to necessary" (46).

Yet, as Damon readily admits, this is the *potential* of schooling, not necessarily the reality. Many times the focus in schooling is in decoding texts rather than comprehending them or putting them to use, memorizing lists of facts rather than gaining any understanding of what may make such facts significant or relevant to the way they live their lives. In his discussion of E. D. Hirsch's treatise on cultural literacy[1] Damon points out the irony of Hirsch's position:

In his book he cites a number of psychological sources . . . most of [which] . . . are either obsolete or tangential to the problems in human learning and development that he addresses. . . .

He deplores the "natural development" theories that liken a child to an "acorn" growing into a tree—theories which he claims have spanned the new kind of teaching and sets himself on the environmental-acculturation side. Whatever rhetorical fruits are to be gathered from such an opposition, it certainly does not represent the current state of thinking in developmental psychology. No serious scholar in child development today could disavow the dynamic interplay between culture and individual growth. . . . No scientific position holds that children develop like acorns. The controversies in the field revolve not around the question of whether interaction occurs, nor even on whether it is critical to development but rather on the form and directions of the interaction. . . . One would think that a scholar who presumes to set an agenda for educational reform—and particularly a

scholar who claims to be committed to the accumulated knowledge of cultures—would attempt to understand and use the best knowledge available
about such matters. But the intricacies of human development elude Mr.
Hirsch, just as I am sure the intricacies of history or geography would elude
any student whose education consisted of learning Mr. Hirsch's lists. A passing acquaintance with facts does not define the depths of literacy, "cultural"
or otherwise. (44–45)

Thus, Damon concedes that while out-of-school literacies may not offer users
the "conventional symbol systems" necessary for "higher" cognitive activities,
neither will the functional or cultural perspectives dominating our schools.
As one student in our basic writing program put it recently: "My teachers
taught me how to write a five-paragraph essay but at the same time to remember that five paragraph essays aren't always the right approach. They taught
me how not to write how you talk, but they never really taught me to think
critically."[2]
   In his now quite controversial "Developing Literacy: Walter J. Ong and
Basic Writing" (1978), Thomas J. Farrell builds on Ong's—his mentor—theory
that cultures can be divided along a continuum, with primarily oral cultures
at one end and those highly literate on the other, making the argument that
"open admissions students . . . are . . . beginning writers because they are still
highly oral and residually oral persons . . . who come from a cultural background in which literacy and literate (i.e., analytic, abstract, detached, scientific) modes of thinking do not predominate" (30). In doing so, he represents the problem of "basic writers" as a deficiency in the cognitive processes
available to their "literate" counterparts:

> The oral person is involved and committed to a given . . . position on mat-
> ters, whereas the fully literate person is capable of being detached and look-
> ing at matters from different points of view. Highly literate persons can
> examine experience and arrange it, can separate themselves from the expe-
> riences instead of just identifying with them, can stand apart from the
> "object" and reconsider it and analyze it and evaluate it. (32)

Several years later, in "Orality, Literacy, and Standard English" (1991),
David Lazere perpetuates this association of basic writing students with "oral
culture" and all others with "literate cultures," highlighting "differences in
stages of cognitive development between students whose language and culture are primarily oral and those who have assimilated the written language,
the body of literate knowledge and codes of academic discourse on which college-level reading and writing depend" (87–88). While accepting that Ferrell's distinction between "oral culture" and written ones may be too reduc-
tive to explain the difficulties basic writing students face, he argues that "oral
culture may indeed be one significant factor, among others, of the difficulties

faced in school by Blacks and other children whose foundation is that of oral culture" (90). The goal of basic writing thus becomes "helping students make the transition from oral to written discourse," which he argues is important to cognitive development as "oral culture tends to be appositional and formulaic, while literate culture tends to be propositional in reasoning, so that writing facilitates a much greater degree of abstract and analytic reasoning" (94, 91).[3]

As Brian V. Street points out, such cognitive functions may seem valuable in school literacies, but they represent an autonomous model of literacy that is, in fact, inappropriate as it forces compliance to the dominant worldviews and thus forces individuals into a passive stance few would contend bears any resemblance to critical thought. Street calls this arbitrary separation between orality and literacy "the Great Divide," describing it as "one of the major means whereby an autonomous model of literacy is internalized and disseminated in contemporary society" (115). Literacy and orality are largely inseparable and attempts to separate them perpetuate the autonomous model of literacy that I hope has already been established as an entirely inappropriate one to describe how literacy actually works in our lives and, therefore, how we should teach it. In fact, as Laura Gray-Rosendale shows us in her provocative study *Rethinking Basic Writing*, the oral skills of basic writing students are often no less complex (and quite similar to) those we associate with academic literacy—especially as they use these same oral moves to help one another negotiate that distance between "home" and the "academy."

In the end, however, the question of whether or not "academic" literacies are more intellectually viable than vernacular ones or whether those activities considered to be "literate" in the traditional sense are more intellectually productive than "oral" ones is moot: The current institutional mechanisms that define some writers as "basic/illiterate" and others as "normal/regular/literate" demand compliance; thus, basic writing teachers and tutors (and our students) have little choice but to comply.

In *Basic Writing as a Political Act*, Linda Adler-Kassner and Susanmarie Harrington (2002) examine the very real "tensions between making basic writing a political act and doing so within institutional and social constraints that essentially work against politicizing the act of literacy development" (8). In their exploration of (1) how basic writing students are portrayed in key scholarship, (2) how basic writing students perceive themselves and their position as basic writers, (3) how they are portrayed in mainstream media, and (4) how their teachers represent them in their syllabi and other course materials, the authors reveal the complex ways in which the confusing "problem" of students called basic writers is generated and perpetuated by multiple artificial and conflicting narratives with narrators who seem largely unaware of one another. While they "ultimately agree with Ira Shor that [in his words] 'find[ing] allies with whom to study, talk, experiment, and plan campaigns against testing, tracking, and against the imposition of skills-based teaching'

(100) is important," they argue that such a "solution ultimately does not address the needs of students who sit in our basic writing classes here and now" (7). They contend that a more practical and at once more *political* solution is to bring all these conflicting narratives into conversation with one another—the basic writing scholarship, the media on basic writers, the basic writers themselves, and their teachers—reminding ourselves "that basic writing, no matter how theorized or studied, is fundamentally a classroom-based enterprise." In doing so, they hope to "raise series questions about the ways literacy is represented in classes and the consequences of these representations for students and teachers" (97).

In developing the *pedagogy of rhetorical dexterity* advocated in this book, I hope I have forged "instruction that enables students to understand how definitions of literacy are shaped by communities, how literacy, power, and language are linked, and how their myriad experiences with language (in and out of school) are connected to writing" (98). In that the preceding pages are designed to convince literacy educators and their basic writing students to think of literacy in new, more contextualized ways, perhaps the book itself and the curriculum it advocates is a "political act."

Save cases of extreme mental disability (and perhaps not even then), no one is illiterate. By virtue of living in the world, speaking a language others can understand, and using a sign system of some sort—such an individual is literate. In that we assume every individual is highly literate in at least one community of practice, especially if that individual is an adult who has had eighteen years or so to develop productive literacies in one or more communities of practice, neither is that person a basic writer, despite the institutionalized label she may receive when she begins college.

I hope the arguments presented in this book have been persuasive in their attempts to reveal the intellectual and cultural complexities communities of practice beyond the academy enable and perpetuate. Once those of us in the academy begin to recognize and validate such communities—church literacies, Star Trek literacies, comic book literacies, autoworker literacies—we enable those marked as basic writers to reimagine the possibilities of academic discourse. This reimagination, in turn, challenges traditional notions of academic discourse and forces changes to emerge—changes that open up the possibility that someday—perhaps some day soon—no one will even be *labeled* "basic writer," as no one really is.

Appendix A

WRITING ASSIGNMENT 3
(THE VIOLENT TENDENCIES OF LITERACY)

"Texts" under exploration and working as evidence for WA3

- WA1 and WA2
- Deborah Brandt's "Sponsors of Literacy" (1998)
- Elspeth J. Stuckey's *The Violence of Literacy* (1991)
- *Central Station*

KEY QUESTIONS TO EXPLORE IN WA3

How might literacy sometimes be considered "violent" or destructive? Can sponsors of literacy—as Brandt defines them—be violent? If so, how? How might people/ institutions/value-sets sponsor this violent or destructive literacy? Who are the sponsors of literacy in *Central Station* and what's their function? How might this function play itself out (or have played itself out) in your own literacy experiences?

BRIEF SUMMERY OF POSSIBLE PROCESS
FOR DEVELOPING A DRAFT OF WA3

- Examine the "violence" possible in literacy, according to Stuckey.
- Respond to this "violence" in class discussions and in your journal.
- Examine "violence" through sponsorship and other methods as you see them portrayed in *Central Station*.
- Respond to this violent sponsorship in class discussions and in your journal.
- Examine WA1, WA2, and notes generated in response to questions and journal prompts for useful information to fold into WA3 through the new lenses provided by this film and Stuckey's arguments.

- Develop a draft of WA3 from this examination and reworking.
- Share this draft with another reader, examine the reader's feedback, and develop plans for revision.
- Deeply revise WA3, before sharing it with your instructor for feedback. As with all the essays written in this course, it is likely this essay will go through several more revisions before it shows up in your Final Portfolio.

Appendix B

PRE-READING LITERACY AT CENTRAL STATION

SETTING THE CONTEXT

We've been reading and writing about your own literacy past for several weeks now. We've even traced what Deborah Brandt calls the "sponsors of literacy" that have made these literacy experiences possible (or *impossible*). In *The Violence of Literacy*, Stuckey told us that literacy education itself may be said to commit the greatest acts of violence, perpetuating the inequities in society even while contending that education is the "great equalizer" in society.

In other words, sponsors of literacy may be, in fact, sponsors of a kind of "violence" against those who were promised access to the American Dream.

In this second part of our discussions in preparation for WA3, I'd like for us to explore these issues in spaces that extend beyond the American context we've been examining thus far.

What makes literacy an inherent "good"? Is the ability to read and write naturally better than an inability to read or write? In other words, Stuckey tells us we are committing "violence" when we treat literacy as more civilized behavior than we do illiteracy, thus privileging literate individuals above illiterate ones. What might be the consequences of this perspective of literacy? What are your thoughts with respect to this?

Before you "read" this film, read yourself. What's your position?

1. Let's imagine illiteracy for just a moment. How does it *feel*? Pretend that you can't read or write in the traditional sense. That is, imagine you can neither write words others can understand nor read the words others have written. How would your life change? Pretend that you must communicate with someone who *can* read and write but the only way to contact them is via letter or not at all. What if just about everyone you knew were in the same position, so you had to rely on a stranger to communicate with this

person (family remember, loved one, close friend) for you. How would you do this? List a couple options for communicating with this person and follow each option with at least one possible negative consequence of employing this option.

2. What about Stuckey's discussion of the "Violence of Literacy" resonated with you the most? What are some of the possible implications of the "Violence of Literacy" you can see at work in a context like this where illiterate individuals must rely so heavily on literate ones?

As you read this film, consider the paper you are writing and the conversations we've been having about literacy thus far. What might this film be saying about literacy, the power of literacy, the objects of literacy, the sponsors of literacy, and/or the violence of literacy? Think about these questions as you watch the film, and spend some time jotting down your thoughts immediately following each viewing day. You should also jot down any questions you may have after the first viewing day so you can ask them before the film begins again that second viewing day.

RESPONDING TO LITERACY AT CENTRAL STATION

Now that you've read Stuckey's article and viewed the film *Central Station*, what do you think? Do not forget to offer readings that both "accept" the arguments and evidence Stuckey offers in her article and "resist" them. That is, share what you know and respect about her arguments before working to resist them or aspects of them (which is the next, very important step).

1. The film doesn't really deal with literacy education per se, but it certainly deals with literacy. Divide a sheet of paper or a page in your journal into two columns. In the first column, make a list of every scene that pops into your head that seems to have something to do with literacy. In fact, list every scene that seemed to resonate with you at all. In the second column, jot down an answer or two to the following questions (for each scene): What does this scene seem to reveal about literacy? Be specific. That is, if the scene reveals something about the power of literacy, describe what it reveals and how it reveals this. If it reveals something about the violence of literacy, describe what it reveals about this *violence* of literacy and how it works to reveal this. If it somehow makes use of the idea that literacy acquisition and/or illiteracy needs *sponsorship*, especially if the possible sponsors of this literacy seem to resonate with you, jot this down. Read over your responses to the "Before You Read" questions and think about what the film disclosed with respect to these issues of literacy and literacy education.

2. After you've completed step 1, read over your notes. Which of these scenes seem to offer the most useful information for your WA3?

3. Describe, in as much detail as possible, two to three key scenes that really seemed to resonate with you—scenes you think you might include in WA3.
4. Why might someone who can read and write feel she has the right to make decisions for those who can't read or write? Are you familiar with anyone who may they feel should make decisions for others—even other adults—based on their assumption that they their literacy skills surpass those of the one for whom they feel it necessary to make decisions? Explain.
5. Consider the following quotation from Stuckey's *The Violence of Literacy* with respect to what it might reveal about the portrayal of literacy in *Central Station*:

> Literary is a social restriction and an individual accomplishment. Individuals read and write, or don't, and individuals do with literacy what they can. The subjectivities of minds and the ways in which people make their lives and thoughts, and the ways in which people are coerced, entrapped, colonized, or freed, must be addressed as *processes*. At the same time, the processes must not become the issue, since the conditions for any process, and especially for the literacy process, determine the possible outcomes. That is why, for example, teaching literacy depends on the circumstances rather than on the textbook. Our attention needs to be focused on the *conditions* in every instance. (64, emphasis mine)

First, what does this quote mean to you? List several of your first responses in your journal. Then, think about what this quote means with respect to your viewing of *Central Station*. Finally, brainstorm some ideas that you think may be useful to you as you prepare for WA3. Bring this quote into conversation with your own ideas and arguments as expressed in WA1 and WA2, those offered by Brandt in "Sponsors of Literacy."

Appendix C

(Sample Writing Assignments)

SAMPLE 1: THE GROUP PRESENTATION

In order to gain an even more productive understanding of what we mean by occupational communities of practice and—eventually—what this exploration may have to do with writing for college, I would like for us to spend some time unpacking these literacies via the various occupations examined in Rose's study, *The Mind at Work*. Each group will be assigned a chapter from Rose's book to review. Some will analyze plumbing, some the work of hair stylists, some the work of the electrician. Rose's study focused on manual and service work, so this exploration may or may not bring up things you will discover yourself as you generate plans for WA4. It will, however, offer a productive analysis of Rose's major claims, which we can then work from in your fourth writing assignment.

Again, please consider the following very carefully:

The work that my uncle [a "railroad man"] and mother [a waitress] did affected their sense of who they were, and, though limiting in so many ways, it provided a means of doing something in the world.

Doing something in the world. I couldn't have expressed it this way when I was growing up, but the work I saw connected in my mind with agency and competence—that's what being an adult meant to me and it was intimately tied to physical work. And, as does any child, I craved competence. Special terminology caught my ear; the idiom of freight trains or food orders, because not everyone could speak it, especially in the right way and it made things happen. Particular movements of the body made things happen, too, in the restaurant and the stockyard. And there was knowledge of tools and services, wrenches and hacksaws and measures and the whirring blender. Tied to this knowledge were tricks of the trade. And what a kick it was when one of my uncles or a cook or a waitress showed me how to do something with a little more efficiently, with a little less effort and a little more finesse. Hold it this way. Move it in, like this. See? I became the work's insider, if just for a moment. (xviii)

You and the other members of your group should read the assigned chapter carefully, generating a handout (one-page) that offers the following information:

- A brief summary of the chapter (in no more than three sentences).
- What did you learn about the "special terminology" used in this occupational community of practice? Offer a word or two only those literate in this occupation know. The "terminology" that "gets things done" (see Rose passage above).
- What particular body movement is necessary for this kind of work? What do you need to be able to *do* (not just with your mind, but with your body—physically)?
- What tools do you need to know (note: even if you are not dealing with manual or service labor, tools will still be involved. As a teacher, I have to know how to use tools like the overhead, the chalkboard, chalk, a word-processing program, and so on).
- What "tricks of the trade" do members know that makes things "more efficient"—enables users to do the work "with a little less effort and a little more finesse"? Those in the community of "college writing teachers" often share tricks of the trade with incoming members—like how to respond to papers more efficiently and more effectively, how to keep track of attendance and paperwork (etc.). What are the "tricks of the trade" in the community of practice you are examining?

You will develop enough copies of this handout to share with the rest of us. We will use these handouts to generate our summaries of Rose and our analysis of a community of practice with which we have much familiarity ourselves.

SAMPLE 2: FIELD RESEARCH PROJECT

PHASE 1

Group Members: _____ and _____
Discipline One: _____ Discipline Two: _____

Step 1: Choose a partner and two disciplines to investigate.

Step 11: Go to the library and pull (from reserve) two books and two journals (each) from each discipline.

Step III: Thumb through the journals and books and find two articles from each discipline to investigate/analyze.

Step IV: At the end of the first library day, you should jot down the title of each article, the page number, and the name of the journal/book that it came from. Hand this to the tutor before you leave.

Step V: Pick up the same articles/books again (from reserve). You might bring (or purchase) a copy card so you can have copies of these articles.

Step VI: On a separate sheet of paper, analyze the articles. Begin by analyzing, comparing, and contrasting the articles representing the first discipline. Write the article title, page numbers, and journal/book title at the top of a separate sheet of paper.

Step VII: Then analyze the first article, using the following questions as a guide: (1) Is the language formal or informal? How can you tell? (2) Do you see "I" in this? "You"? Contractions? (3) Read the article. What argument is the author trying to make? Summarize the main argument in one-two sentences. (4) Do you see graphs, charts, and/or other illustrations? Surveys? Polls? Statistics? Interviews? (5) What terms do you see used several times in this article that you haven't seen in or heard in other communities of practice (specialized terminology)? Write down at least two.

Step VIII: Compare your findings from this article with another in the same discipline. In other words, what are the similarities between the two disciplines as represented in the articles you examined? What are the differences? In order to determine this, you should use the following questions as a guide in your analysis of the second article: (1) Formal or informal language? How does that compare with the other article? Did the other article have a similar feel? Explain what you mean. (2) What argument is the author trying to make, and how does this compare with the argument made in the previous article? (3) Graphs? Charts? Other illustrations? Surveys? Polls? Statistics? Interviews? How does this compare with the other article and what conclusions can you draw from any similarities and/or differences you find? (4) Do you find any of the same specialized terminology at work in this article? Which terms are repeated, and what are we to make of this? Explain.

Step IX: Work through steps VII and VIII in response to the articles in the second discipline.

Step X: Compare and contrast your findings from one discipline with the findings from the second. What are the similarities between the two disciplines as represented in the articles you examined? What are the differences?

The next phase of this Field Research Project will be to prepare the presentation.

PHASE 2

You are responsible for understanding and presenting the literacy requirements of *two* disciplines (or three if you are working in groups of three). You
have completed the first phase of this project as a group. You and your part-
ner(s) should now prepare a presentation that will reveal your findings to the
rest of us.

Step I: You should have found the similarities and the differences between the
literacy requirements for each discipline you analyzed. Write the biblio-
graphic information at the top of a separate sheet of paper, and divide it in
half. Place the similarities on one side and the differences on the other side
of the page.

Step II: Use this sheet to generate your presentation. In this step, you will be
developing a handout for your presentation, which you will share with your
tutor. Your handout should present carefully articulated responses to the following questions and requirements:

> What two (or three) disciplines did you analyze and why? What did you
> expect to find (did you expect to find differences)? Did you find what you
> expected?
>
> In one sentence (each), explain what each article was about.
>
> What are the similarities between these disciplines (name at least three)?
>
> What are the differences (name at least two)?
>
> How is evidence presented in each discipline? Is it formal? Informal?
>
> What kinds of evidence did the author use? Look at all your findings
> from the first phase of this field research project.
>
> Is the language formal? Informal?

Step III: Meet with your tutor to receive feedback on your handout and discuss presentation plans.

Step IV: Revise it to address tutor's concerns.

Step V: Prepare some sort of visual aid. I suggest: Bring copies of the first couple pages of each article you analyzed. Share them with the group so they can
see what you mean as you present your findings.

Step VI: Practice, practice, practice! You need to run through your presentation at least once before you give it to the group more formally, making sure
you know who will speak to which discovery. You cannot have one person
doing all the talking. You may decide to have one person speak to all the similarities and one person speak to all the differences. This is up to you. And

you also need to be sure you will be able to complete the presentation in the time allotted. A practice run will help you meet this time constraint. Time limits: ten minutes for a group of two, fifteen for a group of three.

Step VI: Make enough copies of your handout for each member of your group to have one. Make sure your visual aids are in order.

We look forward to your presentation!

SAMPLE 3: CULMINATING PROJECT

WA6: WHAT VERNACULAR LITERACIES
HAVE TO TEACH US ABOUT ACADEMIC ONES

> We are all highly literate in at least one other context—even those writers who struggle in contexts demanding standard written English. It is therefore important to understand, articulate, and negotiate the" points of contact" and "points of dissonance" between a community of practice with which you have much familiarity and another, less familiar one. Rhetorical dexterity encourages writers to use their own lives and interests—what they know and really care about—to make sense of what they don't yet understand

Description: An essay that compares and contrasts a community of practice seemingly unrelated to school with those literacies required of writers at the college level. Why? Doing so may reveal what literacies beyond the school may have to teach us about writing for school.

Page-length Requirement: five to six pages

Content Requirements: You must include (a) a detailed description of the community of practice (or communities) you are comparing/contrasting with the literacies required of us in school; (b) a detailed discussion of at least five SPECIFIC strategies literate users employ in that community of practice in order to be considered "literate" insiders; (c) a detailed description (with specific examples) of at least three commonalities ("points of contact") between the strategies required of members in this community of practice and those required of members of an academic community of practice; (d) a detailed description (with specific examples) of at least *two* areas of conflict ("point of dissonance") between the strategies required of members of this community of practice and those required of members of an academic community of practice. That is, at least two strategies (or tool, value, etc.) that are required of literate members of one community of practice yet will not work at all in an academic community of practice (and/or vice versa).

PREPARING FOR WA6 BY PREPARING FOR
INDIVIDUAL PRESENTATION TO INSTRUCTOR

Directions: (1) I would like for you to examine again (through the essays you've already written) a very familiar literacy that is not school-based. From this exploration, you should develop a list of at least five "strategies" literate users employ in that particular community of practice (in order to be considered "literate"). From these, (3) articulate at least three "points of contact" between the literate practices of the community studied and those considered typical of the academic community of practice. (4) Finally, identify at least one area of conflict between these two literacies ("points of dissonance").

Suggestions: You should review WA3, WA4, and/or WA5, settling on one specific community of practice and developing a list of at least five "strategies" literate users employ in that particular community (in order to be considered "literate"). Next, review WA2 and your Field Research Project to generate a list of possible similarities and differences between these two communities of practice (a school-related community and one less closely associated with school). Finally, develop a chart that contains the following information:

- A brief summary of the community of practice you are comparing and contrasting with a school-related community. In no more than three sentences, define this community of practice for us.
- A list of at least five "strategies" literate users employ in that community of practice in order to be considered "literate" insiders.
- A list of at least three commonalities ("points of contact") between the strategies required of members in this community and those required of members of an academic community of practice.
- A list of at least one area of conflict ("point of dissonance") between the strategies required of members of this community of practice and those required of members of an academic community. That is, at least one strategy (or tool, value, etc) that is required of literate members of one community of practice yet will not work at all in an academic community (and/or vice versa).

You will bring this chart to a meeting with me on Monday, 11/20. It is our hope that you will be able to use the ideas and information generated for and during this session to generate a draft of WA6.

PREPARING FOR THE INDIVIDUAL PRESENTATION

Due Monday, 11/20, during your assigned conference time.

What might the "rules" for literacy in spaces associated with leisure activities ("play") and work have to do with the rules for writing in school?

Activity 1 (in pairs): In preparation for WA6, I have asked you to review the essays you've written throughout these last few months. Let's do this again in pairs. Take out a pen and paper, ask your partner the following questions, and jot down his/her responses. You are going to give your responses to your partner, so try to make them as legible and clear as possible.

Interviewer's Name:

_____

Interviewee's Name:

_____

1. What did you write about in WA5 (in-class essay from Friday, 11/10)? What did you say separates "insiders" from "outsiders" in this community of practice? What strategies must one use to be heard, understood, and taken seriously within the rhetorical spaces of this community? What "rules" do literate members of this community know and follow? How did you learn them? Where did these rules come from?
2. What did you write about in WA4 ("Literacies at Work")? What did you say separates "insiders" from "outsiders" in this community of practice? What strategies must one use to be heard, understood, and taken seriously within the rhetorical spaces of this community? What "rules" do literate members of this community know and follow? How did you learn them? Where did these rules come from?
3. What did you write about in WA3 ("Literacies Beyond the School")? What did you say separates "insiders" from "outsiders" in this community of practice? What strategies must one use to be heard, understood, and taken seriously within the rhetorical spaces of this community? What "rules" do literate members of this community know and follow? How did you learn them? Where did these rules come from?
4. How might the rules and expectations for literate behavior in school relate to that in other communities of practice, especially those about which you wrote in WA3–WA5?
5. Are these rules and expectations the same in every class at every level? Why not? Consider your Field Research Project in determining the answer to this question.
6. Choose a class and talk about the rules and expectations for literate behavior within that class. How'd you learn these rules? How do they differ from other classes? Why do they differ? How are they the same? Why might they be somewhat similar?
7. What special knowledge do you have to know in order to meet the rules and expectations of school literacies? Is this knowledge always the same, regardless of for whom you are writing (in school)? Why not?

8. What special terminology do you have to know in order to meet the rules and expectations of school literacies? Is this knowledge always the same, regardless of for whom you are writing (in school)? Why not?
9. What tools do literate users know how to use in the communities of practice associated with school?
10. Choose a class and/or a high-stakes writing situation like TASP/TAAS/TAKS and answer the following questions: What would you say separates "insiders" from "outsiders" in this community of practice? What strategies must one use to be heard, understood, and taken seriously within the rhetorical spaces of this community of practice? What "rules" do literate members of this community know and follow? How did you learn them? Where did these rules come from?

Activity 2 (individually): Go back to your responses to these questions and use them to come up with (a) the community of practice you will be comparing with an academic community, (b) five strategies literate users (insiders) make use of in this community of practice (those that distinguish insiders from outsiders), (c) at least three ways in which these strategies compare with those required of literate members of an academic community, and (d) at least one way in which the strategies required in this community of practice are unlike those required of users in an academic community.

Activity 3 (in pairs again): Compare your responses with your partners. At the end of class today, you should both have the information required to complete the following chart (Figure 2). I offer these requirements here (again) for your convenience—

FIGURE 2
WA6 Chart ("Preparing to Write WA6")

1. Offer a brief summary of the community of practice you are comparing and contrasting with a school-related community of practice. In no more than three sentences, define this community for your reader.	

2. List at least five "strategies" literate users employ in that community of practice in order to be considered "literate" insiders.

3. Prepare a list of at least three commonalities ("points of contact") between the strategies requires of members in this community and those required of members of an academic community of practice.

4. List at least one area of conflict ("point of dissonance") between the strategies required of members of this community of practice and those required of members of an academic community. That is, at least one strategy (or tool, value, etc.) that is required of literate members of one community of practice yet will not work at all in an academic community (and/or vice versa).

Out-of-School Literacy	In-School Literacy
Point of Contact 1:	
Point of Contact 2:	
Point of Contact 3:	
Point of Dissonance:	

Appendix D

CRITICAL REFLECTIONS

This last assignment asks you to look back over the reading, writing, and thinking you've done this term so you can tell your reader (specifically) how your Final Portfolio should be read. You want your reviewer to understand exactly how this portfolio works as evidence of your growth as. a reader, writer, and critic this term. What have been the key moments in your work this term? How are you writing differently now than you were at the beginning of the term? What new things have you learned about yourself as a writer and reader? I also want you to examine each of the pieces you have written: think about the *story* each assignment tells, from your earliest invention, to your peer, tutor, and instructor responses, to your final choices for revision. How did your writing change within and across these different assignments? What did you learn about writing? Play a "movie of your mind" for us so we may learn what you were thinking and feeling when you pulled your portfolio together and/or developed these final revisions. What is your reaction to the collection of work that your portfolio represents? If you see this process as important to your development or growth as a thinker (or something else), why do you see it this way, and what have you gained from the process? This is your chance to wow us!

To complete this assignment successfully, you must reflect on and quote from selected writing you've done this term, as well as from the readings. You choose what you want to quote and use, determine how to best use it, and make sure your reader understands how everything you quote works as evidence in support of your growth as a writer. Think of this as your final exam. Show us what you learned.

The best places to locate information from which to draw:

1. Your Dialogue Journals have been specifically created to give you loads and loads of ideas and text you can then use to generate this final assignment. The more effectively and extensively you have used these DJs, the

more useful they will be to you as you create your critical reflections. You may also consider using these journals as a place to jot down your thoughts as you develop revisions, work through future readings, discuss writing projects, and receive/offer feedback during group workshops.

2. Any place in which you described your writing process, reflected on your own essays, answered questions that asked you to share a bit about your writing process and your thoughts about a particular essay before your next reader responds to it.

This essay serves as an introduction to the most important work you will develop this term: Your Final Portfolio. The most effective essays will

- be filled with very specific information that shows your reader how (*exactly!*) your portfolio illustrates your growth as a writer this term;
- include many, many very specific and detailed accounts of your experiences with writing and deeply revising two or more specific essays;
- offer a smart, specific, and elaborate exploration of the importance of (and strategies for) effective revision;
- share some of the very specific ways that you used peer feedback to generate these smart, thoughtful revisions;
- share some of the very specific ways that you used your instructor's feedback to generate smart, thoughtful revisions of specific writing assignments;
- share some of the very specific ways that you used your tutor's feedback (and the Writing Center) to generate thoughtful revisions of specific writing assignments;
- reveal your understanding of the importance of and strategies for managing the complexities of writing through multiple drafts;
- include a detailed description of the specific ways in which your multiple readings and discussions about literacy have affected your understanding of literacy and its role in society;
- offer a detailed illustration of the ways in which your experiences with these various writing assignments have prepared you for future writing classes.

DRAFT 1: FIRST REVIEW OF CRITICAL REFLECTIONS

Student: This draft has been reviewed by at least two expert readers to determine the sorts of things you should consider in your revision of this important essay. Please review the following rubric carefully.

If you received 1–3 in any category listed above, you *must*: (1) deeply revise this assignment to effectively address the readers' major concerns and (2) work with a tutor in the Writing Center before turning the final revision (completed form [attached] must accompany this revision). If you received 4–5 in *every single category listed in Figure 3*, you are strongly encouraged to deeply revise this assignment but not required to.

171

FIGURE 3
Rubric for Critical Reflections

CONTENT				
Reveals how student has grown as a reader (providing ample evidence from specific reading experiences)				
1	2	3	4	5
Reveals how student has grown as a writer (providing ample evidence from specific writing experiences)				
1	2	3	4	5
Includes many, many very specific and detailed accounts of the student's experiences with writing and deeply revising two or more specific essays.				
1	2	3	4	5
Offers a smart, specific, and elaborate exploration of the importance of (and strategies for) effective revision				
1	2	3	4	5
Shares some of the very specific ways the student has used peer feedback to generate smart, thoughtful revisions (referring to one or more specific writing experiences)				
1	2	3	4	5
Shares some of the very specific ways the student has used instructor feedback to generate smart, thoughtful revisions				
1	2	3	4	5
Shares some of the very specific ways the student has used his/her tutor's feedback (and the Writing Center) to generate smart, thoughtful revisions				
1	2	3	4	5
Shares some of the very specific ways the student has used instructor feedback to generate smart, thoughtful revisions ·				
1	2	3	4	5
Reveals student's understanding of the importance of and strategies for managing the complexities of writing through multiple drafts				
1	2	3	4	5
Includes a detailed description of the specific ways in which your multiple readings and discussions about literacy have affected your understanding of literacy and its role in society				
1	2	3	4	5
Includes a detailed description of the specific ways in which your investigations of familiar literacies have affected the way you now approach less familiar ones—especially school-based ones				
1	2	3	4	5
RHETORICAL CONCERNS				
Organization				
1	2	3	4	5
Focus				
1	2	3	4	5
Length				
1	2	3	4	5
Surface features				
1	2	3	4	5

Notes

CHAPTER ONE. THE WAY LITERACY TEXTS

1. According to the CCCC Position Statement on Assessment, "standardized tests, usually developed by large testing organizations, tend to be for accountability purposes, and when used to make statements about student learning, *misrepresent disproportionately the skills and abilities of students of color*. This imbalance tends to decrease when tests are directly related to specific contexts and purposes, in contrast to tests that purport to differentiate between 'good' and 'bad' writing in a general sense" ("Writing Assessment").

2. The new TASP Law would require anyone enrolling in their first college coursework *after* August 1989 to take the test. Thus, most college-bound seniors from the class of '89 took college-level coursework the summer before so we wouldn't be required to take and pass TASP. It's what our teachers and counselors suggested, as no one yet knew much about the test itself or what would be expected of test takers.

3. According to Stephen Klein et al. (2001), Walt Haney (2000), Linda McNeil and Angela Valenzuela (2001), among others, test preparation regularly dominates school curriculum in this "TAAS system," especially in poorer and minority schools. I grew up white and middle class and my high school was one of the two in Corpus Christi that residents of wealthier neighborhoods were most likely to attend. Still, test preparation dominated the curriculum for us, too. I can only imagine what happened in the poorer schools. According to Rich Haswell and Glenn Blalock's study of Texas A&M-Corpus Christi student attitudes toward TAAS more than ten years later, little has changed in that respect. As one student put it in their 2001 survey, "Throughout probably ten out of the twelve years in school, I probably spent a quarter to two-thirds of that time going over TAAS practice tests and reviews."

4. Throughout the current study, I will refer to the students in our program as "basic writers," even though I disagree with this assessment. I do so in order to draw attention to their label, not the validity of the label "basic writer."

5. In a recent article for *Rethinking Schools*, a long-time teacher of Texas fifth graders concurs:

If anyone had tried to convince me ten years ago how drastically high-stakes testing would change my teaching, I would have laughed. No health education? Worksheets instead of writing journals? No staging of mock campaigns—complete with voter registration and staffing polling booths—to teach about national elections? No way.

Yes, I would have laughed. Except it isn't funny anymore. These are precisely the changes I've been asked to make in my fifth-grade classroom since our district began equating success with scores on Texas's standardized tests. (Beam-Conroy)

6. As Barbara Gleason points out in "Evaluating Writing Programs in Real Time: The Politics of Remediation" (2000), basic writing program evaluation should always pay close attention to context, especially the political and institutional forces that limit and shape program development.

7. For a fascinating exploration of the ways composition professionals might better position arguments for access ("horizontal discourse with a qualitative emphasis") amid policymakers' decisions that, more often then not, utilize "vertical discourse with a quantitative emphasis," see Stanford T. Goto's "Basic Writing and Policy Reform: Why We Keep Talking Past Each Other" (2002).

8. For a provocative discussion of the negative effects of such standards on student writers—especially those from minority groups and who may speak English as a second (or third) language—and how we can provide space for writers to write against these effects, see Susan Naomi Bernstein's "Teaching and Learning in Texas" (2004).

9. TAAS= the Texas Assessment of Academic Skills

10. TASP = the Texas Academic Skills Program

11. State law also precludes—at least it did until the TASP Law was repealed in 2003—any public college or university in the state from offering credit for remediation programs serving students who failed one or more sections of TASP (or the Texas Higher Education Assessment [THEA], the exam that replaced TASP in 2004).

12. In addition to the curricular choices described in this study, the 2006–2007 texts included Martha Kolln's *Rhetorical Grammar* in a further attempt to placate those who worry about our choice to focus on issues beyond "grammar." The tutors working with these students read and discuss Laura Micchiche's "Making a Case for Rhetorical Grammar" before making use of Kolln's text in their classes. In 2007–2008, we replaced Kolln with Gerald Graff's *They Say, I Say*.

13. As noted above, TASP is the Texas Academic Skills Program, which was renamed THEA (Texas Higher Education Assessment). While THEA continues, in 2003 it was replaced with TAKS (Texas Academic Knowledge and Skills) and will eventually be phased out.

14. Though we do not believe these tests are accurate measures of what our students can actually do, I have not pushed for changes to such measures and I will not until I am absolutely sure that (a) such discussions won't again raise the issue of whether or not we should be raising admission "standards" rather than continuing to "accommodate" those who some see as "not ready for college" and (b) new measures will be adequately funded and theoretically sound. Until both of these conditions are

in place, I am leery of fighting for change at levels of program and placement. Instead, we focus our efforts on change at the levels of curriculum, training, and exit criteria.

15. This method appears to be more in keeping with Ed White's arguments for effective measures for portfolio assessment (2005).

16. Of course, some of these activities may be considered "work" more than "play" and vice versa.

17. According to Street, "the further these usages get away from the social practices of reading and writing, the more evident it is that the term 'literacy' is being used in a narrow, moral, and functional sense to mean cultural competence or skills" (135).

18. The term has been most popular in managerial and organizational studies, and in recent years many larger, more progressive corporations have made extensive use of the learning theories that have emerged from it.

CHAPTER TWO. THE WAY LITERACY OPPRESSES

1. Because this population (often referred to in literacy studies as the "Vai people") invented their own script that, unlike Western systems, was taught at home rather than school, researchers were able to separate the consequences of schooling from literacy and schooling, concluding that "the persistent claims that deep psychological differences divide literate and non-literate persons" are false (Scribner and Cole, 251).

2. The authors use the term "'limited literacy skills' to describe people whose English language skills would likely be below high school level if they were tested with conventional literacy assessments" (2). They do not trust such measurements to portray the rich complexities of how literacy actually functions in their lives, but they use this definition nonetheless.

3. I do not wish to imply that taking government assistance is a negative social choice; I only wish to work against the assumption promoted by many that those who cannot read or write are a drain on the nation's resources.

4. Throughout this study, I will present these students' words just as they were presented to us via the texts they generated in our basic writing program.

5. Source: National Center for Education Statistics, National Institute for Literacy, 1992 National Adult Literacy Survey.

6. In the case of over-the-counter medication they may rely on the ways in which such medication was dispensed to them when they were children and—if it is new to them—they may depend on the pharmacist or a friend or the doctor. Perhaps they will call a local clinic, a strategy an older relative of mine relied on for most of her life since she never learned to read in English—through she spoke perfect "standard" English and wrote—I am told—flawless prose in Spanish.

7. I am grateful to David Bartholomae who, in a keynote address for EGAD (the graduate student conference hosted by our department), told us we should read our own student's prose with as much patience and generosity as we would read something written by a poet or a novelist, even a poet as complicated as Gertrude Stein ("Gertrude Stein in the Writing Center," July 2003).

CHAPTER THREE. THE WAY LITERACY LIBERATES

1. In "A Common Ground," Kurt Spellmeyer calls this perspective "language-as-filter."

2. The New London Group includes many of the scholars in New Literacy Studies I cite several times throughout this book, including Gunther Kress, Mary Kalantzis, J. P. Gee, and Bill Cope. Accordingly,

The New London Group is named after the place where we first met, in New London, New Hampshire, USA. During this first meeting, from 6 to 11 September 1994, the group developed the ideas that became the core of the jointly authored paper, "A Pedagogy of Multiliteracies: Designing Social Futures," which was published in the Spring 1996 issue of the *Harvard Educational Review*. The ideas were also presented over a series of plenaries to 800 participants at the Literacy and Education Research Network Conference on Learning, held in Townsville from 29 June to 2 July 1995. The group met for another three days at this time and finalised the joint paper for publication in the *Harvard Educational Review*. Most recently, the team gave plenary presentations at the Domains of Literacy Conference at London University, 7–8 September 1996, and met for another three days to plan a book-length version of the multiliteracies argument.

"About the New London Group and the International Multiliteracies Project." *Education Australia Online*. <http://edoz.com.au/educationaustralia/archive/features/mult3.html>. 10 August 2005.

3. I am grateful to my colleague and friend Donna Dunbar-Odom (former director of First-Year Composition at my university) for assisting me in designing this sequence—especially for introducing me to Deborah Brandt's "Sponsors of Literacy" by including it in the first-year assignment sequence two years previously.

4. In "What Happens When Basic Writers Come to College?" Patricia Bizzell hypothos[izes that] basic writers are those who are least well prepared for college. They may be defined in absolute terms, by features of their writing, or in relative terms, by their placement in a given school's freshman composition sequence but, either way, their salient characteristic is their "outlandishness"—their appearance to many teachers and to themselves as the students who are most alien to the college community (164).

5. Early in the term—and for some, even later in the term—the rhetorical use of scholarship via quotations among most writers is not terribly sophisticated. The use of the concepts articulated in this scholarship, however, is quite impressive already.

6. I am grateful to my colleague and friend Dick Fulkerson for introducing me to Durst's work and encouraging the analysis that follows.

7. This dichotomy seems most problematic in his concluding chapter. It may not invalidate his overall argument, but this reader felt it affected his ethos in ways I'm certain he did not intend.

8. Ana easily passed English 100, by the way. We focused on her extensive work, her smart revisions, and the sheer volume of work she was able to accomplish in fifteen weeks.

CHAPTER FOUR. THE WAY LITERACY STRATIFIES

1. In *Understanding Comics* (1993), Scott McCloud makes an argument like this, though he applies it to the world of comic books—naming the various strategies comic book makers and their readers use to communicate with one another. Interesting enough, his entire argument is made in comic book form. As McCloud points out in his overview of the book, it's "a 215–page comic book about comics." Matt Groening, creator of *The Simpsons*, offers this telling review (blurb from back cover): "If you've ever felt bad about wasting your life reading comics, then check out Scott McCloud's classic book immediately. You might still feel you've wasted your life, but you'll know why, and you'll be proud."

2. See James Paul Gee, especially *What Video Games Have to Teach Us About Literacy and Learning* (2003) and *Situated Language and Learning* (2004).

3. See Jabari Mahiri.

4. As I understand it, Mrs. Arachi was actually trained in Montessori methods by Maria Montessori herself.

5. See chapter two for more on this topic of the "pedagogization of literacy."

6. At this time in Texas—at least in the places we lived—no Montessori schools existed, and other educational choices were largely limited to private, religious schools that—though not forced to comply to the standards-based assessments mandated by the State of Texas—were no less likely to be shaped by an autonomous model of literacy education that was standards-based and, above all, "functional."

7. Interestingly enough, 1982 is also about the same year my family brought our first console gaming system (*Intellivision*) into our home

8. Basic is the very same language my brother used to program the computers at our local computer stores to read "Help! Let me out of here!"

9. See "Raaka-Tu Introduction" (full citation in Works Cited) for more about this game and the complex literacies required to negotiate it.

CHAPTER FIVE. THE WAY LITERACY (RE)PRODUCES

1. The proceedings for this conference, including Hirch's presentation on "Literacy and Culture," were published later that year in the *Journal of Basic Writing*, which Mina Shaughnessy herself began just a few years earlier. The conference theme was "A Literate Democracy."

2. This experiment was just one in a series of related experiments that were part of his own research, quite a bit of which was funded by a major grant from the National Endowment for the Humanities.

3. Comic book literacy also requires a very different skill-set, as Scott McCloud argues in *Understanding Comics* (1993).

4. According to Stephen Foote, a friend and avid comic book fan, "The original publication of the story was 'America Vs. The Justice Society', a mini-series published in 1985. It was pre-Crisis. This post-Crisis flashback was published in 'JSA', a regular series, in 2005 (if that date is correct)."

5. Again, according to DC fan Stephen Foote, "This year's mini-series 'Infinite Crisis' has again rewritten history. This is called *retconning* (or, a retcon [retroactive continuity]), a term popularized by Roy Thomas, the writer of *All-Star Squadron*. (That was a comic published in the 1980s, pre-Crisis, about the Earth-2 heroes in World War II.)"

6. The students in Marilyn Sternglass's *Time to Know Them*, however, appeared to use "writing to learn" in some effective ways.

7. Russell suggests not only that writing instruction be moved into the disciplines, but that the GWSI course be replaced with a course "*about* writing, its uses and its power—for good or ill—in the cultures and activity systems that employ it" (73). I argue that such a course can exist in the basic writing program and that it can, in fact, function as a writing course in the traditional sense if the writers write about literacy as it lives within a variety of communities. That's what rhetorical dexterity is all about.

8. The theoretical premise is articulated most thoroughly in *Facts, Artifacts, and Counterfacts*, with many of their corresponding and quite popular textbooks, including *Ways with Words* and *Ways with Images*.

9. To be fair, several years later Bartholomae does speak quite directly to the issue of conflict that one experiences in moving from one discourse to another (see especially, "The Tidy House: Basic Writing in the American Curriculum," 1993).

10. See especially *Representing the "Other": Basic Writers and the Teaching of Basic Writing* (Urbana, IL: NCTE, 1999).

11. In the graduate-level course, we read several ethnographic studies designed to expand this concept of rhetorical dexterity beyond basic writers and their teachers to include society at large as portrayed in the field of composition and literacy studies by Deborah Brandt (*Literacy in American Lives*), Cynthia Selfe and Gail Hawisher (*Literate Lives in the Information Age: Narratives on Literacy from the United States*), James Paul Gee (*What Video Games Have to Teach Us About Learning and Literacy* and *Situated Language and Learning: A Critique of Traditional Schooling*), Mike Rose (*The Mind at Work: Valuing the Intelligence of the American Worker*), and Katherine Shultz and Glenda Hull's collection *School's Out!: Bridging Out-of-School Literacies with Classroom Practice*. We began with Debra Dickerson's memoir *An American Story* as it complicates the myth of meritocracy in some fascinating ways.

12. "Jake Pichnarcik." Unpublished paper (2005).

13. According to Bizzell, scholars working from this perspective include C. H. Knoblauch and Lil Brannon.

14. Scholars working from this perspective include, according to Bizzell, Mina Shaughnessy, Elaine Maimon, and David Bartholomae.

15. Those Bizzell associates with this perspective include Frank D'Angelo and Andrea Lunsford.

16. In her article written for *College English* a few years earlier ("Translating Self and Difference Through Literacy Narratives"), Soliday takes on a similar task: "By foregrounding their acquisition and use of language as a strange and not a natural process, authors of literacy narratives have the opportunity to explore the profound cultural force language exerts in their everyday lives" (511).

CHAPTER SIX. THE WAY LITERACY LIVES

1. As described in chapter three, a prior sequence included excerpts from Elspeth Stuckey's *The Violence of Literacy* and Deborah Brandt's "Sponsors of Literacy" and focused on the ways in which the autonomous model that shapes standardized tests like TASP and TAAS is largely inappropriate and even unfair to many marginalized populations. In many ways, the sequence was a great success; however, while many students did seem empowered by this perspective, a large percentage continued to define literacy in terms no less problematic and were, therefore, unable to display the linguistic and rhetorical flexibility required to succeed in the variety of rhetorical contexts extending beyond the basic writing classroom.

2. In a recent presentation for CCCC and an article for *College English*, I explore the ways in which my own Christian illiteracies have complicated my work with some of my most religious students (see "Living Inside the Bible (Belt)").

3. See Appendix C for a detailed description of this project.

4. We also viewed Trekkies as an interesting example of how fandom functions as a community of practice, as well as an episode of the British reality show *Faking It* in which a fry cook learns what he needs to pass as a master chief at a top restaurant in London. Future sequences may make use of the cult film *Heavy Metal Parking Lot* as it examines the value-sets, activities, language, clothing, and other elements that mark the activities associated with heavy metal fandom (at least in the mid-1980s). The film is a strange documentary in which an amateur filmmaker simply records the activities of fans "hanging out" in the parking lot before a Judas Priest concert.

5. See Appendix C for a more detailed description of this assignment.

6. Again, this system appears to me to be in keeping with Edward White's suggestions for portfolio assessment at the programmatic level.

7. In the past, the librarians on our campus have been incredibly helpful with similar activities. I have already spoken with at least one librarian about our curriculum change, and he tells me that what I suggest can be easily accommodated.

CONCLUSION

1. Hirsch defines "cultural literacy" as "the basic information needed to thrive in the modern world" (*Cultural Literacy*).

2. "Seeking to find a Lost Treasure" (WA1, 1–2).

3. In *Rethinking Basic Writing*, Laura Gray-Rosendale works from a similar assumption (though decidedly more socially and culturally aware) that basic writers are much more proficient orally than they are on paper. However, she contends that this discrepancy is not, in fact, evidence of any cognitive deficiency on their part. In fact, as her detailed study of peer writing groups reveals, the oral, in this case, regularly mimics the rhetorical and intellectual moves we want from their academic prose. Simply talking about academic writing (their own and that of their peers) encourages them to use the language of academic writing.

Works Cited

"About the New London Group and the International Multiliteracies Project." *Education Australia Online*. <http://edoz.com.au/educationaustralia/archive/features/mult3.html>. 10 August 2005.

Adler-Kassner, Linda, and Susanmarie Harrington. *Basic Writing as a Political Act: Public Conversations about Writing and Literacies*. Cresskill, NJ: Hampton P, 2002.

A Generation of Failure: The Case for Remediation and Testing in Texas Higher Education. Texas Higher Education Coordinating Board. 17 July 1986. <http://www.thecb.state.tx.us/reports/PDF/0006.PDF>. 25 June 2006.

Anderson, Gary L., and Patricia Irvine. "Informing Critical Literacy with Ethnography." *Critical Literacy: Politics, Praxis, and the Postmodern*. Ed. Colin Lankshear and Peter L. McLaren. Albany: State U of New York P, 1993. 81–104.

August, Bonne, and Rebecca Mlynarczyk. "Editor's Column." *Journal of Basic Writing* 23.1 (Spring 2004): 1–3.

Baron, Dennis. "No Students Left Behind: Writing and the Secretary of Education's Commission on the Future of Higher Education." *Conference on College Composition and Communication*. March 2006. *NCTE Podcast*. <http://www.ncte.org/announce/124236.htm>. 16 June 2006.

Bartholomae, David. "Inventing the University." *Journal of Basic Writing* 5.1 (1986): 4–23.

———. "The Tidy House: Basic Writing in the American Curriculum." *Journal of Basic Writing* 12.1 (1993): 4–21.

Bartholomae, David, and Anthony Petrosky. *Facts, Artifacts, Counterfacts: Theory and Method for a Reading and Writing Course*. Portsmouth, NH: Heinemann, 1986.

———. "Introduction." *Ways of Reading: An Anthology for Writers*. New York: Bedford/St. Martin's, 2002. Rpt. in *Writing on the Margins: Essays in Composing and Teaching*. Palgrave: Macmillan, 2005. 272–288.

———. *Ways of Reading: An Anthology for Writers*. 7th ed. New York: Bedford/St. Martin's, 2005.

————. *Ways of Reading Words and Images.* New York: Bedford/St. Martin's, 2005.

Barton, David, and Mary Hamilton. *Local Literacies: Reading and Writing in One Community.* New York: Routledge, 1998.

Beam-Conroy, Teddi. "Bamboozled by the Texas Miracle." *Rethinking Schools: Online* 16.1 (Fall 2001). <http://www.rethinkingschools.org/archive/16_01/Tex161.shtml>. 16 June 2006.

Beck, John C., and Mitchell Wade. *Got Game: How the Gamer Generation Is Reshaping Business Forever.* Cambridge: Harvard Business School P, 2004.

Bernstein, Susan Naomi. "Teaching and Learning in Texas: Accountability Testing, Language, Race, and Place." *Journal of Basic Writing* 23.1 (Spring 2004): 4–24.

Berthoff, Ann. *The Making of Meaning: Metaphors, Models, and Maxims for Writing Teachers.* Montclair, NJ: Boynton/Cook, 1981.

Bizzell, Patricia. "Arguing About Literacy." *College English* 50 (1988): 141–153.

————. "Introduction." *Academic Discourse and Critical Consciousness.* Pittsburg: U of Pittsburg P, 1992. 3–30.

————. "The Intellectual Work of 'Mixed' Forms of Academic Disourse." *AltDis: Alternative Discourses and the Academy.* Ed. Christopher Schroeder, Helen Fox, and Patricia Bizzell. Portsmouth, NH, 2002. 1–10.

————. "What Happens When Basic Writers Come to College?" *College Composition and Communication* 37 (1986): 294–301.

————. "William Perry and Liberal Education." *College English* 46 (1984): 447–454.

Bowe, John, Marisa Bow, and Sabin Streeeter. *Gig: Americans Talk About Their Jobs.* New York: Three Rivers P, 2000.

Boylan, Hunter R. *An Evaluation of the Texas Academic Skills Program.* (Director of the National Center for Developmental Education, under contract with the Texas Higher Education Coordinating Board). 30 September 1996. <http://www.thecb. state.tx.us/reports/PDF/0282.PDF>. 25 June 2006.

Brandt, Deborah. "Accumulating Literacy: Writing and Learning to Write in the Twentieth Century." *College English* 57 (1995): 649–668. 651.

————. *Literacy in American Lives.* Cambridge: Cambridge UP, 2001.

————. "Sponsors of Literacy." *College English* 49.2 (1998): 165–185.

Brodkey, Linda. *Academic Writing as Social Practice.* Philadelphia: Temple UP, 1987.

————. "Writing on the Bias." *College English* 56.5 (September 1994): 527–547.

————. *Writing Permitted in Designated Areas Only.* Minneapolis: U of Minnesota P, 1996.

Bruffee, Kenneth A. "Collaborative Learning and the 'Conversation of Mankind.'" *College English* 46 (1984): 635–652.

Burke, Kenneth. *The Philosophy of Literary Form.* Berkeley: U of California P, 1941.

Carter, Eric. Telephone interview. 22 June 2005 and 16 July 2005.

Carter, Shannon. "Living inside the Bible (Belt)." *College English* 69.6 (July 2007): 572–595.

———. "Living Inside the Bible (Belt)." *College English* 69.6 (July 2007): 572–95.

———. "Redefining Literacy as a Social Practice." *Journal of Basic Writing* 25.2 (Fall 2006): 94–125.

———. "The Prisoner's Body." Thomas R. Watson Conference on Rhetoric and Composition. Louisville, KY. October 2004.

———. "The Writing Center Goes to Jail: Composition Matters in a Prison Literacy Program." Conference on College Composition and Communication. San Antonio, Texas. March 2004.

———. "What Is a Community of Practice?" <http://faculty.tamu-commerce.edu/scarter/CofP.htm>. 30 November 2006.

Choi, Mina. "Communities of Practice: An Alternative Learning Model for Knowledge Creation." *British Journal of Educational Technology* 37.1 (2006): 143–146.

Cooper, Marilyn. *Writing as Social Action*. Portsmouth, NH: Boynton/Cook, 1989.

Cope, Bill, and Mary Kalantzis, eds. *Multiliteracies: Literacy Learning and the Design of Social Futures*. New York: Routledge, 2000.

Cushman, Ellen. *The Struggle and the Tools: Oral and Literate Strategies in an Inner City Community*. Albany: State U of New York P, 1998.

Damon, William. "Reconciling the Literacies of Generations." *Literacy: An Overview by Fourteen Experts*. Ed. S. R. Graubad. New York: Hill and Wang, 1991.

DeAngelo, Frank. "Luria on Literacy: The Cognitive Consequences of Reading and Writing." *Literacy as a Human Problem*. Ed. James C. Raymond. Tuscaloosa: U of Alabama P, 1982. 154–169.

Del Principle, Ann. "Paradigm Clashes Among Basic Writing Teachers: Sources of Conflict and a Call for Change." *Journal of Basic Writing* 23.1 (Spring 2004):64–81.

"Developing Critical Consciousness in an Age of Oppression." <http://www.hermes-press.com/freire1.htm>. 19 August 2005.

DeVoss, Danielle, Gail Hawisher, Charles Jackson, Joseph Johansen, Brittney Moraski, and Cynthia L. Selfe. "The Future of Literacy." *Literate Lives in the Information Age: Stories from the United States*. Mahwah, NJ: Erlbaum, 2004.

Dickerson, Debra. *An American Story*. New York: Anchor, 2001.

DiPardo, Anne. *A Kind of Passport: A Basic Writing Adjunct Program and the Challenge of Student Diversity* (Research Report No. 24). Urbana, IL: NCTE, 1993.

Durst, Russell K. *Collision Course: Conflict, Negotiation, and Learning in College Composition*. Urbana, IL: NCTE, 1999.

Ehrenreich, Barbara. *Nickel and Dimed: On (Not) Getting By in America*. New York: Owl Books, 2002.

Eleanor, Suzy Groden, and Vivian Zamel. *The Discovery of Competence: Teaching and Learning with Diverse Student Writers*. Portsmouth, NH: Boyton/Cook, 1993.

Emig, Janet. "Mina Pendo Shaughnessy." *College Composition and Communication* 30.1 (February 1979): 37–38. Rpt. *Journal of Basic Writing.* 13.1 (1994): 9–94.

Farrell, Thomas J. "Developing Literacy: Walter J. Ong and Basic Writing." *Journal of Basic Writing* 2 (Fall/Winter 1978). 30–51.

Fingeret, Arlene. "Social Network: A New Perspective on Independence and Illiterate Adults." *Adult Education Quarterly* 33.3 (1983): 133.

Flower, Linda. "Revising Writer-Based Prose." *Journal of Basic Writing* 3.3 (1981): 62–74.

Fox, Tom. *Defending Access: A Critique of Standards in Higher Education.* Portsmouth, NH: Boynton/Cook, 1999.

Freire, Paulo. *Pedagogy of the Oppressed.* New York: Penguin Books, 1972.

Freire, Paulo, and Donaldo Macedo. *Literacy: Reading the World and the Word.* South Hadley, MA: Bergin & Garvey, 1987.

——— . *Pedagogy of the City.* New York: Continuum International Publishing Group, 1992.

Fulkerson, Richard. "Composition at the Turn of the Twenty-First Century." CCC 56.4 (2005): 654–687.

Gee, James Paul. "Literacy, Discourse, and Linguistics." *Journal of Education* 171.1 (1989): 5–17.

——— . "Quality, Science, and the Lifeworld: The Alignment of Business and Education." *Difference, Silence, and Textual Practice: Studies in Critical Literacy.* Ed. Peter Freebody, Sandy Muspratt, and Bronwyn Dwyer. Cresskill, NJ: Hampton P, 2001. 359–382.

——— . *Situated Language and Learning: A Critique of Traditional Schooling.* New York: Routledge, 2004.

——— . *The Social Mind: Language, Ideology, and Social Practice.* New York: Bergin and Garvey, 1992.

——— . "What Is Literacy?" *Literacy: A Critical Sourcebook.* Ed. Ellen Cushman, Mike Rose, Barry Knoll, and Eugene Kintgen. New York: Bedford/St. Martin's, 2001.

——— . *What Video Games Have to Teach Us About Literacy and Learning.* New York: Palgrave, 2003.

Geisler, Cheryl. *Academic Literacy and the Nature of Expertise: Reading, Writing, and Knowing in Academic Philosophy.* Mahwah, NJ: Erlbaum, 1994.

——— . "Writing and Learning at Cross Purposes in the Academy." *Reconceiving Writing, Rethinking Writing Instruction.* Ed. Joseph Petraglia. Mahwah, NJ: Erlbaum, 1995. 101–120.

Ginsberg, Debra. *Waiting: The True Confessions of a Waitress.* New York: Perennial, 2001.

Giroux, Henry. *Ideology, Culture, and the Process of Schooling.* Philadelphia: Temple UP, 1984.

———. "Literacy and the Politics of Difference." *Critical Literacy: Politics, Praxis, and the Postmodern*. Albany: State U of New York P, 1993.

———. *Theory and Resistance: A Pedagogy for Opposition*. South Hadley, MA: J. F. Bergin, 1983.

Gleason, Barbara. "Evaluating Writing Programs in Real Time: The Politics of Remediation." *College Composition and Communication* 51.4 (2000): 560–588.

Gold, David. "'Where Brains Had a Chance': William Mayo and Rhetorical Instruction at East Texas Normal College, 1889–1917." *College English* 67.3 (January 2005). 311–330.

Goody, Jack, ed. *Literacy in Traditional Societies*. New York: Cambridge UP, 1968.

———. *The Domestication of the Savage Mind*. New York: Cambridge UP, 1977.

Goto, Stanford T. "Basic Writing and Policy Reform: Why We Keep Talking Past Each Other." *Journal of Basic Writing* 21.2 (2002): 4–19.

Graff, Gerald, and Cathy Birkenstein. *They Say/I Say: The Moves That Matter in Academic Writing*. New York: W. W. Norton, 2005.

Graff, Harvey. *The Labyrinth of Literacy*. London: Falmer P, 1987.

———. *The Literacy Myth: Cultural Integration and Social Structure in the Nineteenth Century*. New York: Academic Press, 1979.

Gray-Rosendale, Laura. *Rethinking Basic Writing: Exploring Identity, Politics, and Community in Interaction*. Mahwah, NJ: Erlbaum, 2000.

Grobman, Laurie. "(Re)Writing Youth: Basic Writing, Youth Culture, and Social Change." *Journal of Basic Writing* 20.1 (2001): 5–26.

Guerra, Juan C., and Marcia Farr. "Writing on the Margins: The Spiritual and Autobiographical Discourse of Two *Mexicanas* in Chicago." *School's Out!: Bridging Out-of-School Literacies with Classroom Practice*. Ed. Glenda Hull and Katherine Schultz. Teacher's College P, 2002. 96–123.

Haney, Walt. "The Myth of the Texas Miracle in Education." *Education Policy Analysis Archives* 8.41 (19 August 2000). <http://epaa.asu.edu/epaa/v8n41/>. 15 June 2006.

Halasek, Kay, and Nels P. Highberg. "Introduction." *Landmark Essays on Basic Writing*. Mahwah, NJ: Erlbaum, 2001.

Harrington, Susanmarie, and Linda Adler-Kassner. "'The Dilemma That Still Counts': Basic Writing at a Political Crossroads." *Journal of Basic Writing* 17.2 (1998): 1–24.

Harris, Joseph. "Negotiating the Contact Zone." *Journal of Basic Writing* 14.1 (1995): 27–43.

Haswell, Rich, and Glenn Blalock. "Student Views of TAAS." February 2003. <http://comppile.tamucc.edu/TAAS/index.html>. 15 June 2006.

Hawisher, Gail E., and Cynthia L. Selfe, eds. *Gaming Lives in the Twenty-First Century: Literate Connections*. Palgrave Macmillan, 2007.

Heath, Shirley Brice. *Ways with Words: Language, Life and Work in Communities and Classrooms*. Cambridge: Cambridge UP, 1983.

Hilgers, Thomas. "Basic Writing Curricula and Good Assessment Practices." *Journal of Basic Writing* 14.2 (1995): 68–74.

Hillocks, George. *The Testing Trap: How State Writing Assessments Control Learning.* New York: Teacher's College P, 2002.

Hindman, Jane E. "Inventing Academic Discourse: Teaching (and Learning) Marginal Poise and Fugitive Truth." *Journal of Basic Writing* 18.2 (Fall 1999). 233–46.

———. "Reinventing the University: Finding a Place for Basic Writers." *Journal of Basic Writing* 12.2 (1993): 55–76.

Hirsch, E. D. *Cultural Literacy: What Every American Needs to Know.* New York: Vintage, 1987.

———. "Culture and Literacy." *Journal of Basic Writing* 3.1 (1980): 27–47.

Hull, Glenda, and Katherine Schultz. "Introduction: Negotiating the Boundaries Between School and Non-School Literacies." *Schools Out!: Bridging Out-of-School Literacies with Classroom Practices.* Ed. Glenda Hull and Katherine Schultz. New York: Teacher's College P, 2002. 1–10.

Huot, Brian. *(Re)articulating Writing Assessment for Teaching and Learning.* Logan: Utah State University.

Ishkur's Guide to Electronic Music. <http://www.di.fm/edmguide/edmguide.html>. 5 July 2005.

Johnson, Steven. *Everything Bad Is Good for You: How Today's Popular Culture Is Actually Making Us Smarter.* New York: Riverhead Books, 2005.

Klein, Stephen P., Laura S. Hamilton, Daniel F. McCaffrey, and Brian M. Stecher. "What Do Test Scores in Texas Tell Us?" *Education Policy Analysis Archives* 8.49 (26 October 2000). <http://epaa.asu.edu/epaa/v8n49/>. 19 July 2006.

Klosterman, Chuck. "Billy Sim." *Sex, Drugs, and Cocoa Puffs: A Low Culture Manifesto.* New York: Scribner, 2003.

———. *Fargo Rock City: A Heavy Metal Odyssey in Rural North Dakota.* New York: Simon & Schuster, 2001.

Knoblauch, C. H., and Lil Brannon. *Critical Teaching and the Idea of Literacy.* Portsmouth, NH: Boynton, 1993.

Knobel, M. *Everyday Literacies: Students, Discourse, and Social Practice.* New York: Peter Lang, 1999.

Kolln, Martha. *Rhetorical Grammar: Grammatical Choices, Rhetorical Effects* 5th ed. New York: Longman, 2007.

Kress, Gunther. "Socio-Linguistic Development and the Mature Language User: Different Voices for Different Occasions." *Language and Learning an Interactional Perspective.* Ed. G. Wells and J. Nicholls. London: Farmer P, 1985.

Krieg, Richard M. "Information Technology and Low-Income Inner City Communities." *Journal of Urban Technology* 3.1 (Fall 1995): 1–17.

Kutz, Eleanor, Suzy Q. Groden, and Vivian Zamel. *The Discovery of Competence: Teaching and Learning with Diverse Student Writers.* Portsmouth, NH: Boynton/Cook, 1993.

Lave, Jean, and Etienne Wenger. *Situated Learning: Legitimate Peripheral Participation*. Cambridge: Cambridge UP, 1991.

Lazere, David. "Orality, Literacy, and Standard English." *Journal of Basic Writing* (1991): 87–98.

Lu, Min-Zhan. "Conflict and Struggle: The Enemies or Preconditions of Basic Writing?" *College English* 54.8 (1992): 887–913. Rpt. in *Representing the "Other": Basic Writers and the Teaching of Basic Writing*. Bruce Horner and Min-Zhan Lu. Urbana, IL: NCTE, 1998. 30–55.

———. "Redefining the Legacy of Mina Shaughnessy: A Critique of the Politics of Linguistic Innocence." *Representing the "Other": Basic Writers and the Teaching of Basic Writing*. Urbana, IL: NCTE, 1998. 105–116.

Lu, Min-Zhan, and Bruce Horner. *Representing the "Other": Basic Writers and the Teaching of Basic Writing*. Urbana, IL: NCTE, 1999.

Maher, Jane. *Mina Shaughnessy: Her Life and Work*. Urbana, IL: NCTE, 1997.

Mahiri, Jabari, ed. *What They Don't Learn in School: Literacy in the Lives of Urban Youth*. New York: Peter Lang, 2004.

Marinara, Martha. "When Working Class Students 'Do' the Academy: How We Negotiate with Alternative Literacies." *Journal of Basic Writing* 16.2 (Fall 1997).

Maxson, Jeffrey. "'Government of da Peeps, for da Peeps, and by da Peeps': Revisiting the Contact Zone." *Journal of Basic Writing* 24.1 (Spring 2005): 24–47.

McCloud, Scott. *Understanding Comics: The Invisible Art*. New York: HarperPerennial, 1993.

McCormick, Kathleen. *The Culture of Reading and the Teaching of English*. New York: St. Martin's, 1994.

McNeal, Linda M. "Creating New Inequalities: Contradictions of Reform." *Phi Delta Kappan* (June 2000): 729–734.

McNeil, Linda, and Angela Valenzuela. "The Harmful Impact of the TAAS System of Testing in Texas: Beneath the Accountability Rhetoric." *Raising Standards or Raising Barriers? Inequality and High Stakes Testing in Public Education*. Eds. M. Kornhaber and G. Orfield. New York: Century Foundation, 2001. 127–150. <http://caracas.soehd.csufresno.edu/whatsnew/valenzuela/Valenzuela1%20.pdf>. 16 June 2006.

McNenny, Gerri, ed. *Mainstreaming Basic Writers: Politics and Pedagogies of Access*. Mahwah, NJ: Erlbaum, 2001.

Merrifield, Juliet, Mary Beth Bingman, David Hemphill, and Kathleen P. Bennett deMarrais. *Life at the Margins: Literacy, Language, and Technology in Everyday Life*. New York: Teacher's College P, 1997.

Micchiche, Laura. "Making a Case for Rhetorical Grammar." *CCC* 55.4 (2004): 716–737.

Miller, Charles, and Cheryl Oldham. "Setting the Context: Issue Paper." *A National Dialogue: The Secretary of Education's Commission on the Future of Higher Education*. 30

March 2006. <http://www.ed.gov/about/bdscomm/list/hiedfuture/reports/miller-old-ham.pdf>. 15 June 2006.

Miller, Richard. *As If Learning Mattered*. Ithaca: Cornell UP, 1998.

Moss, Gemma. "On Literacy and the Social Organisation of Knowledge Inside and Outside School." *Language and Education* 15.2&3 (2001): 146–161.

Mutnick, Deborah. "The Strategic Value of Basic Writing: An Analysis of the Current Moment." *Journal of Basic Writing* 19.1 (2000): 69–83.

———. *Writing in an Alien World: Basic Writing and the Struggle for Equality in Higher Education*. Portsmouth, NH: Boynton/Cook, 1995.

"National Assessment of Adult Literacy: FAQs." *National Center for Education Statistics*. <http://nces.ed.gov/naal/faq/faqpurpose.asp#8>. 23 July 2005.

National Commission on Excellence in Education. *A Nation At Risk: The Imperative for Educational Reform*. April 1983. <http://www.ed.gov/pubs/NatAtRisk/index.html>. 12 June 2006.

Odell, Lee. "Basic Writing in Context: Rethinking Academic Literacy." *Journal of Basic Writing* 14.1 (1995): 43–55.

Ong, Walter. *Orality and Literacy: The Technologizing of the World*. New York: Routledge, 1982.

Pena, George. "Literacy Becoming Even More Important." *Dallas Morning News*. 25 September 1999. <http://www.dallasreads.org/events/viewpoints.htm>. 30 July 2005.

Perl, Sondra. "A Look at Basic Writers in the Process of Composing." *Basic Writing: Essays for Teachers, Researchers, and Administrators*. Ed. Lawrence N. Kasden and Daniel R. Hoeber. Urbana, IL: NCTE, 1980. 13–32.

———. "The Composing Processes of Unskilled College Writers." *Research in the Teaching of English* 13.4 (1979): 317–36.

Petraglia, Joseph. "Introduction." *Reconceiving Writing, Rethinking Writing Instruction*. Ed. Joseph Petraglia. Mahwah, NJ: Erlbaum, 1995. xi–xvii.

popo1. Online post. *The Dancing Sausage Web Journal*. 18 April 2004. <http://gus.protest.net/MT2archive/0000676.html>. 25 October 2004.

Purves, Alan C., and W. C. Purves. "Viewpoints: Culture, Text Models, and the Activity of Writing." *Reading in the Teaching of English* 20.2 (1986): 174–197.

"Raaka-tu Introduction." *An Interactive Fiction Game for the TRS-80 and TRS-80 Color Computer*. August 2003. <http://www.figmentfly.com/raakatu/raakatu.html#coco%20instructions>. 19 November 2006.

Resnick, Lauren B. "Literacy in School and out." *What Counts as Literacy: Challenging the School Standard*. Ed. M. A. Gallego and S. Hollingsworth. New York: Teacher's College P, 2000. 27–41. <http://pickle.ed.psu.edu/moodle/file.php/33/literacy/resnick.pdf>. 15 September 2005.

Rhodes, Keith. "Developmental Administration: A Pragmatic Theory of Evolution in Basic Writing." *Discord and Direction: The Postmodern Writing Program Administrator*. Ed. Sharon James McGee and Carolyn Handa. Logan: Utah UP, 2005. 84–94.

Rich, Adrienne. "The Burning of Paper Instead of Children." <http://www.sccs. swarthmore.edu/users/99/jrieffel/poetry/rich/children.html>. 19 August 2005.

Rogers, Alan. "Afterword: Problematising Literacy and Development." *Literacy and Development*. Ed. Brian V. Street. New York: Routledge, 2001. 205–221.

Rose, Mike. "Remedial Writing Programs: A Critique and a Proposal." *College English* 45 (February 1983): 109–128. Rpt. in *A Sourcebook for Basic Writing Teachers*. New York: Random House, 104–124.

———. *The Mind at Work: Valuing the Intelligence of the American Worker*. New York: Penguin, 2005.

Royster, Jacqueline Jones. "Academic Discourses or Small Boats on a Big Sea." *AltDis: Alternative Discourses in the Academy*. Ed. Christopher Schroeder, Helen Fox, and Patricia Bizzell. Portsmouth, NH: Boynton/Cook, 2002.

Russell, David R. "Activity Theory and Process Approaches: Writing (Power) in School, and Society." *Post-Process Theory: Beyond the Writing Process Paradigm*. Ed. Thomas Kent. Carbondale: Southern Illinois UP, 1999.

———. "Activity Theory and Writing Instruction." *Reconceiving Writing, Rethinking Writing Instruction*. Ed. Joseph Petraglia. Mahwah, NJ: Erlbaum, 1995. 51–77.

Saxe, Geoffrey. *Culture and Cognitive Development: Studies in Mathematical Understanding*. Hillsdale, NJ: Erlbaum, 1991.

Schrag, Peter. "Too Good to be True." *The American Prospect* 11:4 (January 3, 2000). <http://www.prospect.org/archives/V11–4/schrag.html>. 17 June 2006.

Schoen, Donald A. *Educating the Reflective Practitioner: Toward a New Design for Teaching and Learning in the Professions*. San Francisco: Josey-Bass, 1990.

Schultz, Katherine, and Glenda Hull. "Locating Literacy Theory in Out-of-School Contexts." *School's Out!: Bridging Out-of-School Literacies with Classroom Practice*. Ed. Glenda Hull and Katherine Schultz. New York: Teacher's College P, 2002. 11–31.

Schuster, Edgar H. "National and State Writing Tests: The Writing Process Betrayed." *Phi Delta Kappan: The Professional Journal for Education* 85.5 (January 2004): 375–378. <http://www.pdkintl.org/kappan/k0401sch.htm>. 8 July 2004.

Scott, T. "Literacies and Deficits Revisited." *Journal of Basic Writing* 12.1 (1993): 46–56.

Scribner, Sylvia, and Michael Cole. *The Psychology of Literacy*. Cambridge: Harvard UP, 1981. 251.

"Section II: TASP Skills." *THEA Test Home Page*. <http://www.thea.nesinc.com/fac_ sec2htm>. 23 July 2005.

Selfe, Cynthia, and Gail Hawisher. *Literate Lives in the Information Age: Narratives on Literacy from the United States*. Mahwah, NJ: Erlbaum, 2004.

Severino, Carol. "Where the Cultures of Basic Writers and Academia Intersect: Cultivating the Common Ground." *Journal of Basic Writing* 11.1 (1992): 4–15.

Shaughnessy, Mina. *Errors and Expectations: A Guide for Basic Writing Teachers*. New York: Oxford UP, 1977.

Shor, Ira. *Empowering Education: Critical Teaching for Social Change*. Chicago: U of Chicago P, 1992.

———. "What Is Critical Literacy?" *Journal of Pedagogy, Pluralism, and Practice* 4.1 (Fall 1999). <http://www.lesley.edu/journals/jppp/4/shor.html>. 24 June 2006.

Skilton-Sylvester, Ellen. "Literate at Home but Not at School: A Cambodian Girl's Journey from Playwright to Struggling Writer." *Schools Out!: Bridging Out-of-School Literacies with Classroom Practices*. Ed. Glenda Hull and Katherine Schultz. New York: Teacher's College P, 2002. 61–90.

Smith, Michael W., and Jeffrey D. Wilhelm. *Reading Don't Fix No Chevys: Literacy in the Lives of Young Men*. Portsmouth, NH: Heinemann, 2002.

Soliday, Mary. *The Politics of Remediation: Institutional and Student Needs in Higher Education*. U of Pittsburg P, 2002.

———. "Toward a Consciousness of Language: A Language Pedagogy for Multi-Cultural Classrooms." *Journal of Basic Writing* 16.2 (Fall 1997). 62–75.

———. "Translating Self and Difference through Literacy Narratives." *College English* 56.5 (September 1994): 511–526.

Spellmeyer, Kurt. "A Common Ground: The Essay in the Academy." *College English* 51 (1989): 262–276.

Stein, Gertrude. "on composition." 6 August 2004. <http://www.english.upenn.edu/~afilreis/88/stein-composing.html>. 9 July 2005.

Street, Brian V. "Autonomous and Ideological Models of Literacy: Approaches from New Literacy Studies." *Media Anthropology Network*. 17–24 January 2006. <http://www.philbu.net/media-anthropology/street_newliteracy.pdf>. 10 July 2006.

———. "Introduction." *Literacy and Development: Ethnographic Perspectives*. Ed. Brian V. Street. New York: Routledge, 2001. 1–18.

———. *Social Literacies: Critical Approaches to Literacy in Development, Ethnography, and Education*. New York: Longman, 1995.

———. "What's 'New' in New Literacy Studies?: Critical Approaches to Literacy in Theory and Practice." *Current Issues in Comparative Education* 5.2 (May 12, 2003). 77–90. <http://www.tc.columbia.edu/CICE/Archives/5.2/52street.pdf>.

Sternglass, Marilyn. *Time to Know Them: A Longitudinal Study of Writing and Learning at the College Level*. Mahwah, NJ: Erlbaum, 1997.

Stuckey, Elspeth J. *The Violence of Literacy*. Portsmouth, NH: Heinemann, 1991.

The Full Monty. Twentieth-Century-Fox, 1997.

Thelin, William. "Understanding Problems in Critical Classrooms." *CCC* 57.1 (2005): 114–41.

Thomas, Karen M. "Literacy Fund-Raiser to Bring Together Parents, Celebrities, Love of Books." *Dallas Morning News*. 2 Nov. 2002.

Toenjes, Laurence A., A. Gary Dworkin, Jon Lorence, and Antwanette N. Hill. "The Lone Star Gamble: High Stakes Testing, Accountability, and Student Achievement in Texas and Houston." The Sociology of Education Research Group (SERG). Department of Sociology. University of Houston. August 2000. <http://www.brookings.edu/gs/brown/bc_report/2000/Houston.PDF>. June 2006.

Trainor, Jennifer Seibel. "Critical Pedagogy's 'Other': Constructions of Whiteness in Education for Social Change." CCC 53.4 (June 2002): 631–650.

Traub, James. City on a Hill: Testing the American Dream at City College. New York: Addison-Wesley, 1994.

Valenzuela, Angela. Leaving Children Behind: Why Texas-Style Accountability Fails Latino Youth. Albany: State U of New York P, 2004.

Watson, Debra. "Education and the 2000 Elections: Texas Miracle Debunked." World Socialist Website. 21 August 2000. <http://www.wsws.org/articles/2000/aug2000/tex-a21.shtml>. 12 June 2006.

White, Edward M. "The Scoring of Writing Portfolios: Phase 2." College Composition and Communication 56.4 (June 2005): 581–600.

William, Damon. "Reconciling the Literacies of Generations." Literacy: An Overview by Fourteen Experts. Ed. Stephen R. Graubard. New York: Hill and Wang. 1991.

Williams, Stephen. "The Literate Lineman." Unpublished essay, 2006.

Williams, Stephen, and Shannon Carter. "The (Il)literate Lineman: Deconstructing the Literacy Myth through Ethnographic Inquiry." Federation Rhetoric Symposium. Commerce, TX. February 2007.

Willingham, W. W., and Cole, N. S. (1997). Gender and Fair Assessment. Mahwah, NJ: Erlbaum, 1997.

"Writing Assessment: A Position Statement." CCCC Position Statement: A Statement Approved by the CCCC Executive Committee. National Council of Teachers of English (March 1995). <http://www.ncte.org/about/over/positions/category/write/107610.htm>.

Yagelski, Robert P. "Abby's Lament: Does Literacy Matter?" Literacy Matters. New York: Teachers College Press, 2000. "Chapter 1." <http://www.albany.edu/~rpy95/chapter1.htm>. 30 June 2006.

Index